COIN DICTIONARY
AND GUIDE

COIN DICTIONARY and GUIDE

By C. C. CHAMBERLAIN
and FRED REINFELD

STERLING PUBLISHING COMPANY, INC. · New York

Distributed to the coin trade by
PRESIDENT COIN CORPORATION

COIN BOOKS BY FRED REINFELD

Cash for Your Coins

A Catalogue of the World's Most Popular Coins

Coin Collectors' Handbook

Coin Dictionary and Guide (with C. C. Chamberlain, co-author)

Coinometry: An Instructive Historical Introduction to Coins and Currency for the Young Collector (with Robert V. Masters, co-author)

How to Build a Coin Collection

The Story of Civil War Money

The Story of Paper Money

Treasury of the World's Coins

Second Printing – November 1960

INTRODUCTION

To Peter Bell, a primrose by a river's brim was—just a yellow primrose, nothing more. To the uninitiate, a coin is just a metal disk, with "heads" on one side, "tails" on the other. To those, however, who have taught themselves to know and understand the art and science of numismatics, a coin can be a great deal more. The study of coins is a magic carpet that takes us not only through all the countries of the world, but carries us back through all the ages. To those blessed with insight and potent powers of imagination, a coin is an amulet that can awaken bygone scenes, and call up spirits from the misty past. Through its spell, the rites and ritual of creeds and myths and legends are evoked.

In the Ancient World coins were of far greater importance and power than they are today. When there were no banknotes, bills of exchange, or even checks, every commercial transaction, even the largest, that was not done by barter, was done by weighing or counting out actual coins. From an early period their power of propaganda was realized. At its lowest, a coin could advertise the basic commodity of some city; politically it could be used to enforce allegiance to some *tyrannos* or to extend the bounds of an augmenting empire. At its highest, it bore the sign, the symbol, even the features of some divinity. It was fitting that such coins should be stored within the precincts of some temple where, it was believed, under the eye of some immortal god, they would be safe from sacrilegious plundering.

Every coin has its setting, its historical background; it has links with the religion, the art, the literature of the period. Obviously the problem here has been not what to put in, but what to leave out. The world of numismatics is so vast that in this book we have had to keep more to the highways than to the byways of collecting. Greek coins must have prime choice. It was in Ancient Greece that coins began; it was there that they achieved perfection. Yet, when we consider that some two thousand cities in the Grecian Empire issued their own coins, and most of these cities struck a great number of differing types in the course of the ages, we realize it needs not one book but a library to deal adequately with such a vast study. In the case of the Roman Empire, the study of its coins must bulk large because of their historical importance. It is on the foundation of Roman currency that our currency of today is based.

Finally, in a book intended for American readers, interest demands that the largest space be allotted to American and English coins. Consequently, the great and imposing corpus of European coinage has had to be by-passed for the most part, while the tangled intricacies of Oriental coinage have been barely touched upon. These and similar fields of study are for the coin specialist, and for such this book is not intended. It is essentially a non-technical work for the beginner, a *vade-mecum* for the small collector who has little Latin and less Greek. It aims to be a simple guidebook to a vast and delectable region where the main pleasure is to see and find out for yourself. Like any other respectable guidebook, it will show you all the high roads through that region, and tell you where they lead; it will point out by the way interesting features of the landscape; it will show you the spots where history was made.

For the sake of quick reference, the information has been set out in alphabetical order, and cross references, often indicated by italics, have helped in saving space. Technicalities have been avoided, wherever possible; and where, for want of a simple word, some numismatic term has been employed, the explanations of such a word will be found in the dictionary itself. Above all, we have endeavored to produce not simply a technical lexicon, but something readable and interesting in itself. Thus its appeal is not solely to the collector, but to those who want to learn something about coins and their story, and in particular to those who realize that to know coins well is to know and to understand world history.

The fascination of collecting coins is at least as old as the Roman Empire. From a curious reference in the Life of Augustus by Suetonius (*c.* 75) we learn that the Romans of that time prized their own antique coins and valued those of foreign nations. Among the earliest known collectors of Europe was Pope Boniface VIII (1294-1303), well known to us from Dante's poem. Petrarch (1304-74), the Italian poet and human-ist, from his enthusiasm for classical antiquity, was an ardent collector. During the Renaissance, numbers of Italian princes and grandees amassed cabinets of Roman and, later, Greek coins. Where original rarities were lacking, the local medalist with his "Paduan" medallions filled up the gaps. Alfonso, King of Naples, was perhaps the greatest collector of the time; he is the first known "specialist": he specialized in the coins of Julius Caesar and the Julian family. Numismatics in those days meant the study of Greek and Roman coins, or "medals" as they were indiscriminately termed. Medieval coins were looked upon as "Gothic" barbarisms.

The first mention of an English collection is in a will dated 1552, that of Edward Beaumont of Oxford. The Stuarts were great collectors of works of art, among which their coin collections held high place. Prince Henry, son of James I, left behind him the valuable collection of coins and medals his father had started for him. This royal collection was greatly increased by Charles I, but the whole was seized and dispersed by the iconoclastic Puritans.

Among other famous collectors were the Duke of Buckingham, Sir Robert Cotton the bibliophile, William Camden the antiquary, Henry Hyde, second Earl of Clarendon, and John Evelyn the diarist. The famous Pembroke collection, formed by Thomas Herbert, Earl of Pembroke, was the first to give English numismatics an equal honor to that previously given to the coins of Greece and Rome. In France, Louis XIV (1638-1715) was so keen a collector that he never passed a day without viewing some portion of his treasures.

The vast collection now contained in the British Museum began with various bequests in the eighteenth century; early in the nineteenth century it was enriched by the acquisition of the royal collection. Glasgow University in 1783 acquired the large and valuable collection formed by the famous surgeon, William Hunter.

Concerning the question as to whether it is better for coins to be gathered together in museums, under glass cases, where only students can handle them and study them closely, or whether it is better for them to circulate freely for the benefit of private collectors, there is much to commend and condemn on both sides. The plea for the private collector has perhaps been put most eloquently in the will of Edmond de Goncourt:

"My wish is that my drawings, my prints, my curiosities, my books— those objects of art which have been the joy of my life—shall not be consigned to the cold tomb of a museum, and so laid out to the foolish glancing of the careless passer-by; but I will that all shall be dispersed by the hammer of the auctioneer, so that the pleasure which the acquiring of each one of them has given me shall be given once again, in every case, to someone, the inheritor of my own tastes."

In forming a collection of coins, there are two golden rules to remember: (i) Avoid diffusion: you cannot study your coins properly unless they are marshaled methodically in serried ranks, for there is no pleasure in looking at a trayful of jumbled coins, old mixed with new, East confused with West, etc. (ii) See that all your pieces are in fine condition: remember that a coin catalogued at $5 in superb condition is worth only a few cents if badly worn, defaced, illegible. Moreover, one shabby specimen in a group of otherwise presentable coins is like a poor relation at a party—it sheds a gloom around!

Apart from the amassing and hoarding of coins, which can hardly be called collecting, there are two main approaches to numismatics: (1) the technical, and (2) the "human." The technical collector is absorbed in the study of coins as coins; his scientific mind divides and subdivides, and everything is classified. Hand him a silver penny of Edward I or II and he will be able to tell you nothing of the Middle Ages or of Medievalism, whereas, from certain secret marks and subtle minutiae, he will be able to tell you to which of the forty-two sub-classes it should be assigned. At the risk of offending many high dignitaries of the numismatic world, we unhesitatingly affirm the "human" approach to coins to be the right approach, of greater interest and of more importance than the technical. The scientific numismatist, like all scientists today, must be a specialist. The danger of specializing is that it tends to contract rather than to enlarge the mind. To the student, with his "human" approach, coins are primarily the picture book of history. "What is the use," asked Alice in Wonderland, "of a book without pictures or conversations?" It is coins that supply us with these pictures, many of them lovely works of art, by contemporary artists; as for their "conversations," coins are unrivaled storytellers, and can speak to us with eloquence if only we learn to understand their language.

Abbreviations: The following abbreviations are used in this book.

Ar. (L. *Argentum*) . .	Silver
Au. (L. *Aurum*) . . .	Gold
C. (L. *circa*) . . .	About, approximately
Cf. (L. *confer*) . . .	Compare
Ob (v)	Obverse
Q.v. (L. *quod vide*) . .	Which see
R(ev)	Reverse
Sc. (L. *scilet*) . . .	Understand, supply
Arab.	Arabic
A.S.	Anglo-Saxon
Dan.	Danish
Fr.	French
Ger.	German
Gr.	Greek
H.	Hindustani
It.	Italian
L.	Latin
L.L.	Late Latin
M.L.	Middle Latin
O. Fr.	Old French
Port.	Portuguese

For other abbreviations, see *condition, rarity.*

A

Accolated: Used to describe a coin which has two portraits facing in the same direction and overlapping. *Conjoined* is a synonym.

Account, Money of : Money existing in name only, and of which no actual coins are struck; thus the English guinea, at one time an actual coin, is now only money of account.

Act of Union: In 1707 England and Scotland were united; coins issued before the Union and after can be distinguished by the arms on the reverse. On post-Union coins the English leopard and Scottish lion, instead of being placed on separate shields, are impaled on the top and bottom shields.

Before the Act of Union, the denominations of Scottish coins represented one-twelfth of the value of the corresponding English coins. By virtue of this Act the values were made equal.

Adams-Woodin (A-W) Numbers: Specialists in collecting U.S. pattern coins attribute their coins according to listings in *U.S. Pattern, Trial and Experimental Pieces,* by Edgar H. Adams and William H. Woodin.

Ae (L. *aes,* bronze, etc.): Numismatic symbol for brass, bronze, copper, or coins of this color.

Aegina (Island of Greece): The first European coins were struck here, in the seventh century B.C., though coins of an even earlier date had been struck in Asia Minor (see *Lydia*). They were of silver. The earliest existing coins of Aegina bear the figure of a turtle, presumed to be a symbol of Aphrodite,* or Astarte, the goddess of fertility; she

Left: Aegina, silver stater. Tortoise on obverse (about 650 B.C.).

Right: Aegina, tortoise on reverse (about 380 B.C.).

presided over the moon and the seas, and hence was the patroness of commerce. An important temple devoted to her worship overlooked the harbor of Aegina. Later coins show a land tortoise in place of the turtle, and it is probable the tortoise represented a standard weight in early Greece. Aegina was an important center of trade, and the Aeginetan system of coin weights and values was the most extensive before that of Corinth and of Athens. (See *Pheidon.*)

Aes: The Latin word for both copper and bronze; the word was also used to signify money of copper or bronze.

Aes Grave (heavy bronze): The earliest form of the *as,* weighing 1 lb.; hence it was also known as the *as libralis.* The weight of the metal represented a real and not a token value. (See *As.*)

Aes Rude (rough bronze): Denoted the earliest pieces of metal, shapeless and unstamped, presumed to be a standard of value and exchange in Ancient Rome. Their intrinsic value could be ascertained only by weighing, and so they cannot be considered as actual coins.

Aes Signatum (stamped bronze): Heavy pieces of cast bronze, in the shape of bars or ingots, impressed with the figure of some animal, or other symbol. Illustration shows a specimen in the British Museum. It is a little more than 6½ in. long, and weighs about 5 lb. It has been attributed to about the year 280 B.C. Such pieces could hardly be

---

* We must not overlook the fact, however, that turtle and tortoise shells were a popular form of currency among certain primitive races, notably in China.

Aes signatum. A bull.

intended for general currency, but their exact purpose is unknown. Pliny attributes their invention to Servius Tullius, the sixth king of Rome.

Agnel (L. *agnellus,* a little lamb): French gold coin, thirteenth to sixteenth century, bearing on the obverse a figure of the Paschal Lamb, hence also known as a *mouton d'or.* It was imitated by Edward III and Henry V in the Anglo-Gallic series.

Alabama Centennial Commemorative Half Dollar: See *Commemorative Coins (U.S.),* p. 61.

Albany, N.Y. Charter Commemorative Half Dollar: See *Commemorative Coins (U.S.),* p. 66.

Alexander the Great (reigned 336-323 B.C.): Coins bearing the name of Alexander are among the commonest of ancient coins. Not only were enormous numbers minted in his own lifetime to cover his vast empire, but also for more than a century and a half after his death coins were struck bearing his name and types. (See also *Portraits on Coins.*)

Alexandria: A prolific mint. From the time of Tiberius, base billon tetradrachms were issued of the value of one denarius. It was the last Roman provincial mint; down to the time of Diocletian (A.D. 296) the familiar dumpy base potin coins of this mint were poured out in vast quantities. The legends are in Greek, though the common late types of Victory and Eagle show they were issued in connection with the Roman garrison there. (For dating these coins see *L.*)

Alliance Coins: A term applied to certain coins of Ancient Greece, which were struck in common by two or more cities or states. They were often issued with some common device. Thus, when Thebes, Ephesus, Iasus, Cnidus, Samos, Rhodes, and Byzantium allied themselves in 394 B.C. to expel the Spartans, all these cities issued coins with various reverses, but bearing in common on the obverse the device of Hercules as an infant strangling serpents, with the inscription ΣΥΝ (*sunmachon,* "allied"). (See *Symbols and Symbolism.*)

Alloy: A combination of gold or silver or copper with one or more other metals. The purpose is to produce a coin of more durable and cheaper

11

composition. Alloys have been used at times to debase coinage. See *Antoninianus, Debasement, Electrum, Pyx, Tolerance.*

Alpha and Omega, A, Ω : The first and last letters of the Greek alphabet, symbolizing "The Beginning and the Ending" (Rev. i. I. 8). A Christian symbol found on Roman coins from the time of Constantius II (*c.* A.D. 350), on a few Anglo-Saxon coins, and on some medieval European coins.

Altered Dates: Dates of common coins are sometimes unscrupulously altered to make them appear as other (and rarer) coins. By way of example, 1944 D cents are often encountered with the first "4" altered to a "1" so as to appear as 1914 D's. These altered dates can be recognized, however, by the "VDB" on the truncation of the bust, which does not appear on the genuine 1914 D cents.

Aluminum: This metal is extremely light in weight and cheap to produce. It is becoming more and more popular as a medium for cheap coins in European countries where currency has depreciated. It is also largely used as an alloy. Abbreviation, Al.

Ambrosino (St. Ambrose): Silver grosso, struck by the Republic of Milan 1230-1310, though the type persisted until the end of the fifteenth century. A few were struck in gold. The patron saint of Milan, St. Ambrose, is figured on the obverse; the reverse bears a cross within a beaded circle.

American Independence Sesquicentennial Commemoratives: See *Commemorative Coins (U.S.)*, pp. 62, 69.

American Numismatic Association: Membership dues in this organization are $7 the first year, and $5 annually thereafter. Membership includes a subscription to *The Numismatist* (a monthly magazine), and access to the association's extensive library of numismatic works. Prospective applicants for membership can communicate with Professor Lewis M. Reagan, General Secretary, P.O. Box 577, Wichita 1, Kansas.

American Numismatic Society: Located at Broadway between 155th and 156th Streets, New York 32, N.Y. Organized in 1858, the Society has one of the world's most comprehensive numismatic collections and a library of more than 50,000 items. It also provides a photographic service for members at moderate cost. Membership dues are $17.50 a year for a Fellow and $7.50 for an Associate Member.

Anchor Money: Small silver coins, struck in 1820 and 1822, for use in Mauritius, the West Indies, and other British colonies. One-half, one-quarter, one-eighth, and one-sixteenth of a dollar were issued. The reverse shows an anchor crowned.

Anepigraphic, Anepigraphous (Gr. *an*, without, *epigraphe*, inscription): The primitive coins of almost all nations are anepigraphic, i.e., they have no legend inscribed upon them.

Angel (originally *angel-noble*): Gold coin introduced by Edward IV in 1465. The noble originally represented half a mark (6s. 8d.), but as it had appreciated in value, it became necessary to strike this new form of noble to retain the old value. It was so called from the obverse showing St. Michael defeating Satan; the reverse shows a ship bearing a large shield. The angel was the chosen coin in "touching" by the Tudors and Stuarts (see *Touch Piece*). Half-angels were popularly known as "angel-halfpennies" and quarter-angels as "angel-farthings." The last angel was struck by Charles I.

Gold angel of Edward IV (1471–83).   Anglesey token (halfpenny) issued by Parys Mine Company, 1791.

Anglesey Pennies and Halfpennies: The first eighteenth-century English tokens, issued in 1787. They bear a Druid's head (commemorating the last stand of the Druids in Anglesey), and on the reverse the cipher of the local mint, the Parys Mine Company.

Anglo-Gallic Coins: Name given to coins struck by English sovereigns for use in their French dominions, from the time of Henry II to Henry VI. The series includes the *angelot, blanc, chaise, denier, florin, gros, guennois, hardi, leopard, mouton, pavillon,* and *salute.* The Anglo-Gallic series does not include coins of the Calais mint, nor the few groats that were struck at Tournay by Henry VIII. The only coins Richard I struck in his own name were Anglo-Gallic coins.

Anglo-Hanoverian Coins: The Hanoverian line of kings, beginning with George I and ending with William IV, struck special coins for their German possessions, Brunswick-Lüneburg and (from 1814) the Kingdom of Hanover. Either the portrait of the English king or his monogram appears on the obverse, whereas the reverse bears a German device.

Anglo-Saxon Coinage: The Anglo-Saxons reckoned their wealth in pounds, shillings, and pence, but pounds and shillings were only monies of account. A few round halfpennies were issued (introduced by the Viking invader Halfdene, 875-77), but the principal coin was the (so-called) penny, in silver, modeled on the New Denarius of Charlemagne. This could be cut for halfpennies and farthings. (See *Penny, Sceat, Scilling.*)

Anna (Hind. *ana*): A modern Indian copper coin, one-sixteenth of a rupee, and worth about $2\frac{1}{2}d$. The two-anna piece was a small silver coin.

Antietam Commemorative Half Dollar: See *Commemorative Coins (U.S.),* p. 67.

Antoninianus (L. relating to Antoninus): Roman silver coin, a double denarius; distinguished from the denarius by its slightly larger size and the radiate head of the emperor. The head of an empress is set on a crescent. The radiate head and the crescent are symbolic of the sun and the moon. Introduced by Caracalla (Marcus Aurelius *Antoninus*) in

Roman Empire, silver antoninianus (A.D. 215). *Left:* Caracalla; *right:* Sun-god.

A.D. 215, it gradually replaced the denarius as the principal silver coin. In course of time, however, the silver became so debased that by the time of Gallienus (A.D. 260-68) it was little more than a copper coin. Many barbarous copies of the antoninianus were struck in Gaul and Britain.

Architecture, Illustrated by Coins: Greek coins, with their idealistic symbolism, rarely depict anything of architectural interest. The head of the Colossus of Rhodes is probably shown on the coins of Rhodes, but rather as an idealistic symbol of the sun-god than as a literal rendering of the actual statue. Of the harbor of Zancle and the Labyrinth of Crete we have some kind of simple diagrams, but here again they are purely symbolical. Roman coins are more realistic in their architectural features. The justifiable pride of the Romans in their buildings is displayed in numerous types of coins, such as those depicting the Capitol (Vespasian), the Forum (Trajan), the Coliseum with its crowd of spectators (Titus), the round Temple of Vesta (Vespasian), the Temple of Janus with its closed gates, signifying the world at peace (Nero), the Circus Maximus (Nero), the great harbor of Ostia (Nero), the Villa Publica in the Campus Martius (P. Fonteius), the Altar of Lyons (Tiberius), the Marcian Aquaduct (P. Fonteius), Trajan's Column (Trajan). Even on very late coins we see the Praetorian or City Gate (see *Gateway*), and on a rare medallion of Constantius we can even see the

Roman sesterces.
Left: Circus Maximus. *Right:* Coliseum.

gate and walls of Roman London. In early medieval Europe the Carlovingian *novus denarius* copied as one of its common devices the Roman temple, but with a Christian cross in place of the heathen god within. It bore the legend XPISTIANA RELIGIO. A later form of stylized ecclesiastical building was the *Châtel Tournois* (q.v.). A number of Anglo-Saxon coins show interesting architectural types, particularly those of Edward the Elder (A.D. 900-25), and the "York Minster" coin of Athelstan (925-39).

On U.S. coins (regular issues) there are two notable architectural reverses—Jefferson's home at Monticello on the Jefferson nickel, and the Lincoln Memorial on the Lincoln Head cent. Architectural motifs appear fairly frequently on commemorative coins (see *Commemorative Coins, Foreign* and *Commemorative Coins, U.S.*). Among outstandingly beautiful architectural coins may be mentioned the Hebrew temple shown on a coin of the second revolt against the Romans (132-35 A.D.), and a coin issued by Pope Alexander VII (1655-67) showing a hall with columns; this is undoubtedly one of the handsomest coins ever struck.

Left: Palestine, Second Revolt (A.D. 132-5), tabernacle with ark and scroll (see page 139).
Right: coin issued by Pope Alexander VII (1655-67).

Arkansas Centennial Commemorative Half Dollar: See *Commemorative Coins (U.S.)*, pp. 64 and 67.

Art: (i) *Greek*. The masterpieces of numismatic art are to be found in the coins of the Ancient Greeks, the period of finest art being that of the fourth century B.C., from the end of the Athenian supremacy to the age of Alexander (*c*. 400-336 B.C.). The great numismatic artists of the period, such as Kimon and Euainetus, attained inimitable perfection in the dekadrachms of Syracuse. Many contemporary masterpieces of Greek sculpture inspired the design of coins; the statue of Olympian Zeus by Phidias originated the head of the god on the tetradrachms of Philip II* and on the coins of Elis; the statue of Athena in the Parthenon,

Top left: Aetna, silver tetradrachm.
Bottom left: Macedon, silver tetradrachm of Philip II.
Top right: Rhegium, silver tetradrachm.
Bottom right: Athens, silver tetradrachm, goddess Athene.

also carved by Phidias, may have originated the head on the later Athenian tetradrachms; on the coins of Cnidos we see the Aphrodite of

* A fairly faithful copy of the complete statue is seen on a stater of Antiochus IV of Syria.

Praxiteles; the head of a statue of Hera by Polycleitus was copied on a coin of Argos; and the radiate head of Helios on the coins of Rhodes must have been imitated from the Colossus of Rhodes, one of the Seven Wonders of the World; the famous Victory of Samothrace (now in the Louvre) figures on a coin of Demetrius Poliorcetes of Macedonia. (See *Nike.*) From the artistic point of view it is disappointing to find that in some of the larger cities commercialism cramped the free development of art; certain popular coins, such as the "Owls" of Athens, were deliberately struck for centuries in their original archaic style, as any innovation would have been unacceptable in foreign and less civilized parts.

(ii) *Roman Art.* The early native coins of Rome in conception and execution were massive, crude, and clumsy, but by the time the early silver denarii were struck, the finer artistry of Greece was recognized and sought. The consular series of denarii are Greek in spirit, if not always in execution. The imperial series are more pedestrian in conception. Roman art was essentially realistic. The deities on the coins are but clumsy-looking mortals, the abundant abstractions and personifications are mundane creatures, lacking any spirit of imagination. Roman art is more at home in depicting architectural objects, but it is in realistic portraiture that it really excels. The virility and vivid characterization of the Roman portrait busts are apparent in coins, especially in those of the first and second centuries A.D. With the decline of Rome in

Portraiture on Roman coins. *Left:* Bronze sesterce, Claudius (A.D. 41–54). *Right:* Bronze sesterce, Nero (A.D. 54–68).

the third century, the portraiture gradually becomes feebler and more debased, and in the fourth century it seems to lack all life and character.

(iii) *European Art.* The early medieval coins of Europe did not aspire to any fine artistic effects. The simple, direct method of striking from a few punches (see *Die*) of lines and curves hampered any attempt at elaboration. The coins—with their saints and symbols, their pious mottoes, and ever-recurring crosses—were the expression of a simple and profound religious faith rather than works of art.

With the Renaissance, a florid splendor of self-conscious art breaks out, and the egotism of realistic portraiture is manifest. Great artists, among them Leonardo da Vinci and Benvenuto Cellini, designed coins as well as medals.* A classical realism triumphs over medieval symbolic

Left: Milan, gold ducat, Giovanni Galeazzo Maria Sforza (1481). *Right:* Mantua, silver testone, Francesco Gonzaga (*c.* 1500).

art. With the seventeenth century comes in the golden age of heraldic splendor, seen especially on the German coins. Eighteenth-century European continental coins are outstanding for their ostentatious display of big-wigged busts (often incongruously displayed over a Roman

Palatinate, silver taler, Count Wolfgang Wilhelm of the Palatinate.

cuirass!), and they abound with laudatory titles. In the nineteenth century, an age of mechanical mass production, utilitarianism takes the place of art. In our own century the designs of our coins are eclectic, illustrating such trends as the pseudo-Gothic, photographic realism and a straining after futuristic style. (See also *Architecture, Engraver, Portraits,* etc.)

(iv) *American and Canadian Art.* For the most part, the early coinage of the United States places no great stress on artistic merit. The ban on personal portraits led to the use of Liberty heads in a diversity of forms and with rather poor execution. The exquisite flying eagle reverse

---

* Da Vinci designed the testone of Johannes Maria Sforza and that of Lodovico il Moro, the rulers of Milan.

of the Gobrecht dollars was a pleasant exception to a depressing general rule. Later in the century, the Barber and Morgan Liberty Head types represented another great advance, as did their predecessor, the Liberty Seated type.

But it was with the beginning of the generally very beautiful commemorative series that a new high standard of artistry was introduced into American coinage. Such examples as the Pilgrim Tercentenary, the Oregon Trail Memorial and the Huguenot-Walloon Tercentenary, to mention only a few, will bear comparison with the finest examples of contemporary coin design and engraving.

The same claim may be made equally convincingly for the magnificent eagles and double eagles designed by Augustus Saint-Gaudens after

U.S.A., Saint-Gaudens double eagle.

the turn of the twentieth century. The handsome Indian Head incuse types of Bela Pratt, issued about the same time, are not unworthy of being ranked in the same illustrious company.

The appearance of the beautiful Lincoln Head cent in 1909 broke with the tradition of never picturing an actual person on U.S. coinage. It is significant that all the current coin types have similar portraits on the obverse—Thomas Jefferson on the nickel; Franklin D. Roosevelt on the dime; George Washington on the quarter; and Benjamin Franklin on the half dollar. The day of the symbolical obverse is apparently finished, and when the present portraits are discontinued, they will undoubtedly be succeeded by other portraits.

Canadian coinage has followed a different path of evolution. The portrait of the living monarch has always furnished the standard motif for the obverse. For a long time the reverses followed a tradition of plain and serviceable design, but since the mid-Thirties a distinct trend toward far more attractive reverses has been noticeable. These admirable reverses have impressively evoked the Canadian scene and the Canadian past: the maple leaf on the cent; the beaver on the five cents nickel; the fishing schooner on the ten cent coin; the caribou head on the

25-cent coin; the Canadian arms on the 50-cent coin; and the canoe-men or *voyageurs* on the dollar. The equally attractive commemoratives of this period have also contributed to an artistic output that has engaged the interest of an ever-growing number of collectors.

As (L. pl. *asses*): Like our English word *pound*, this Latin word was originally the name of an actual weight; the name became transferred to an equivalent weight of metal, and later to the coin which was intended to represent the value of that weight of metal. As a unit of weight it represented twelve *unciae* (whence our word "*ounce*"). As a coin it was first issued about 300 B.C., and weighed almost 12 oz. It was crudely cast, and showed on the obverse the double head of *Janus* (q.v.), the god of beginnings; on the reverse the prow of a ship, symbolizing the growing power of the Empire overseas. The following is a table giving the *as*, and its principal divisions, showing the marks of value that figure on the coins, and the heads of the different deities that are represented on them:

Marks of Value.	Name of Coin.			Divinity.
I.	As			Janus
S.	Semis	($\frac{1}{2}$ of the *as*)		Jupiter
. . . . (four pellets)	Triens	($\frac{1}{3}$,, ,, ,,)	(4 unciae)	Minerva
. . . (three pellets)	Quadrans	($\frac{1}{4}$,, ,, ,,)	(3 unciae)	Hercules
. . (two pellets)	Sextans	($\frac{1}{6}$,, ,, ,,)	(2 unciae)	Mercury
. (one pellet)	Uncia	($\frac{1}{12}$,, ,, ,,)	Roma or (?)	Bellona

The *as* was continually being reduced in weight; in the time of Augustus it had dwindled to about the size, weight, and value of the English halfpenny. As a unit of monetary reckoning it was superseded in the third century B.C. by the *sestertius*.

Assarion (Gr. diminutive of Latin *as*: a little *as*): The Greek name for the *as* in its reduced form; but it seems to have been used loosely for any small copper coin of trifling value, as in Matthew X. 29 (translated in our Bible as "farthing"), the price of a couple of sparrows.

Assay: An analytical test or trial to ascertain the purity, weight, and consistence of precious metal in coin or bullion. Formerly known as *touch*. (See *Pyx*, *Trial*.)

Assignat: Term for *paper money* issued during the French Revolution from 1790 to 1795. Though ostensibly secured by confiscated church land, the notes dwindled steeply in value.

Attribution: The process of identifying a coin by reference to all relevant details, such as country of issue, language of inscription, date, composition of metal, designs on obverse and reverse, mint marks, etc.

Augg., Auggg., etc.: A peculiar form of abbreviated plural found on Roman coins. The number of the final letter indicates the number of Augusti in whose name the coin was struck. (See also *Britt.*)

Augustus (usually abbreviated on Roman coins to Avg.) (L. majestic, venerable): Originally a title of honor bestowed on Octavius Caesar and afterwards on all the succeeding emperors. Diocletian (283-305) decreed the Empire should be governed by two Augusti, and two sub-Emperors, or Caesars (see *Augg.*).

Aureus (L. the *golden*, sc. *denarius*—the golden denarius): The standard gold coin of Ancient Rome, equal to 25 denarii or 100 sestertii (about the same weight and value as the gold sovereign). Originally struck by certain generals in the provinces, it was introduced into Rome by Julius Caesar *c.* 49 B.C. It was the principal Roman gold coin from Augustus to the reign of Constantine. In common with other Roman coins, it decreased in weight and value, and in the time of Constantine was replaced by the *solidus* (q.v.).

B

Bactrian Coins: Bactria was a kingdom corresponding roughly to the modern *Balk*, in Afghanistan. Conquered by Alexander the Great in 328 B.C. A form of Hellenic civilization spread to this country, and numerous coins are found here and in northwest India with debased Greek types and inscriptions. Later coins are bilingual. (See *India, Coinage of.*)

Baiocco (It. *baio*, bay color): A copper or white metal coin of the Papal States, worth about a cent. 100 *baiocchi* = 1 *scudo*.

Bank of England Dollars and Tokens: A silver token five-shilling piece was issued in 1804. It was struck on the Spanish dollar. Two millions of these dollars were used for this purpose. It replaced the

Great Britain, Bank of England Dollar, Seated Britannia (1804).

countermarked Spanish dollar (see *Dollars, Countermarked*). The marks of the original Spanish coin are occasionally discernible on the over-struck coin. In 1811, Bank of England tokens for three shillings and for one shilling sixpence were issued. The dollar and these tokens were current up to the time of the re-issue of the regal currency in 1816.

Banknote: A form of legalized paper currency, issued by a bank, being a promise to pay a specified sum on demand. Banknotes may have originated from the receipts which goldsmiths gave for specie and other valuables entrusted to them. When gold was scarce in England during the Napoleonic wars Bank of England notes were made legal tender in 1799 for amounts over one pound. They are still legal tender. (See *Broken Bank Note, Paper Money*.)

Bar Cent: See *Colonial and Pre-Mint Coinage*.

Barbarous Radiates: A prolific issue by the Gauls, the Ancient Britons, and other barbarian races of the third century A.D., consisting of imitations of Roman coins. The coins most frequently imitated were those of Postumus, Victorinus, Tetricus I, and Tetricus II (from A.D. 259 to 273). These emperors were always depicted with a radiate crown. Most of these barbarous radiates are crudely designed and carelessly struck, but some are close copies, and are often mistaken for the original Roman coins. (See also *Minim*.)

Barber Head Coins: Any coins or patterns designed by mint engraver Charles E. Barber but used specifically to refer to the Liberty Head dime, quarter and half dollar of the 1892-1916 issue. (See entries for these denominations.)

Baronial Coins: In Germany, France, and Italy the coinage is complicated by the fact that the privilege of minting coins in the early Middle Ages was farmed out to innumerable dukes, counts, earls, lords, and barons. Such coins are known as seignorial or baronial coins. In England, however, the prerogative of the royal mint was jealously upheld, the only exception being made in the case of a few privileged ecclesiastics.

Barter: A direct exchange of commodities, without the intermediary of coins. The derivation of this word from O. Fr. *barater*, signifying not only to *barter*, but also to *cheat*, seems to point to the fact that this primitive method of trade was not always satisfactory to both parties concerned. (See *Cattle Used as Money*.)

Base Metal: A metallurgical term for any metal not classified as "noble." Lead, zinc, copper, and iron are base metals.

Beistle Numbers: Specialists in collecting half dollars issued in the period 1794-1921 refer to die varieties and attribute their coins according to listings in *A Register of U.S. Half Dollar Die Varieties*, by M. L. Beistle.

Bezant (L. *Byzantius*, i.e., *Byzantius nummus* = the Byzantine coin): Gold coin of Constantinople, which freely circulated over all Europe (including England) from the fourth to the fifteenth century. The bezant was a late form of the *solidus* (q.v.). Also spelled *besant*.

Biblical Coins: See *Israel*.

Biga (late L. pl. form of *bigae*): A chariot drawn by two horses abreast (cf. *Quadriga*). A frequent type of the early Republican Roman denarii, where Diana or Victory is the charioteer.

Bilingual: A coin bearing words in two different languages is said to have a bilingual inscription.

Billon (Fr.): An alloy of copper and silver (cf. *potin*). Billon coins contain more than half copper. Large quantities of billon coins were minted at Alexandria in imperial times; though Roman coins, they bear Greek inscriptions.

Bimetallism: An economic term, borrowed from modern French, to denote any system of currency which is based on a fixed relative value of any two metals (in practice, nearly always gold and silver); under a *bimetallic* system both metals are legal tender for any amount. (See also *Gold Standard*.)

Bit: A "bit" cut off from the edge or from the center of a Spanish piece of eight, and countermarked for currency in the West Indies. They were in circulation until the early years of the nineteenth century. A

Left: Piece of Eight.
Right: 2 bits and 4 bits.
(See also page 180.)

"bit" is equivalent in value to one *real*. It was a common custom to divide an 8-*reales* piece into quarters—hence our expression "two bits" to denote a quarter dollar. (See *Peso*.)

Black Money: A general term for base-silver pennies; also applied to jetons, counters, or tokens in brass which imitate silver coins. (See *Spurious*.)

Blanc (Fr. white): French silver coin, first struck in the fourteenth century; also the Anglo-Gallic coin copied from this, struck by Henry VI.

Blank: See *Flan*.

Bolender Numbers: Specialists in collecting silver dollars issued during the period 1794-1803 refer to die varieties and attribute their coins according to listings in *The United States Early Silver Dollars from 1794 to 1803*, by M. H. Bolender.

Bonnet-piece: Scottish gold coin, first issued by James V in 1539; value at the time, forty shillings Scottish; so called from the large flat bonnet which appears on the portrait of the king.

Bonnet Type: One of the eight types of pennies ascribed to William I (Type II). The king's head is shown full-face, and bears a jewelled and tasselled crown of inordinate size.

Boone (Daniel) Bicentennial Commemorative Half Dollar: See *Commemorative Coins (U.S.)*, p. 63.

Boulton, Matthew: He was born at Birmingham in 1728, and at an early age devoted his energies to improving steam power and introducing it into factories to take the place of the very limited power hitherto provided by human hand, or horse-mills or waterwheels. He founded the Soho works near Birmingham in 1762, and this was later recognized by the Government as an authorized mint. In 1777 he became a partner with James Watt, the famous engineer and inventor. In 1788 he began work on his new steam coining press, and grouped around him many famous numismatic artists, such as Droz and Küchler. The latter artist produced the dies for the re-coinage of 1797 (see *Cartwheel*). Coins were struck for some of the colonies, and for foreign countries. The 5s. Bank of England token was struck by Boulton, and later other Bank tokens for both England and Ireland were struck by the firm. Boulton died in 1809, but the firm continued until 1898. Ruding, writing in 1840, describes the mint as:

"adapted to work eight machines, each of which is capable of striking from seventy to eighty pieces of money, the size of a guinea, per minute. . . . Every piece becomes perfectly round, and of equal diameter, which is not the case with any other national money ever put into circulation."

Box-coins: A small box formed by hollowing out and joining together the obverse and reverse of two similar coins. The two halves are usually threaded so that the top may be unscrewed. Many box-coins were made in the sixteenth century at Augsberg and Nuremburg from the large thalers of the German States. These are known as "box-thalers" (Ger. *schraubthaler*), and contained colored miniatures and other small objects. Such boxes have often been made from the larger English Georgian coins, particularly from the 1797 "cartwheel." This was also often done with American Trade Dollars.

Bracteate (L. *bractea*, a thin plate of metal): (i) Thin, uniface disks, strung together and used as body ornaments and amulets by northern

Frankfurt am Main, bracteate (silver denarius), Frederick Barbarossa.

nations in the Viking period. They appear to have been imitated originally from Roman gold coins, but were apparently not used as currency.

(ii) Flimsy silver or gold-leaf coins, popular in central Europe in the twelfth and thirteenth centuries. They originated in Thuringia, and were of such thin fabric that it was only possible to show the design on one side, the reverse remaining incuse. They were issued by emperors, barons, dukes, counts, palatine electors, and largely by ecclesiastics, hence the name *pfaffen-pfennige* (parsons' pennies).

Braided Hair Type: See *Cent* (*U.S.*), *Half Cent*.

Brass: Modern brass is an alloy of copper and zinc, though the word is loosely used to include all alloys of copper. The Romans called their brass *orichalcum*. In Old English the Latin word *aes* (q.v.) was rendered "brass," hence in early literature "brass" became synonymous with "money" (*Piers Plowman iii.* 189, Matt. x. 9.); the word in this sense persists in English slang of today.

Brass, First, Second, and Third: A somewhat loose way of classifying Roman coins by *size*, big, medium, and small; abbreviated to *Ae*. I, *Ae*. II, *Ae*. III. Usually, *Ae*. I is a *sestertius*, *Ae*. II, a *dupondius*, and *Ae*. III, an *as* or its division.

Bridgeport, Conn. Centennial Commemorative Half Dollar: See *Commemorative Coins* (*U.S.*), p. 66.

Britain, Allusions to on Roman Coins: Many Imperial Roman coins allude to Britain, either directly or indirectly, in both legends and types. The first direct allusion is a gold coin of Claudius, showing the triumphal arch erected to celebrate his conquest and which bears the words DE BRITANN. The coins of Hadrian and Antoninus Pius showing the figure of Britannia are mentioned and illustrated under *Britannia*. Hadrian also inscribed coins ADVENTUI AVG. BRITANNIAE, where the Emperor and the Genius of Britain join in sacrificing to the Roman gods. Septimius Severus and his sons struck coins relating to victories in Britain. There is a unique gold medal of Constantius struck to commemorate the defeat of Allectus (A.D. 296) and the restoration of Britain to the Roman Empire. The emperor is shown on horseback about to enter the City of London. The Genius of the City welcomes him, and below we see a galley manned with soldiers, symbolizing the relieving force. The medal bears the legend REDDITOR LVCIS AETERNAE ("Restorer of the light eternal"). (See *Roman Mints in England, Roman Coins Relating to Britain.*)

Britannia: Both Hadrian (117-38) and Antoninus Pius (138-61) commemorated their achievements in Britain, and in particular the building of two great walls, by striking coins on which the Genius of the country, Britannia, figures. The attitude and the attributes of Britannia on the sesterius of Antoninus resemble so closely those of Britannia on many

Seated Britannia on a coin of Antoninus Pius (138–61).

modern coins that almost certainly the new must have been modeled on the old. Britannia was introduced on English coins in the time of Charles II, on the halfpence and farthings. Frances Stewart (afterwards Duchess of Richmond), sat as model for Britannia.

British Museum (London): Originated by the purchase in 1753 of the great collection of books, MSS., antiquities, natural history specimens, etc., of Sir Hans Sloane. The collection included 23,000 coins and medals.

Valuable guides, handbooks, and catalogues of coins are issued by the Museum. Personal attention is given to any numismatic query, although, for obvious reasons, no valuations will be given.

Britons, Coins of the Ancient: The earliest, struck as early as 150 B.C., were gold coins, copied from Gaulish imitations of the stater of Philip of Macedon. They were uninscribed, and were current in southeast England. As they were copied and re-copied, in course of time, the original design became almost lost; the head of the divinity on the obverse (originally Apollo or Hercules) became a mass of meaningless but highly decorative waves, dots, and lunettes; the horse on the reverse (originally a biga) became disjointed and distorted, until it was quite unrecognizable as an animal. About the period of Augustus, however, the influence of Rome became apparent in the more realistic art, the more varied design. Roman lettering was used, giving the initial abbreviation of the British king or the town where the coin was struck. The silver, bronze, and tin coins of the Ancient Britons are of considerably later date than the gold. (See also *Currency Bars; Gaul, Coins of; Tin Money*.)

Britt. and Britt. Omn.: These abbreviated legends on English coins are not, as is often supposed, an error in spelling. BRITT. is the peculiar form of abbreviated plural, standing for *Britanniarum* (of the Britains, i.e., Great Britain and the British possessions overseas). In the same way we write *pp.* for *pages* (vide *Augg.*). BRITT. was first placed on Victorian coins, and the OMN. was added by Edward VII in 1901, as an appreciation of the assistance rendered by the colonies in the Boer War. In conformity with the new conception of the Commonwealth, this legend has now been omitted from coins struck after 1953.

Broad (so called because they are larger and thinner than the later milled coins): A hammered gold coin, first struck under James I in 1604, and originally worth twenty shillings. At that period it was called a *Unite*, from the motto it bore—*Faciam eos in gentem unam* ("I will make them one nation"—Ezek. xxxvii. 22.). This was an allusion to the union of Scotland with England. The broad of 1619 is known as a *Laurel*, from the laureated bust of the king. The unite of James I is also known as a *Jacobus*, and that of Charles I as a *Carolus*, these words being derived from the Latin forms of the names of the respective monarchs.

Brockage (allied to *breakage*): On a brockage coin one side is struck perfectly and the other side becomes a mirror image—i.e., *incuse* (q.v.).

Broken Bank Note: Many of the State Banks which came into existence in the United States before the passage of the National Banking Act of 1863 became insolvent—they went "broke" and their notes became worthless. Such a note is termed a "Broken Bank Note."

Broken Die: In the early days of American coinage, it frequently happened that the dies from which coins were struck broke because of improper hardening or flaws in the dies. On coins struck from such dies we find evidence in the form of raised lines of metal corresponding to the cracks in the die or extra lumps of metal where a whole chip had fallen out of the die. The rare 1804 large cent is usually found struck from broken dies.

Bronze: An alloy of copper and tin, etc., usually consisting of 80–95 per cent copper. It is the world's earliest artificial alloy, and, in fact, was manufactured in prehistoric days. The "brass" of the Bible was actually bronze.

Browning Numbers: Specialists in collecting 1796–1838 quarters refer to die varieties and attribute their coins according to listings in *Early Quarter Dollars of the U.S.*, by A. W. Browning.

Bryan Dollars: These satirical tokens and medals were issued privately during William J. Bryan's "free silver" crusade during the period 1896–1900.

Buffalo Type: See *Nickel Five-Cent Piece (U.S.).*

Bullion (M.L. *bulliona,* an ingot, allied to *billon*): Uncoined gold and silver, in the form of bars, ingots, plate, etc.

Bun Penny: Popular name of the Victorian bronze penny, struck 1860–94, so called from the prominent "bun" of hair on the queen's bust. Great numbers were issued, and are still in circulation, but 1869 is a rare date, and scarce issues are those of 1864, 1870, 1871, and 1894.

Bungtown Copper or Bungtowns (derivation uncertain): A crude imitation of the English copper halfpenny; spurious and illegal pieces that circulated in Pennsylvania and other American states in the late eighteenth century.

Bust: The head, including all or part of the collar bone. Almost invariably shown in profile.

Bust Type: See *Dime; Dollar, U.S. Silver; Half Dime; Half Dollar; Quarter Dollar.*

Byzantine Coinage: In 395 the Roman Empire was split between the sons of Theodosius: Honorius ruled the Western Empire at Rome, and Arcadius the Eastern Empire at Constantinople. The Western Empire came to an end overwhelmed by hordes of barbarians, and the last Emperor, Romulus Augustulus, was deposed in 476. The Eastern Empire, however, preserved for nearly a thousand years something of the culture and traditions of the Graeco-Roman civilization. The Byzantine emperors claimed to be the direct successors of the Caesars, and held their empire intact until the fall of Constantinople in 1453. The early coins of Constantinople copied closely the prevailing style of the West, but gradually Greek, Oriental, and Christian influences evolved that peculiarly distinctive form of art we call Byzantine. Greek lettering gradually replaced Latin in the legends of the coins. Under Anastasius (491–518) and Justinianus (527–65) sweeping reforms in the currency carried it far beyond the conventional Roman style and tradition. (See *Bezant, Follis, Nummus.*)

C

Cabinet: This word may refer to the box, drawer, file, case, or other receptacle in which we house our coins, or to an entire *collection* of any size, apart from any such receptacles. A favorite wood for coin cabinets is mahogany; cedar-wood cabinets should be shunned, as the fumes from the oil in this wood discolor base-metal coins, sometimes beyond reparation. (See *Storing Coins*.)

Caesar: Originally a personal name, the cognomen of the Julia family, to which family Julius Caesar belonged. Nero was the last emperor entitled to bear this family name, but, with succeeding emperors, the name became a title equivalent to ruler. In A.D. 136 Hadrian adopted Aelius Verus, and gave him the title of *Caesar*; henceforth it was adopted as the official title of the heir-apparent to the throne. (See *Augustus*.)

Caesars, The Twelve:

Julius Caesar . . .	Dictator 49–44 B.C.
Augustus	29 B.C.–A.D. 14
Tiberius	A.D. 14–37
Caligula	A.D. 37–41
Claudius	A.D. 41–54
Nero	A.D. 54–68
Galba	A.D. 68–69
Otho	A.D. 69
Vitellius	A.D. 69
Vespasian	A.D. 69–79
Titus	A.D. 79–81
Domitian	A.D. 81–96

Only the first six were of the family of Julius.

The coins of the Twelve Caesars, covering practically the whole of the first century A.D., form an interesting series for a collector who may wish to restrict himself to a compact and limited group of Roman types. Coins bearing fine and realistic portraits of all these emperors are readily obtainable.

Calais Mint: Calais was an English possession from the time of Edward III (1247) until the end of the reign of Queen Mary (1558); as such, the ordinary English coins of the realm were struck there by Edward III, Richard II, Henry IV, and Henry VI. They can be distinguished from the English mints by the provenance mark "C" on the gold and the words VILLA CALESIE on the silver. The mint was opened in 1363, but ceased striking coins in the reign of Henry VI. (See also *Anglo-Gallic Coins*.)

California Diamond Jubilee Commemorative Half Dollar: See *Commemorative Coins (U.S.)*, p. 62.

California-Pacific Exposition Commemorative Half Dollar: See *Commemorative Coins (U.S.)*, p. 64.

Canadian Coinage: Under the French regime there was always a shortage of coins, despite some issues of silver, copper and billon (q.v.). The use of "playing-card money" for almost a century helped to relieve the situation. After Canada became a British colony the shortage continued and this led in time to large and extensive issues of private tokens.

Nova Scotia started issuing bronze coinage (cents) in 1817. Other provinces followed suit: Province of Canada in 1858, New Brunswick in 1861, Newfoundland in 1865, and finally the official coinage was extended and standardized when the Dominion of Canada came into existence in 1870. This coinage has always carried the portrait of the reigning British monarch on the obverse. So far five rulers have been featured:

Victoria	1858–1901
Edward VII	1902–10
George V	1911–36
George VI	1937–52
Elizabeth II	1953 to date

Canadian coins have appeared in the following denominations:

large cents	1858–1920
small cents	1920 to date
5 cents silver	1858–1921
5 cents nickel	1922 to date
10 cents silver	1858 to date
20 cents silver	1858
25 cents silver	1870 to date
50 cents silver	1870 to date
silver dollars	1935 to date
gold sovereigns	1908–19
5 dollars gold	1912–14
10 dollars gold	1912–14

Up to 1948 the monarch's title read REX ET IND: IMP ("King and Emperor of India"). In Victoria's time the legend was REGINA ET IND: IMP for "Queen and Empress of India." In 1948 ET IND: IMP disappeared from the coinage as a result of India's change in status.

In Canadian coinage mint marks play a far less important role than they do in U.S. coinage. Canadian coins have been struck at three different mints, but the striking of the same denomination at more than one mint in a single year has been rare. Consequently Canadian coinage lacks the notable disparities in value that one finds in U.S. coinage when coins of the same denomination have been struck in the same year at more than one mint. On the other hand, the quantities in which

Canadian coins were struck in the past were so small that the premium value of many issues has already increased substantially.

Two years of Canadian coinage were struck with special marks after completion of the regular coinage for those years. In 1937, new dies not being available, the mint added a tiny dot under the 1936 date to indicate the later issue of the cent, ten-cent and twenty-five-cent coins. This "dot coinage" produced outstanding rarities in the two lower denominations.

Again in 1948 the mint struck some coins from the 1947 dies, adding a tiny maple leaf after the date to show that 1948 was the real date of the coins.

Beginning with the 1935 commemorative dollar and then continuing with the lesser denominations, the Canadian mint introduced a series of colorful reverses which make Canadian coins among the most attractive that have been struck in modern times.

In addition to individual entries for the denominations, see also *Canadian Tokens; Gold Coins; Mints, Canadian; Mint Marks; Paper Money; Proof.*

Canadian Currency: See *Paper Money.*

Canadian Mints: See *Mints, Canadian.*

Canadian Numismatic Association: Membership dues in this organization are $5 the first year, and $4 annually thereafter. Membership includes a subscription to the *Canadian Numismatic Journal* (a monthly magazine), and access to the Association's library of numismatic works. Prospective applicants for membership can communicate with the General Secretary, Mrs. Louise Graham, 23 Hollywood Avenue, Willowdale, Ontario, Canada.

Canadian Numismatic Journal: See *Canadian Numismatic Association.*

Canadian Tokens: After Canada passed into British control in 1763, almost a century elapsed before an official coinage system was introduced. From 1738 to 1763 the French authorities had brought over quantities of jetons (q.v.) for general use. After 1763 the circulating medium was made up of British money as well as foreign currencies.

Early in the nineteenth century an urgent need for more coinage developed. This took the form of an enormous output of private tokens from a variety of sources—banks, transportation firms, merchants. In 1837 the famous Bouquet Sous appeared and proved very popular because of their French inscriptions. During the aftermath of the Rebellion of that year, the sous were suppressed by the government.

The two great fur-trading organizations, the Hudson's Bay Company and the North West Company, issued tokens that were still in use during the twentieth century. The most valuable of all Canadian tokens were issued in British Columbia in 1862 at the height of the gold rush there. These coins are $10 and $20 pattern gold pieces and in 1960 were valued up to $3500 in some catalogues.

The introduction of official coinage in 1858 did not fully replace tokens for a long time, but the need for the private coinage was greatly reduced.

Cancelled Note: A banknote that has been paid or redeemed, and marked to call attention to this payment. Such cancellation may be in the form of writing or stamping on the note, or of holes of various shapes cut in the note.

Canopy Type: A type of English penny struck by William I. Eight different types are ascribed to William, and the Canopy Type is type III. It is easy to recognize from the shrine-like structure in which the king's head is framed.

Capita aut Navia: The "heads-or-tails?" of Roman coins. *Capita* ("Heads") refers to the double head of Janus seen on the *As* (q.v.), and *Navia* ("ship") refers to the vessel prow seen on the reverse of the *As*. Long after the Roman coins had departed from these early types, however, the phrase was still retained in the popular language to signify a "toss-up."

Carat (Arabic *qirat*, a pod, Gr. *keration*, the seed of the locust tree): Originally a small weight, and still so used by jewelers in weighing diamonds, etc. Applied to gold, it indicates the degree of fineness or purity, pure gold being reckoned as 24 carats. Gold coins are usually precisely .900 fine, approximately 22 carats, which means that they consist of 2/24 alloy. (See *Crown Gold*.)

Carolingian Dynasty (or **Carlovingian**) (L. *Carolus*, Charles): The second dynasty of the Frankish kings, following the *Merovingian Dynasty* (q.v.). The title is derived from Charles Martel, the "Hammer" of the Franks, whose son, Pepin, in 751 deposed the feeble king of the Merovingians and made himself king. Pepin was succeeded by Charlemagne (Charles the Great) in 768. In 800 Charlemagne was crowned Emperor of France, Germany, and Italy by the Pope, thus giving birth to the Holy Roman Empire. For the *Novus Denarius*, introduced by Pepin, which had such enormous influence on the coinage of early medieval Europe, see under *Denier*.

Charlemagne reorganized the coinage of the Empire; in place of the confused number of private mints of the preceding dynasty, the coinage was made a royal prerogative. The dynasty ended in 984 by the accession to the throne of Hugh Capet.

Carolus (L. Charles): (i) French billon coin, first struck by Charles VIII (1483–98). It bore on the reverse a large Gothic X, denoting its value, ten deniers tournois. The value varied, however, and eventually it became merely money of account. It was current in England, being valued at fourpence in the time of Henry VIII.

(ii) An English gold coin of Charles I (see *Broad*).

Cartouche: A oval-shaped panel which contains an *inscription* or decoration.

Cartwheel: The massive copper twopenny-piece of George III, struck in 1797 by Matthew Boulton (q.v.) at the Soho Mint, Birmingham. It weighs exactly two ounces; the corresponding "cartwheel" penny-piece, struck the same year, weighs one ounce. The metal content of these coins was intended to correspond with their actual value. Proofs were issued of a halfpenny and a farthing in the series (weighing one-quarter ounce and one-sixteenth of an ounce respectively), but the coins were

Great Britain: "Cartwheel" twopenny.

never issued as currency. The 1797 penny was the first English copper penny. A magnifying glass will show the word SOHO engraved on the rocks on the reverse. The initial "K" on the bust of the king indicates Küchler, the designer of the coin.

Cash: Chinese coins of copper alloy, with a large hole in the middle so they can be strung on a thread; they are usually strung together in fifties or hundreds or multiples of a hundred. Sometimes they are threaded together in the shape of a sword, presumably as a talisman. For many centuries the cash was the only coin of China. The design was standardized from the time of the Tang Dynasty (seventh century A.D.) up to A.D. 1900. In the field are four characters, the two at the side read "Current Money," and the two at the top and bottom give the name of the Emperor's reign. The name of this coin has no connection with the English word "cash," which is derived from the French *caisse*, a box or treasure chest. The Chinese word is from the Tamil *Kas*, a small Indian coin. The name given to the coin in China is *tsien*.

Certain small copper coins still current in Travancore are also known as *cash*.

Cast Coins: Coins produced by pouring molten metal into a mold, usually of clay, though certain Ancient British coins show traces of having been cast in wooden molds.

The earliest and the commonest method of producing coins was by hammering, but some coins, especially in the Roman series, were always cast. In Roman Britain a common way of making the molds was by pressing an existing hammered coin into the clay. It was a cheap and easy way of producing an abundance of coins, rather crude specimens, but good enough for a semi-barbarous province.

Casting is a cheap and common method of making forgeries. Cast coins may be distinguished from struck coins by the blunt and blurry edges of the design; this is especially noticeable in the lettering. In the angles of the lettering, and on the whole surface of the field, little pit-marks of the sand used in the casting can nearly always be discerned.

Cattle Used as Money: The *Iliad* of Homer reflects the civilization of the Late Mycenaean period, long before the invention of coins. In those days barter was the only method of commercial transactions, and for this purpose the standard of value agreed upon was the value of an ox. In Homer we find female slaves valued at four to twenty oxen, and a tripod, the prize for wrestling, valued at twelve oxen (*duodekaboios*— worth twelve oxen). It is, however, a debatable point whether actual beeves were exchanged for goods, or whether lumps of metal stamped with animal figures were used for the purpose. Ingots of bronze have been found in Greece in the shape of an oxhide, which seems to have been used there as currency in primitive times, and the *aes signatum* of the Romans sometimes bore the figure of an ox. It is significant that our English word "pecuniary" is from the Latin word for cattle (*pecus*), and the word "fee" is from a Teutonic root with a similar meaning. The word "chattels" ("goods and chattels") retains in curious fashion this bovine derivation.

Cent, Centime, Centimo, Centavo (L. *centisimus*, a hundredth part): In countries where the decimal system of currency has been adopted this is a small coin, usually of copper or nickel. It represents the hundredth part of a unit such as the *dollar* (U.S.A., Canada), *franc* (France, Belgium, Switzerland), *peso* (Spain, South America), *lira* (Italy).

Cent (Canadian): Large cents were issued during 1858–1920; small cents have been issued from 1920 to date. The obverses and years of issue of this bronze coin are as follows:

Large cents	Victoria	1858–1901
	Edward VII	1902–10
	George V	1911–20
Small cents	George V	1920–36
	George VI	1937–52
	Elizabeth II	1953–

On all the large cents the reverse design is made up of the value and date enclosed in a wreath. The H mint mark appears on some dates. On the 1876, 1881, 1882, 1890 and 1907 issues it appears under the date on the reverse. On the 1898 and 1900 issues it can be found above the bottom rim on the reverse. The outstanding rarity of this series is the 1891 small-date variety. The 1907 H is also quite a scarce issue. The first coin of the George V series (1911) is interesting because the words DEI GRATIA ("by the grace of God") were omitted, probably to avoid overcrowding in the obverse legend. After this "Graceless" or "God-less" issue the phrase was restored.

When the small cents were introduced in 1920 a simpler and more artistic design was adopted for the reverse, providing a small maple leaf at each side of the value.

The death of George V in 1936 necessitated the preparation of new dies with an obverse portraying George VI. The new dies were not ready at the beginning of 1937. The mint therefore decided to issue 1936 cents for the time being. In order to show the later origin of these coins, the mint placed a small dot under the "1936" of the old dies. According to the official records some 680,000 of these standby coins were issued. Yet only 8 specimens of this dot coinage have been discovered to date, making them extremely valuable. The best explanation of what happened is that the old dies must have been worn and that this resulted in the dot getting filled up.

Beginning with the 1937 cents of George VI the reverse underwent another transformation, the main item of the design being a large maple leaf. This was retained on all subsequent cents.

Cent (U.S.): This copper coin, authorized by the Mint Act of 1792, has been issued from 1793 to date. Large cents were struck through 1857, after which a smaller size was adopted with far more satisfactory results.

Large Cents. This denomination has more types, varieties and die breaks than any other American coin issued for a comparable period.

CENT

The types are as follows:

Chain	1793
Wreath	1793
Liberty Cap	1793–96
Draped Bust	1796–1807
Turban Head	1808–14
Coronet	1816–39
Braided Hair	1839–57

The large cents suffered from much of the unpopularity that the half cents encountered. The early specification for the weight of the cent had to be scaled down, as the price of copper made the original weight prohibitive.

The Chain (or Link) cent got its name from the circular chain of links enclosing the value on the obverse. A bust of Liberty with free-flowing hair and facing right appeared on the obverse. The combination of these motifs came in for harsh criticism for, as a letter in the Boston *Argus* pointed out, "the American Cents do not answer our expectations. The chain on the reverse is but a bad omen for Liberty, and Liberty herself appears to be in a fright."

The reverse design was changed to a wreath (Wreath type). The planchets for these were heavy enough for a thick edge; in some cases lettering appeared on the edge, for example ONE HUNDRED FOR A DOLLAR. On other varieties vines and bars appeared on the edge. There are two strawberry leaf varieties for 1793 which are the outstanding rarities in the whole coinage of cents.

The Wreath type was soon replaced by the Liberty Cap type. The bust of Liberty (facing right) on the new coins is believed to have been derived from originals inspired by the French Revolution. At the beginning of 1796 the weight of the cent was reduced. This resulted in a thinner coin, so that the lettering on the edge was dropped and replaced by a plain edge as on the modern cent.

The 1794 cents alone appeared in almost 60 varieties due to the lack of a master die or hub. One great cause of confusion was that the mint had no reliable source of copper. Some of it came from scrap, some from melted-down tokens, copper nails, copper imports and various private firms.

In 1796 the Draped Bust (Liberty facing right) appeared and continued to be struck through 1807. Some of the 1801 coins have three errors (see *Three-Error Large Cent*). On some of the reverses of this period the wreath lacks a stem—see *Stemless Wreath*. A clumsy forgery of the 1804 cent was made by mint employees about 55 years later. The deception is easily recognized, as the obverse die was in very bad condition, while an 1818 reverse die was used instead of the noticeably different 1804 reverse.

The Turban Head type (Liberty facing left) was struck 1808–14. No cents were issued in 1815 because of a copper shortage resulting from the War of 1812. The Coronet type (Liberty facing left) first appeared in 1816 and was struck through 1839. A fire at the mint in

U.S.A., large cent, Turban Head type.

1816 led to the introduction of more efficient machinery and the adoption of improved methods. The 1839 issue includes the "Booby Head" and "Silly Head" varieties.

The last type to be used on the large cents, the Braided Hair (Liberty facing left) was struck from 1839 through 1857, the last year of this coinage. During this period the large cent fell on evil days. Not being legal tender, it could be refused by storekeepers, and often was. Private firms that supplied copper to the mint also acted as distributors of the coins. When demand for the large cents weakened, the distributors would get rid of their stock of coins at a slight discount. This made the large cents more undesirable than ever.

To add to the confusion, the price of copper rose to a point in 1851–53 where the coinage of the large cents actually cost the government more than the face value of the coins. For all these reasons Congress stopped the coinage of large cents in 1857, substituting a much smaller, lighter and cheaper copper-nickel alloy. See *Controller Coins*.

Small Cents. These come in three types, as follows:

Flying Eagle	1856–58
Indian Head	1859–1909
Lincoln Head	1909–

The Flying Eagle cent was designed by J. B. Longacre, the engraver at the mint. The beautiful obverse (eagle in flight) was adapted from the reverse of the Gobrecht dollars. On the reverse the value is encircled by a wreath of corn, wheat, cotton and tobacco. Longacre borrowed this wreath from the reverse he had designed for the three-dollar gold piece. Since the issue of this coin was authorized by the Act of February 21, 1857, the 1856 Flying Eagle cents are sometimes placed in the category of patterns. It is impossible to know exactly how many were issued, but it seems that about 500 were struck in 1856, with perhaps a like number restruck in later years with the 1856 date. This is the most valuable coin in the whole small-cent series. It is said that a hoard of several hundred of these coins is in existence; in any event, if the coins really exist they have never been made available to collectors.

The 1858 Flying Eagle cents come in two varieties involving the obverse legend UNITED STATES OF AMERICA. In the "small-letter" variety the A and the M are detached; in the "large-letter" they are joined.

The small cents were struck in an alloy made up of 88 per cent copper and 12 per cent nickel. The rather large proportion of nickel had two consequences. It gave the coins a whitish appearance that was hard to imitate. What was even more forbidding to counterfeiters was the high cost of nickel, which brought the intrinsic cost of the metal in a coin to 4/5 of a cent. The high cost was due to primitive mining methods.

U.S.A., small cents.
Left: Flying Eagle type.
Right: Indian Head type.

The last year of the Flying Eagle design was 1858. Longacre then designed the Indian Head obverse, which was first issued in 1859. According to a legend now largely discredited, Longacre's little daughter was the model for the Indian head. The idea of putting an Indian war bonnet on a girl is incongruous; but if some modern authorities are right, Longacre did something even more incongruous: he put a feathered headdress on a Greco-Roman Venus and called the result "symbolic of America." The heads for the gold dollar and the three-dollar gold piece are said to have come from the same source.

The Indian Head Cent also had a new reverse, a laurel wreath being substituted for the wreath on the Flying Eagle reverse. Beginning with the 1860 issue the laurel wreath was replaced by an oak wreath and a small shield was added at the top of the reverse. Weight and composition remained the same.

For a number of reasons nickel soon proved unsatisfactory. There was excessive die breakage on the nickel planchets. With the coming of the Civil War the government was cut off from foreign nickel supplies, so that it became increasingly difficult to maintain the coinage of the cupro-nickel cent. Worse yet, the official cent had to compete with several hundred varieties of privately issued bronze tokens.

The passage of the Act of April 22, 1864 solved these difficulties. The government adopted an alloy similar to that of the tokens—95 parts copper to 5 parts tin and zinc. This bronze composition is still in use, having been suspended for several years during World War II. The new bronze coin—reduced to 48 grains—received the same ready acceptance that had been accorded to the unofficial tokens. The circulation of the bronze cent was facilitated by a provision in the Mint Act of 1864 which stipulated that the coin was to be accepted as legal tender.

Late in 1864 a further change was made in the obverse of the new Indian Head cent. The designer's initial "L" was placed on the bonnet ribbon. As 1864 coins with the initial are scarce, this type is also quite valuable. After 1864 the initial appears as a regular feature of subsequent issues. See *Controller Coins*.

The most valuable of these later issues is the one of 1877, which was struck in an abnormally small quantity. Only two dates of the Indian Head cent carry a mint mark—those of 1908 and 1909, struck at San Francisco. The mint mark appears at the bottom of the reverse under the wreath.

The Lincoln Head cent has been struck from 1909 to date. The 1909 and 1910 issues were issued at Philadelphia and San Francisco. Beginning with the 1911 issue these cents were also struck at the Denver mint. The mint mark appears on the obverse under the date. The Lincoln Head coin was the first cent to carry the motto IN GOD WE TRUST. It appears around the upper curve of the obverse. The motto E PLURIBUS UNUM appears on the reverse.

On the early 1909 and 1909 S cents the initials of the designer, Victor D. Brenner, appeared at the bottom of the reverse. The initials were removed from the subsequent coins of that year, but, as San Francisco had produced a relatively small number of coins, the VDB 1909 S cents became one of the most eagerly sought rarities in American coinage. Actually in the better conditions this coin is much less valuable than the 1914 D cent, of which only about a million were struck (upwards of 75,000,000 cents were struck that year at Philadelphia). The designer's initials were restored to the Lincoln Head cent in 1918, appearing from then on at the left bottom of the obverse. Knowledge of this helps a collector to detect the altering of the 1944 D date to 1914 D (see *Altered Dates*).

In 1943 the wartime shortage of copper necessitated a change in composition to steel with a thin zinc coating. These cents were very unpopular, possibly because people confused them with dimes. In 1944–45 the government salvaged enough copper from discarded shell cases to mint cents with a composition of 70 parts copper to 30 parts zinc. Because of the large proportion of zinc these coins were a bit lighter in color than the familiar cents of previous years, but they were quite satisfactory. In 1946 the mint returned to the prewar composition. Beginning with the 1959 issue the reverse was redesigned, with the Lincoln Memorial replacing the wreath and the description inside it. See *Controller Coins*.

Cententionalis (L. *centum*, one hundred): Late Roman "third brass" coin, the hundredth part of the *solidus*. Introduced by Diocletian as a silver coin, it soon became brass with a thin washing of silver.

Chain Type: See *Cent (U.S.)*.

Chaise (Fr. chair): A French gold coin, first struck in the thirteenth century; so called from the large and ornate throne on the obverse whereon the king is seated. It is also the name given to an Anglo-Gallic coin copied from this and struck by Edward III.

Channel Islands: Although since the time of William the Conqueror the Channel Islands have been British territory, French coins were current there until 1830, especially the *double tournois*. In that year a one double and a four double piece were struck in England for Guernsey, bearing the arms and name of that island. In 1834 an eight double piece was struck, and a two double piece in 1858. In 1864–68 all four denominations were struck in smaller sizes in bronze in place of copper. The coinage has been revived recently, with the addition (1956) of a cupro-nickel threepenny piece with scalloped edge showing the famous Guernsey cow.

In Jersey, where the English shilling was valued at thirteen pence, coins were struck in 1841 for $\frac{1}{52}$, $\frac{1}{26}$, and $\frac{1}{13}$ of a shilling (Obv/head of Queen Victoria, Rev/the arms of the States of Jersey). These represented the farthing, halfpenny, and penny, respectively, and equated the currency to the French system, in which twenty-six sous were valued at one shilling. These copper coins were replaced by bronze in 1866.

Charon's Fee: Charon was the aged ferryman of the Greeks who ferried the souls of the dead across the River Styx to Hades. As his fee it was customary in the fifth and fourth centuries B.C. to place a small coin, such as an obolus, in the mouth of the dead. The custom never quite died out, and in comparatively recent times coins have been known to have been placed in tombs in Greece and even in Britain. The custom was also popular with the Romans. When the body of Canute was discovered in Winchester Cathedral in 1766 the hand was found to be clasping a silver penny.

Châtel Tournois (O. Fr. the Chateau of Tours): A conventional and highly stylized representation of an ecclesiastical building, supposed to have represented originally the Abbey of Tours. A common type of the later Roman coins was that of a temple on the reverse. The Carlovingian deniers of the ninth century copied this type, but the temple is on the obverse; moreover, the temple has become a Christian building; this is symbolized by a large cross within the building, and the legend XPISTIANA RELIGIO (the Christian religion).

The *gros tournois*, introduced by Louis IX (1226–70), shows also this *châtel tournois*, but so changed that it can hardly be recognized as the representation of a building. The classical pediment has become a Gothic steeple, and two turrets are plainly discernible on the flanks; but beyond this it is merely a decorative symbol.

Check Numbers: On English coins, a minute figure by which the die from which any individual coin was struck can be traced. It was first placed on gold and silver coins in 1864.

China: See *Cash, Knife Money, Spade Money*.

Chi-Rho Monogram: A monogram formed thus: ☧, consisting of the two Greek initial letters of *Christos*. It figures on coins struck by the successors of Constantine (see *Labarum*), and is usually placed between A (alpha) and Ω (omega), the first and last letters of the Greek alphabet. Also known as a Christogram. (See *Alpha and Omega*.)

Chisel Cuts: Small nicks are often found in the edges of ancient coins, e.g., on Roman denarii and ancient Greek staters. They were probably made by merchants and money-changers to discourage counterfeiting (q.v.).

Chop-marks (Hind. *chhap*, an official mark on weights and measures; a customs-house stamp or seal showing duty paid): Up to recent times, the native merchants of Hong Kong and other south China ports impressed their private marks on all the dollars that passed through their hands, as a guarantee of genuineness. Such marks are known as "chop-marks" and a coin so marked is called a "chopped" coin. An unchopped dollar is known as a "clean" dollar. Trade dollars (q.v.) are often found with "chop-marks."

Christian Types on Roman Coins: In the time of Constantine, when Christianity became the official religion of the Roman Empire, little innovation was made in the coins to indicate the recognition of the new faith. In fact, the old pagan types were repeated. Occasionally, however, we find the *Chi-Rho Monogram* appearing, very small and insignificant, on the helmet of Constantine; sometimes small crosses appear in the field of the coin, or a letter X in the legend is exaggerated in size to indicate a surreptitious Christian cross. Coins of later emperors show us the emperor bearing the *labarum* in place of the legionary eagles, and on coins of Magnentius (A.D. 350–53) the sacred monogram fills the whole of the reverse.

Roman Empire: Coin of Magnentius (350–53) with sacred monogram on reverse.

Chuckram (Hind. *chackram*): A very small silver coin, current in Southern India from the eighteenth century. It is still current in Travancore, being the equivalent of 16 *cash*. Four chuckrams are equal to one fanam.

Cincinnati Musical Center Commemorative Half Dollar: See *Commemorative Coins* (*U.S.*), p. 65.

Cistophorus (Gr. name of coin, lit. *chest-bearer*): A Greek silver coin, worth three or four drachmas, first issued by the kings of Pergamum in the second century B.C. Under the Roman domination of Asia Minor it

Pergamum, silver stater with cistophorus (*c.* 190 B.C.).

became the principal coin of Western Asia Minor and was struck at various mints. So called from the *cista mystica*, intertwined with serpents, that was represented on it. This was a chest, or rather basket, used in the Dionysiac and other mysteries. The serpent seems to allude to the worship of Asklepius, the god of healing. There was an important temple of this god at Pergamum. The Romans continued to strike the cistophorus as a coin equal in value to three denarii.

Civil War Tokens: During the early years of the Civil War the Indian Head cent had a premium value because of the high price of copper. Thus there was a tendency for the coins to disappear as soon as they came into circulation. To make up for the deficiency in the supply of cents, private organizations issued tokens known as "Copperheads."

The tokens were the same size as the government cent, and often used an Indian Head obverse which made the resemblance even more striking. The coins were made of copper alloyed with brass, nickel, copper-nickel, white metal, lead, zinc, tin, German silver or silver.

U.S.A., Civil War token.

There were two predominant types, the "storecard" and the patriotic token. The first carried the name and address of the issuing store and an advertising message on the reverse. Since the metal content had some intrinsic value, all tokens were accepted readily. In some cases the advertising slogan was dropped in favor of the portrait of a famous American or a patriotic motto—sometimes given a cynical twist. For example, an Indian Head token had a reverse with the inscription NOT ONE CENT—to which the designer had added: FOR THE WIDOW.

Some 8000 varieties of storecard tokens have been identified as originating in 400 cities and towns spread over 23 states. In 1864 the issue of the new-composition government cents, aided by a new legal-tender provision, led to the disappearance of the tokens from circulation. See the discussion of Indian Head cents under *Cent (U.S.)*.

Classification of Coins: The classification of modern coins is a simple matter; they fall naturally into their respective nationalities, and can be grouped chronologically under the successive rulers whose effigies they usually bear. With the coins of the ancient world, however, many complications arise; the same type was often struck in different parts of the world, and it is often impossible to assign an exact date to them.

Greek coins have been grouped by the British Museum authorities into certain fairly well-defined periods of art, as follows:

I. *Circa* 700–480 B.C. Period of *Archaic Art*, ending with the Persian Wars.

II. *Circa* 480–400 B.C. Period of *Transitional and Early Fine Art*, to the end of the Athenian supremacy.

III. *Circa* 400–336 B.C. Period of *Finest Art*. Age of the Spartan and Theban supremacies.

IV. *Circa* 336–280 B.C. Period of *Later Fine Art*. Age of Alexander and the Diadochi.

V. *Circa* 280–190 B.C. Period of the *Decline of Art*. Age of the Epigoni.

VI. *Circa* 190–100 B.C. Period of *Continued Decline of Art*. Age of the Attalids.

VII. *Circa* 100–1 B.C. Period of *Late Decline of Art*. Age of Mithridates the Great and of Roman dominion.

But there remains the problem of a geographical classification. In the Greek world almost every city and state issued its individual coins, so we have to deal with coins from most parts of Europe, Asia, and North Africa. The usual geographical classification adopted is that of Eckhel, as set out in his great work on ancient coins *Doctrina numorum veterum* (eight volumes, published 1798). The starting point of this classification is at the west, that is Spain; we pass through Gaul to Britain, then down to Italy and Sicily; from here we go to the northern parts of Greece— Macedon and Thrace—and work southwards to Athens. With the Aegean Islands, Europe is left behind, and we pass to the eastern parts of Asia. Still going east, we work our way through the whole of Asia, ending up at India. In Africa we start with Egypt, this time working from west to east; we end up with Mauretania, immediately opposite the point where we started.

Roman coins fall naturally into main groups—the Republican series and those struck under the Empire. The dating of the various denarii of the Republic is an intricate problem; the uninitiated collector will therefore find the simplest way to classify these coins is alphabetically by the various names of the families whose types and legends they bear.

Cleaning Coins: Where a copper coin has a fine *patina* (q.v.) or a silver coin is richly "toned," it is best left alone. A badly corroded coin, however, can be improved by brushing with sawdust soaked in diluted sulphuric or citric acid. Ammonia will remove green oxide.

Because of the stress laid on superb condition, collectors are often tempted to apply some cleaning agent to coins in inferior condition.

Copper or bronze coins, for example, are affected by oxygen in the atmosphere. This causes them to take on a patina—they turn green or black or blue, or brown or red, or some combination of these colors. The color of the patina is determined by the amount of moisture present and the chemical composition of the local soil. These processes explain the appearance of ancient copper and bronze coins. (See *Patina*.)

No silver coins—not even the most brilliant proofs—can hold out against tarnish. Some woods aid the tarnish process; a collector must be careful to avoid them if he plans to store his coins in a wooden cabinet.

There are various tarnish-removers and coin-cleaners on the market, but they should never be used without the advice of an expert. Even then it is wise to test them on a coin of no great value.

Also available are lacquer preparations that protect silver coins against tarnish. The problem this involves is that possible buyers of a collection may not care for the lacquered appearance.

Cleveland Great Lakes Exposition Commemorative Half Dollar: See *Commemorative Coins (U.S.)*, p. 65.

Clipping: The old hammered coins, before the process of reeding (q.v.) was introduced, were often sheared round the edges by unscrupulous persons. Pots have sometimes been unearthed in which quantities of the shavings from coins have been stored, proving that, despite sundry laws, decrees, and fulminations of authorities,* a brisk traffic went on in this nefarious form of gain. In 1247, to prevent this abuse, the short cross on the reverse of the penny was extended to the edge of the coin (see *Long-cross Penny*). This did not stop clipping, however.

Cob Money (Span. *Cabo de barra*, "cut from a bar"): Crude silver coins issued in the Spanish colonies of the New World. These were made by slicing off parts of crude silver bars, which resulted in highly irregular borders. The pieces of metal were then struck from rough dies. The design was ugly, the coins often undated.

The first cob money is thought to have been issued about 1580 (in the reign of Philip II of Spain) or about 1600 (in the reign of Philip III). Specialists enjoy collecting "cobs" because they are the only ones adept at determining the date at which an individual coin was issued, or at least assigning it to a fairly definite period.

Coin (O. Fr. *coin*, a coin die, from L. *cuneus*, a wedge, the early Medieval coin dies being built up from wedges): Piece of metal impressed with an official mark guaranteeing its just weight and fineness and value.

Coin World: A weekly newspaper published by the Sidney Printing & Publishing Co., P.O. Box 150, Sidney, Ohio. Annual subscription $3.

Coinage: (*a*) The process of making coins.

(*b*) A collective term for coins. The term, of course, does not include paper currency, or privately issued tokens.

Coining Press: Any form of *machine* used for producing coins by striking or pressure; it thus includes the *Screw Press* (q.v.), as well as the highly intricate machinery of the modern mint.

---

* By statute of Henry V, clipping, washing, and filing money of the land was held to be treason, the penalty for which was death. This statute was reaffirmed in the time of Elizabeth I. See *Mottoes on Coins* (Cromwell).

Coining, Process of : The process of coining the old "hammered" coins was to melt the metal in crucibles, pour it on a slab to cool, then, when the metal had been beaten into a thin sheet on an anvil, it was cut up with shears into blanks of the requisite sizes and weights. These blanks were then held between the dies and the impression of the obverse and reverse were driven simultaneously into the coin with a few blows of the hammer. (See *Die, Pile, Trussel.*)

Colonial and Pre-Mint Coinage: In the early days of New England, trade was carried on by barter or by the use of wampum. In 1652 the first coinage appeared; it was made up of the "N.E." shilling, sixpence and threepence. (See *New England Money.*) The silver for these coins was obtained from the West Indies, and John Hull, the mint-master at Boston, received the generous pay of one shilling sixpence for every 20 shillings struck by him. These exceedingly crude pieces were easily counterfeited or clipped; they were therefore replaced by the oak tree, willow tree and pine tree coinages (see *Tree Money*).

The Good Samaritan Shilling, struck at Boston in 1652, was apparently a pattern as it never entered general circulation. This is a very valuable coin.

For the early coinage of the Maryland colony, see *Lord Baltimore Coins.*

In New Jersey the coins brought to the colony from Dublin in 1681 (see *Saint Patrick's Money*) received general acceptance. They came in denominations of a halfpence, farthing (copper) and a silver farthing. On both sides there are rather artistically executed designs depicting incidents in the life of the popular saint.

Another popular series was the group of coins struck by William Wood—see *Rosa Americana.* These appeared in the colonies in the period 1722–24. Somewhat earlier the "elephant" coinage (see *Elephant Coin*) had made its appearance in New England and Carolina.

With the coming of the Revolution, Congress authorized the issue of the Continental Dollar, which appeared in 1776. According to some authorities it was struck at Philadelphia, while others believe it originated in London! The obverse has the legend FUGIO ("I fly") and the inscription MIND YOUR BUSINESS (in the sense of "tend your business diligently"). The reverse shows a chain of 13 links; inside this there is the inscription WE ARE ONE. This coin was struck in silver, pewter and brass. In some cases the obverse inscription CONTINENTAL CURRENCY appears as CONTINENTAL CURENCY. A great rarity, quoted at over $3000, is the variety with the legend E.G. FECIT ("E.G. made it").

During the war and after, a good deal of coinage, both official and

Continental Dollar (1776).

private, appeared in a number of states—Connecticut, Massachusetts, New Hampshire, Vermont, New York, New Jersey. (Strictly speaking, Vermont should not be included in this state coinage, as it was not one of the original 13 colonies and remained an independent republic until 1791, when it joined the Union). Some of the motifs that were to appear frequently on the official U.S. coinage may be seen on these coins. These include the eagle and the American shield.

Beginning with 1783—the year when the Revolutionary War was formally concluded—a number of pattern pieces for a new coinage system made their appearance. Among these were the Nova Constellatio coins, the Immune Columbia cents, the Confederatio cents and the doubloon and half doubloon struck by Ephraim Brasher. The Brasher coins are extremely valuable, and a well-known detective story by Raymond Chandler centers about the fictional theft of one of these rare coins.

The undated Bar Cent, probably issued during the 1780's, gets its name from the reverse which is made up of 13 horizontal bars representing the original 13 states. Another contemporary series was devoted to the Washington coins and tokens struck from 1783 to 1795. All of these had portraits of George Washington on the obverse, and many of them are believed to have been struck in England. Finally the Fugio cents appeared in 1787 (see *Fugio Cent*) in several varieties. The legends and most of the design on this famous coin are taken from the Continental Dollar described above.

Columbia, S.C. Sesquicentennial Commemorative Half Dollar: See *Commemorative Coins (U.S.)*, p. 66.

Columbian Exposition Commemorative Half Dollar: See *Commemorative Coins (U.S.)*, p. 59.

COMMEMORATIVE

Commemorative Coins (Foreign): Following is a list of some outstanding commemorative issues, arranged by country of issue.*

Australia

1927 florin (opening of Parliament at Canberra). Crowned bust of George V/Buildings.

1927 florin (centenary of Victoria and Melbourne). Crowned bust of George V/Rider on horseback.

1951 florin (50-year jubilee of the Commonwealth). Bust of George VI/Crowned crossed swords.

1954 florin (royal visit). Bust of Elizabeth II/Kangaroo.

Australia, silver florin commemorating 50-year jubilee of the Commonwealth (1951).

Austria

1626 double taler (marriage of Archduke Leopold). Conjoined busts of Leopold and Claudia de' Medici/Eagle.

1854 double taler (marriage of Franz Joseph). Conjoined busts of Franz Joseph and Elizabeth/Marriage scene.

1857 double taler (opening of South Austrian railways). Laureated head/Lighthouse, engine, boat and shields.

1879 2 florins (silver wedding anniversary). Accolated heads of Franz Joseph and Elizabeth/Seated female figure.

1887 2 florins (reopening of Kuttenberg mines). Laureated head of Franz Joseph/Cathedral.

1908 5 corona (60th year of reign). Bust of Franz Joseph/Running figure of Fame.

1928 2 schillings. Value within circle of 11 shields/Bust of Schubert.

1929 2 schillings. Rev. Bust of Dr. Billroth.

1930 2 schillings. Rev. Seated figure of Walther von der Vogelweide.

1931 2 schillings. Rev. Bust of Mozart.

1932 2 schillings. Rev. Bust of Haydn.

1933 2 schillings. Rev. of Dr. Seipel.

1935 2 schillings. Rev. of Dr. Lueger.

1934 2 schillings. Arms with double-headed eagle/Bust of Doctor Dollfuss.

---

* For illustrations of many of these coins see Reinfeld: *A Catalogue of the World's Most Popular Coins*, Sterling Publishing Company.

1936 2 schillings. Rev. Bust of Prince Eugene of Savoy.

1937 2 schillings. Rev. Karlskirche in Vienna.

1955 25 schillings (reopening of Bundestheater). Muse with mask, two girls drawing curtains/Value in circle of 9 shields.

1956 25 schillings (bicentennial of Mozart's birth). Statue of Mozart/Value in circle of 9 shields.

1959 50 schillings (sesquicentennial of Hofer's revolt against Napoleonic rule). Facing bust of Andreas Hofer/Eagle within circle of 8 shields.

1959 25 schillings (centenary of death of Archduke Johann). Bust of Archduke Johann/Lion of Styria within circle of 8 shields.

Belgium

1930 10 francs (centenary of the kingdom). Conjoined busts of three rulers of modern Belgium/Value.

1935 50 francs (railroad centenary). St. Michael and the Dragon/Exhibition hall.

1939–40 50 francs. Bust of Leopold III/Shields of 9 provinces.

1948–51 100 francs (dedicated to the Belgian dynasty). Conjoined busts of the four kings/Crowned arms.

1958 50 francs (Brussels Fair). Bust of Badouin I/Cathedral.

Belgium, 100 franc piece commemorating the Belgian dynasty (1948).

Bermuda

1959 crown (350th anniversary of Bermuda's founding as a British colony). Bust of Elizabeth II/Sloop and dinghy.

Brazil

1900 400 reis (fourth centennial of discovery). Cross/Value.

1900 1000 reis. Liberty head, plow/Value.

1900 2000 reis. Ship/Value.

1900 4000 reis. Cabral with banner/Shields and value.

1932 100 reis (fourth centennial of colonization). Bust of Cazique Tiberica.

1932 200 reis. Globe/Ship.

1932 400 reis. Map of South America.

COMMEMORATIVE

Brazil (*continued*)

1932 500 reis. Bust of Ramalho.

1932 1 milreis. Da Sousa.

1932 2 milreis. Bust of John III of Portugal.

Canada

1939 dollar (royal visit). Bust of George VI/Parliament buildings in Ottawa.

1949 dollar (Newfoundland commemorative). Bust of George VI/ Sailing vessel.

1951 5 cents (12-sided coin for bicentennial of nickel industry). Bust of George VI/Refining plant.

1958 dollar (British Columbia centennial). Totem pole/Arms.

1958 Silver Dollar commemorating British Columbia's centenary as a crown colony.

Ceylon

1957 rupee (2500 years of Buddhism). Buddhist wheel and other symbols/Inscription.

1957 5 rupees (2500 years of Buddhism). Animals in circular pattern / Inscription.

Colombia

1956 peso (bicentennial of Mint). Building/Semicircular wreath.

Cuba

1952 10, 20, 40 centavos (fiftieth anniversary of the republic). Morro Castle/Star, tree and wheel.

1953 1 peso (Marti centenary). Bust of Marti/Rising sun.

1953 50 centavos. Rev. Scroll with inscription.

1953 25 centavos. Rev. Liberty Cap.

1953 1 centavo. Rev. Star in triangle.

Czechoslovakia

1923 2 ducats (fifth anniversary of the republic). Lion on shield/St. Wenceslaus.

1928 10 koruny (tenth anniversary of the republic). Bust of Pres. Masaryk/Arms.

1937 20 koruny (death of Masaryk). Bust of Masaryk/Arms.

1948 100 koruny (600th anniversary of Charles University in Prague). Lion/Kneeling figure and standing figure.

1948 50 koruny (third anniversary of liberation from the Germans). Lion/Standing figure.

1948 100 koruny (thirtieth anniversary of the republic). Rev. Figure with wreath.

1949 100 koruny (700th anniversary of granting of mining privileges of Jihlava). Lion/Miner.

1949 100 koruny (Stalin's 70th birthday). Bust of Stalin/Arms.

1951 100 koruny (thirtieth anniversary of Communist Party). Bust of Gottwald/Arms.

1954 25 koruny (tenth anniversary of Slovak uprising). Arms within scalloped shield/Armed worker.

Denmark

1848 speciedaler (accession of Frederick VII to the throne). Bust of Frederick VII/Bust of Christian VIII.

1863 2 rigsdaler (accession of Christian IX to the throne). Bust of Christian IX/Bust of Frederick VII.

1888 2 kroner (twenty-fifth year of reign). Bust of Christian IX/ Motto in wreath.

1892 2 kroner (golden wedding of Christian IX). Accolated heads of king and queen/Date in wreath.

1903 2 kroner (fortieth year of reign). Bust of Christian IX/Seated figure.

1906 2 kroner (coronation of Frederick VIII). Bust of Frederick VIII/ Bust of Christian IX.

1912 2 kroner (coronation of Christian X). Bust of Christian X/Bust of Frederick VIII.

1923 2 kroner (silver wedding of Christian X). Accolated heads of king and queen/Crowned arms.

1930 2 kroner (sixtieth birthday of Christian X). Bust of Christian X/ Crowned arms.

1937 2 kroner (twenty-fifth year of rule). Bust of Christian X/ Crowned arms.

1945 2 kroner (seventy-fifth birthday). Bust of Christian X / Dates in wreath.

COMMEMORATIVE

Egypt

1956 50 piastres (British evacuation of Eygpt). Allegorical figure breaking chains and holding Liberty torch/Winged sun with two serpents on either side.

Estonia

1932 2 krooni (tercentenary of University of Tartu). Facade of university/Arms in wreath.

Finland

1951–52 500 markkaa (Olympic games). Chain links/Value in wreath.

German States

Baden

1836 kronen taler (customs union of the German states). Bust of Duke Leopold/Inscription in a circle of shields of ten German states.

Bavaria

1871 taler (victorious conclusion of Franco-Prussian War). Bust of Ludwig II/Seated female.

Bremen

1863 taler (50th anniversary of War of Liberation). Inscription/Crowned and supported arms.

1864 taler (opening of the new Bremen Bourse). Inscription in wreath/Building.

1871 taler (victory in Franco-Prussian War). Inscription/Crowned and supported arms.

Prussia

1861 taler (coronation issue). Accolated crowned busts/Crowned monograms.

1866 taler (victory in the Austro-Prussian War). Laureated head of Wilhelm I/Eagle.

1871 taler (victory in the Franco-Prussian War). Rev. Seated female figure.

1901 5 marks (bicentennial of the kingdom). Bust of Wilhelm II/Bust of Frederick I.

1910 3 marks (centennial of University of Berlin). Accolated busts of Frederick William III and Wilhelm II/Eagle.

1911 3 marks (centennial of the University of Breslau). Obv. Accolated busts of Frederick William III and Wilhelm II/Eagle.

1913 3 marks (centennial of the War of Liberation). King on horseback/Eagle on snake.

1915 3 marks (centennial of uniting Mansfeld with Prussia). Rev. St. George and dragon.

Saxe-Weimar

1908 5 marks (350th anniversary of the University of Jena). Obv. Facing bust of Duke Johann Friedrich.

1915 3 marks (centennial of the grand duchy). Accolated busts of Dukes Wilhelm Ernst and Carl August.

Saxony

1871 taler (victorious conclusion of the Franco-Prussian War). Bust of Duke Johann/Victory on horseback.

1909 5 marks (500th anniversary of the University of Leipzig). Obv. Accolated busts of Duke Friedrich the Pugnacious and Duke Friedrich August III.

1913 3 marks (dedication of the National Battle Monument at Leipzig). Obv. View of the monument.

Wurtemburg

1871 taler (victorious conclusion of Franco-Prussian War). Duke Karl/Angel standing on cannon and flags.

German Republic

1925 3, 5 marks (1000th year of the Rhineland). Knight in armor with shield/Value in wreath.

1926 3 marks (700th year of Lubeck as a free city). Arms/Value.

1927 3, 5 marks (centennial of Bremerhaven). Sailing ship/Eagle on shield.

1927 3, 5 marks. (450th anniversary of the University of Tuebingen). Bust of Eberhard/Eagle with outspread wings.

1927 3 marks (1000th anniversary of founding of Nordhausen). Two seated crowned figures facing each other/Value.

Germany, 3 marks commemorating 1000th anniversary of the founding of Nordhausen (1927).

1927 3 marks (400th anniversary of the University of Marburg). Arms/Eagle with outspread wings.

1928 3 marks (400th anniversary of Albrecht Durer). Bust of Durer/Eagle.

1928 3 marks (900th anniversary of founding of Naumburg). Man with shield/Eagle.

COMMEMORATIVE

German Republic (continued)

1929 3, 5 marks (bicentennial of birth of Lessing). Bust of Lessing/ Eagle.

1929 3, 5 marks (1000th anniversary of founding of Meissen). Man with two shields/Eagle.

1929 3, 5 marks (tenth anniversary of Weimar Constitution). Bust of Hindenburg/Upraised hand.

1929 3 marks (1000th anniversary of Dinkelsbuhl). Medieval statue/ Eagle.

1929 3 marks (union of Waldeck with Prussia). Eagle/Eagle.

1930 3, 5 marks (Graf Zeppelin's world flight). Zeppelin encircling world/Eagle.

1930 3, 5 marks (evacuation of the Rhineland). Eagle on bridge/Eagle on shield.

1930 3 marks (700th anniversary of Walther von der Vogelweide). Bust of Von der Vogelweide/Eagle on shield.

1931 3 marks (tercentenary of the rebuilding of Magdeburg). View of city/Eagle on shield.

1931 3 marks (centennial of death of Freiherr von Stein). Bust of Von Stein/Eagle.

1932 3, 5 marks (centennial of death of Goethe). Bust of Goethe/ Eagle.

1933 5 marks (450th anniversary of birth of Martin Luther). Bust of Luther/Eagle.

1934 2, 5 marks (anniversary of Nazi rule). Potsdam Military Church/ Eagle.

1934 2, 5 marks (175th anniversary of birth of Schiller). Bust of Schiller/Eagle.

1952 5 marks (centennial of Nuremburg Museum). Eagle/Franconian Eagle.

1955 5 marks (150th anniversary of the death of Schiller). Bust of Schiller/Eagle.

1955 5 marks (tercentenary of birth of Margrave of Baden). Bust of Margrave/Eagle.

1957 5 marks (centennial of Baron von Eichendorff's birth). Bust of Eichendorff/Eagle.

1958 2 marks (centennial of Max Planck's birth). Bust of Max Planck/Eagle.

Great Britain

1935 Crown (Silver Jubilee of George V). Bust of George V/ Modernistic St. George and dragon.

Great Britain, crown commemorating Silver Jubilee of George V (1935).

Hungary

1907 5 korona (jubilee issue for Franz Joseph). Bust of Franz Joseph/ Coronation scene.

1930 5 pengo (tenth year of Horthy regency). Bust of Admiral Horthy/Hungarian arms.

1935 2 pengo (University of Budapest commemorative). Three figures/Hungarian arms.

1935 2 pengo (Rakoczi commemorative). Bust of Rakoczi/Hungarian arms.

1936 2 pengo (Liszt commemorative). Bust of Franz Liszt/ Hungarian arms.

1938 2 pengo (900th anniversary of death of St. Stephen). Bust of St. Stephen/Hungarian arms.

1943 5 pengo (Admiral Horthy's seventy-fifth birthday). Bust of Admiral Horthy/Hungarian arms.

1948 20 forint (centennial of Revolution of 1848). Bust of Tancsics/ Value.

1948 10 forint (centennial of Revolution of 1848). Bust of Szechenyi/ Value.

1948 5 forint (centennial of Revolution of 1848). Bust of Petofi/ Value.

Iceland

1930 10 kronur (1000th anniversary of the Althing). King of Thule seated/Shield with supporters.

1930 5 kronur (1000th anniversary of the Althing). Ulfliot the Law-maker/Interlocked dragons.

1930 2 kronur (1000th anniversary of the Althing). Seated female figure/Icelandic Cross with designs in the angles.

Iceland, 10 kronur commemorating 1000th anniversary of the Althing (1930).

Israel

1958 pound (tenth anniversary of the republic). Menorah/Value and inscription.

1959 5 pounds (ingathering of the exiles). People forming a chain in semicircle/Inscription and value.

1960 pound (fiftieth anniversary of the first collective settlement). Kibbutz scene/Value and dates.

Italy

1928 20 lire (tenth anniversary of the end of World War I). Helmeted bust of Victor Emmanuel III/Fasces and lion's head.

Luxemburg

1946 100 francs (600th anniversary of John the Blind). King John mounted/Bust of Prince John.

Mexico

1950 5 pesos (opening of Southern Railway). Locomotive, rising sun, palm trees/Eagle.

1951 50 pesos (centenary of independence). Winged victory/Eagle.

1953 5 pesos (bicentennial of Hidalgo's birth). Bust of Hidalgo/Eagle.

1957 1, 5, 10 pesos (centennial of Constitution of 1857). Bust of Benito Juarez/Eagle.

New Zealand

1935 crown (commemorating Treaty of Waitangi). Crowned bust of George V/Maori and naval officer.

1940 half crown (New Zealand centennial). Bust of George VI/Maori woman.

1949 crown (proposed royal visit). Bust of George VI/Leaf with four stars.

Norway

1906 2 kroner (independence commemorative). Norwegian arms/ Inscription.

1914 2 kroner (centenary of the Constitution). Crowned shield/ Standing figure.

Panama

1953 1 balboa (50th anniversary of the republic). Helmeted bust of Balboa/Female figure and arms.

Philippine Islands

1936 1 peso (establishment of Commonwealth). Accolated busts of President Roosevelt and President Quezon/Arms of Commonwealth.

1936 1 peso (establishment of Commonwealth). Accolated busts of Governor General Murphy and President Quezon/Arms of Commonwealth.

1936 50 centavos (establishment of Commonwealth). Facing busts of Governor Murphy and President Quezon/Arms of Commonwealth.

1947 half peso (MacArthur commemorative). Bust of General MacArthur/Shield of republic.

Poland

1930 5 zlotych (centenary of Revolution of 1830). Flags and inscription/Eagle.

1933 10 zlotych (250th anniversary of relief of siege of Vienna). Bust of Jan Sobieski/Eagle.

1933 10 zlotych (70th anniversary of 1863 insurrection). Bust of Traugutt/Eagle.

1934–39 10 zlotych (20th anniversary of Rifle Corps' entry into field in 1914). Bust of Pilsudski/Eagle.

Poland, 10 zlotych commemorating 20th anniversary of Rifle Corps' entry into field in 1914 (1934–39).

1959 10 zlotych (Copernicus commemorative). Facing bust of Nickolas Kopernik/Eagle.

1959 10 zlotych (Kosciuszko commemorative). Bust of Thaddeus Kosciuszko/Eagle.

COMMEMORATIVE

Portugal

1898 200, 500, 1000 reis (400th anniversary of the discovery of the route to the Indies). Accolated busts of king and queen/Cross with motto.

1910 1000 reis (centenary of the Peninsular War). Bust of Manuel II/Crowned shield.

1910 500 reis (Marquis de Pombal commemorative). Bust of Manuel II/Figures with shield.

1914 escudo (founding of the republic). Republic/Arms in wreath.

1928 10 escudos (Battle of Ourique, 1139). Mounted knight/Shield with cross.

1960 5, 10, 20 escudos (fifth centennial of the death of Prince Henry the Navigator). Facing bust of Prince Henry/Arms.

Rhodesia and Nyasaland

1955 crown (Rhodes commemorative). Bust of Elizabeth II/Portrait of Cecil Rhodes and arms.

Russia

1912 rouble (centenary of victory over Napoleon). Crowned double eagle/Inscription.

1913 rouble (tercentenary of the Romanov dynasty). Busts of Nicholas II and Michael Feodorovich/Crowned double eagle.

Serbia

1904 5 dinars (centenary of the Karageorgeviches). Busts of two kings/Crowned arms in mantle.

South Africa

1947–51 5 shillings (commemorative crown). Bust of George VI/Springbok.

1952 5 shillings (tercentenary of founding of Cape Town). Bust of George VI/Sailing ship.

Sweden

1821 rigsdaler (tercentenary of the Reformation). Bust of Charles XIV John/Medallion portraits of Gustavus Vasa, Gustavus II Adolphus and Frederick I.

1921 2 kronor (four hundredth year of political liberty). Bust of Gustavus Vasa/Arms.

1932 2 kronor (tercentenary of death of Gustavus II Adolphus). Bust of Gustavus II Adolphus/Inscription.

1935 5 kronor (five hundredth anniversary of Parliament or Riksdag). Bust of Gustavus V/Arms.

1938 2 kronor (tercentenary of Swedish settlement in Delaware). Bust of Gustavus V/Sailing ship.

Sweden, 2 kronor commemorating tercentenary of Swedish settlement in Delaware (1938).

1959 5 kronor (sesquicentennial of Swedish constitution). Bust of Gustavus VI/Four men in nineteenth-century costume standing at a table with arms of Sweden and a volume containing the constitution.

Switzerland

1939 5 francs (Zurich exposition). Farm scene above, clasped hands below/Shield and inscription.

1939 5 francs (Laupen commemorative). Male figure/Helvetian cross.

1939 5 francs (650 years of Confederation). Three figures swearing oath/Helvetian cross and inscription.

1944 5 francs (five hundredth anniversary of the Battle of St. Jakob an der Birs). Male figure/Helvetian cross and inscription.

1948 5 francs (centenary of the Swiss Constitution).

United Arab Republic

1958 ½ pound (founding of republic). Pharaoh Ramses II standing in biga/Value and inscription.

1959 50 piastres (founding of republic). Eagle with two-star shield/Value and inscription.

1960 5 pounds (Aswan High Dam). View of Dam/Winged sun with snakes.

Commemorative Coins (U.S.): As the name indicates, these coins are issued to mark special occasions and to honor great men and outstanding historic events. American commemorative coins make up the handsomest and most varied series in all our coinage. Almost all buying and selling of these coins are for the uncirculated state; the commemoratives have never been intended for general use. As of 1960 there were 50 silver commemorative types, of which 48 are half dollars. There were also several gold coins, mostly dollars.

SILVER COMMEMORATIVE COINS

Columbian Exposition half dollar. Issued to commemorate the 400th anniversary of the discovery of America. Obverse (designed by Charles E. Barber): bust of Columbus; reverse (designed by George T. Morgan): *Santa Maria* above two hemispheres. Quantities issued: 1892, 950,000; 1893, 1,550,405. This was the first American commemorative coin. After the exposition the unsold coins went into general circulation.

Isabella quarter. Issued for the Columbian Exposition. Designed by Barber. Obverse: crowned bust of Queen Isabella; reverse: kneeling woman with distaff and spindle. Quantity issued: 1893, 24,191.

Lafayette dollar. Issued to help finance the work of the Lafayette Memorial Commission to provide for a statue of Lafayette in Paris as a gift of the American people. Designed by Barber. Obverse: busts of Washington and Lafayette; reverse: equestrian statue of Lafayette. Quantity issued: 1900, 36,000. This was the first official American coin to carry a portrait of one of our presidents.

Panama-Pacific Exposition half dollar. Issued to commemorate the opening of the Panama Canal. Designed by Barber and Morgan. Obverse: Columbia, with Golden Gate in background; reverse: eagle above shield. Quantity issued: 1915 S, 27,134. Together with the gold coins of this issue, this was the first commemorative coin to carry the motto "In God we trust."

Illinois Centennial half dollar. Issued to commemorate the centennial of Illinois's admission into the Union. Obverse (designed by G. T. Morgan): bust of Abraham Lincoln, from a statue by Andrew O'Connor; reverse (designed by J. R. Sinnock): portion of the Illinois State Seal. Quantity issued: 1918, 100,058.

Illinois Centennial Half Dollar (1918).

Maine Centennial half dollar. Issued to commemorate the admission of Maine into the Union. Prepared by Anthony de Francisci from specifications. Obverse: arms of Maine, with inscription *Dirigo* ("I direct"); reverse: inscription in wreath. Quantity issued: 1920, 50,028.

Pilgrim Tercentenary half dollar. Issued to commemorate the landing of the Pilgrims in 1620. Prepared by Cyrus E. Dallin from previous designs. Obverse: Governor Bradford; reverse: the *Mayflower*. Quantities issued: 1920 (no date on obverse), 152,212; 1921 (date on obverse), 20,053. Of these issues some 148,000 were returned to the Philadelphia mint and melted down.

Missouri Centennial half dollar. Issued to commemorate the admission of Missouri into the Union as the twenty-fourth state. Designed by Robert Aitken. Obverse: bust of frontiersman; reverse: frontiersman and Indian. Quantities issued: 1921 (with 24 in field of obverse— figures separated by star), 5,000; 1921 (no 24 in field of obverse), 15,400.

Alabama Centennial half dollar. Issued to commemorate the admission of Alabama into the Union as the twenty-second state. Designed by Laura Gardin Fraser. Obverse: busts of W. W. Bibb, first governor of Alabama, and T. E. Kilby, governor when this coin was issued; reverse: eagle holding arrows in talons. Quantities issued: 1921 (with 22 in field of obverse—figures separated by St. Andrew's Cross), 6,006; 1921 (no 22 in field of obverse), 49,038. This is the first American coin to carry a likeness of a living person.

Grant Memorial half dollar. Issued to commemorate the centennial of Ulysses S. Grant's birth. Designed by Laura Gardin Fraser. Obverse: bust of Grant; reverse: Grant's boyhood home at Point Pleasant, Ohio. Quantities issued: 1922 (with star in obverse field), 4,250; 1922 (no star in obverse field), 67,411. The star variety is worth about ten times the other variety.

Monroe Doctrine Centennial half dollar. Issued to commemorate the centennial of the promulgation of the Monroe Doctrine. Designed by Chester Beach. Obverse: busts of James Monroe and John Quincy Adams; reverse: two female figures representing the Western Hemisphere. Quantity issued: 1923 S, 274,077.

Huguenot-Walloon Tercentenary half dollar. Issued to commemorate the 300th anniversary of the settlement of New Netherlands. Designed by Morgan. Obverse: busts of Admiral Coligny and William the Silent; reverse: the ship *Nieu Nederland.* Quantity issued: 1924, 142,080.

Lexington-Concord Sesquicentennial half dollar. Issued to commemorate the 150th anniversary of the battles of Concord and Lexington. Designed by Chester Beach. Obverse: Minute Man, from the famous statue by Daniel Chester French; reverse: old Belfry at Lexington. Quantity issued: 1925, 162,099.

Stone Mountain Memorial half dollar. Issued to defray the expenses of carving the portraits of Generals Robert E. Lee and Thomas Jonathan ("Stonewall") Jackson on Stone Mountain in Georgia. Designed by Gutzon Borglum. Obverse: Lee and Jackson on horseback; reverse:

eagle and inscription reading, "Memorial to the Valor of the Soldier of the South." Quantity issued: 1925, 1,314,709.

California Diamond Jubilee half dollar. Issued to commemorate the 75th anniversary of California's admission into the Union. Designed by Jo Mora. Obverse: kneeling Forty-Niner; reverse: walking grizzly bear (state emblem). Quantity issued: 1925, 86,594.

Fort Vancouver Centennial half dollar. Issued to commemorate the centennial of the building of Fort Vancouver, Designed by Laura Gardin Fraser. Obverse: bust of John McLaughlin; reverse: pioneer settler holding musket. Quantity issued: 1925, 14,994. A curious feature of this coin is that although it was struck at the San Francisco mint, it has no mint mark.

American Independence Sesquicentennial half dollar. Issued to commemorate the 150th anniversary of the signing of the Declaration of Independence. Designed by J. R. Sinnock. Obverse: Washington and President Coolidge; reverse: Liberty Bell. Quantities issued: 1926, 141,120. The only American coin to portray a living president.

Oregon Trail Memorial half dollar. Issued to honor the memory of the pioneers who traveled on the Oregon Trail. Designed by James Earle Fraser and Laura Gardin Fraser. Obverse: Indian with war bonnet and bow; reverse: covered wagon. Quantities issued:

1926	48,030	1937 D	12,008
1926 S	86,354	1938	6,006
1928	6,028	1938 D	6,005
1933 D	5,008	1938 S	6,006
1934 D	7,006	1939	3,004
1936	10,006	1939 D	3,004
1936 S	5,006	1939 S	3,005

Oregon Trail Memorial Half Dollar (1933).

The 1933 D coin is the first commemorative coin struck at the Denver mint. The coins of the 1939 issue are the most valuable of the Oregon Memorial group.

Vermont Sesquicentennial half dollar. Issued to commemorate the 150th anniversary of the battle of Bennington and Vermont's independence. Designed by Charles Keck. Obverse: bust of Ira Allen, founder of Vermont; reverse: catamount on pedestal. Quantity issued: 1927, 28,142.

Hawaiian Sesquicentennial half dollar. Issued to commemorate the 150th anniversary of Captain Cook's discovery of Hawaii. Designs sketched by Juliette May Fraser and executed by Chester Beach. Obverse: bust of Captain James Cook; reverse: native chief. Quantity issued: 1928, 10,008. This is the most valuable of all the commemorative half dollars.

Maryland Tercentenary half dollar. Issued to commemorate the 300th anniversary of the founding of Maryland by Lord Baltimore. Designed by Hans Schuler. Obverse: bust of Lord Baltimore; reverse: arms of Maryland. Quantity issued: 1934, 25,015. Lord Baltimore's portrait is full-face instead of the usual profile.

Texas Centennial half dollar. Issued to commemorate the centennial of Texan independence from Mexico. Designed by Pompeo Coppini. Obverse: eagle on large five-pointed star (the "Lone Star"); reverse: kneeling figure of winged Victory, with medallion of General Sam Houston at one side and medallion of Stephen Austin at the other side. Quantities issued:

1934	61,350	1937	6,571
1935	9,994	1937 D	6,605
1935 D	10,007	1937 S	6,637
1935 S	10,008	1938	3,780
1936	8,911	1938 D	3,775
1936 D	9,039	1938 S	3,816
1936 S	9,064		

The 1938 coins are the most valuable of the Texas Centennial group.

Daniel Boone Bicentennial half dollar. Issued to commemorate the 200th anniversary of Daniel Boone's birth. Designed by Augustus Lukeman. Obverse: bust of Daniel Boone; reverse: Boone and Chief Black Fish. Quantities issued:

1934	10,007	1935 D	2,003
1935	10,010	1935 S	2,004
1935 D	5,005	1936	12,012
1935 S	5,005	1936 D	5,005
1935	10,008	1936 S	5,006
with small "1934" added		1937	9,810
to reverse		1937 D	2,506

1937 S	2,506	1938 D	2,100
1938	2,100	1938 S	2,100

The 1938 coins are the most valuable of the Daniel Boone Bicentennial group.

Connecticut Tercentenary half dollar. Issued to commemorate the 300th anniversary of the founding of Connecticut. Designed by Henry Kreiss. Obverse: Charter Oak; reverse: eagle on pedestal. Quantity issued: 1935, 25,018.

Arkansas Centennial half dollar. Issued to commemorate the centennial of the admission of Arkansas into the Union in 1826. Designed by Edward Everett Burr. Obverse: accolated heads of an Indian chief of 1836 and an American girl of 1936, although one issue (listed on page 67) carries a portrait of Senator Joseph T. Robinson; reverse: eagle in flight. Quantities issued:

1935	13,012	1937 S	5,506
1935 D	5,505	1938	3,156
1935 S	5,506	1938 D	3,155
1936	9,660	1938 S	3,156
1936 D	9,660	1939	2,104
1936 S	9,662	1939 D	2,104
1937	5,505	1939 S	2,105
1937 D	5,505		

The 1939 coins are by far the most valuable of the Arkansas group.

Hudson, N.Y. Sesquicentennial half dollar. Issued to commemorate the 150th anniversary of the founding of Hudson, N.Y. Designed by Chester Beach. Obverse: Hudson's flagship the *Half Moon;* reverse: seal of Hudson, N.Y. Quantity issued: 1935, 10,008.

California-Pacific Exposition half dollar. Issued in connection with the exposition. Designed by Robert Aitken. Obverse: seated woman with spear, and at left a bear in the foreground; reverse: observation tower and the State of California building at the exposition. Quantities issued: 1935 S, 70,132; 1936 D, 30,092.

Old Spanish Trail half dollar. Issued to commemorate the 400th anni-

Old Spanish Trail Commemorative Half Dollar (1935).

versary of Cabeza de Vaca's expedition. Executed by L. W. Hoffecker from models by Edmund J. Senn. Obverse: cow's head (literal translation of the Spanish *cabeza de vaca*); reverse: yucca tree and a map of the Old Spanish Trail through the gulf states. Quantity issued: 1935, 10,008.

Providence, R. I. Tercentenary half dollar. Issued to commemorate the 300th anniversary of the founding of Providence. Designed by Arthur Graham Carey and John Howard Benson. Obverse: Roger Williams being welcomed by an Indian; reverse: anchor of Hope within a shield. Quantities issued:

1936	20,013
1936 D	15,010
1936 S	15,011

A curious feature is that the coin contains no reference to Providence.

Cleveland Great Lakes Exposition half dollar. Issued to commemorate the centennial of the founding of Cleveland. Designed by Brenda Putnam. Obverse: bust of Moses Cleaveland; reverse: map of the Great Lakes region with a compass pointing toward Cleveland. Quantity issued: 1936, 50,030. Although all the coins are dated 1936, about half were struck in 1937.

Wisconsin Territorial Centennial half dollar. Issued to commemorate the centennial of the founding of Wisconsin's territorial government. Designed by David Parsons and Benjamin Hawkins. Obverse: Territorial Seal, featuring a forearm holding a pickaxe over a mound of lead ore, and inscription; reverse: badger, the state emblem and an allusion to the early fur trade. Quantity issued: 1936, 25,015.

Cincinnati Musical Center half dollar. Issued to commemorate the 50th anniversary of Cincinnati as a musical center. Designed by Constance Ortmayer. Obverse: bust of Stephen Foster; reverse: kneeling figure of a woman holding a harp. Quantities issued:

1936	5,005
1936 D	5,005
1936 S	5,006

Long Island Tercentenary half dollar. Issued to commemorate the 300th anniversary of the settling of Long Island, N.Y. Designed by Howard K. Weinman. Obverse: accolated heads of a Dutch settler and an Indian; reverse: Dutch sailing vessel. Quantity issued: 1936, 81,773.

York County, Maine Tercentenary half dollar. Issued to commemorate the 300th anniversary of the founding of York County, Maine. Designed by Walter S. Rich. Obverse: York County seal (adapted); reverse: stockade. Quantity issued: 1936, 25,015.

Bridgeport, Conn. Centennial half dollar. Issued to commemorate the 100th anniversary of the incorporation of Bridgeport. Designed by Henry Kreiss. Obverse: bust of P. T. Barnum; reverse: modernistic eagle. Quantity issued: 1936, 25,015.

Lynchburg, Va. Sesquicentennial half dollar. Issued to commemorate the 150th anniversary of the granting of a charter to the city of Lynchburg in 1786. Designed by Charles Keck. Obverse: bust of Senator Carter Glass; reverse: Liberty standing, Lynchburg court-house in background. Quantity issued: 1936, 20,013.

Elgin, Ill. Centennial half dollar. Issued to commemorate the centennial of the founding of Elgin. Designed by Trygve Rovelstad. Obverse: bust of a pioneer; reverse: replica of Pioneer Memorial Statue by the designer. Quantity issued: 1936, 20,015. The dates 1673–1936 on the obverse refer to the year of Joliet and Marquette's entry into Illinois territory.

Albany, N.Y. Charter half dollar. Issued to commemorate the 250th anniversary of the granting of a charter to Albany. Designed by Katherine K. Lathrop. Obverse: beaver gnawing on a maple branch; reverse: Governor Dongan, Peter Schuyler, Robert Livingston. Quantity issued: 1936, 16,887.

San Francisco-Oakland Bay Bridge half dollar. Issued to commemorate the opening of the San Francisco-Oakland Bay Bridge. Designed by Jacques Schnier. Obverse: grizzly bear; reverse: the bridge. Quantity issued: 1936 S, 71,369.

San Francisco-Oakland Bay Half Dollar (1936).

Columbia, S.C. Sesquicentennial half dollar. Issued to commemorate the 150th anniversary of the founding of Columbia in 1786. Designed by A. Wolfe Davidson. Obverse: Justice with sword and scales, with 1786 capitol at left and 1936 capitol at right; reverse: palmetto (state emblem). Quantities issued:

1936	9,007
1936 D	8,009
1936 S	8,007

Arkansas Centennial half dollar (see page 64). New obverse with bust of Senator Joseph T. Robinson. Quantity issued: 1936, 25,265.

Delaware Tercentenary half dollar. Issued to commemorate the 300th anniversary of the landing of the Swedes in Delaware. Designed by Carl L. Schmitz. Obverse: church; reverse: the ship *Kalmar Nyckel.* Quantity issued: 1936, 25,015.

Battle of Gettysburg half dollar. Issued to commemorate the 75th anniversary of the battle of Gettysburg, fought in July 1863. Designed by Frank Vittor. Obverse: accolated busts of a Union and Confederate soldier; reverse; shields of the Union and Confederacy separated by double-bladed fasces (see page 107). Quantity issued: 1936, 26,928. The coin was issued in 1936, although 1938 is the anniversary date.

Norfolk, Va. Bicentennial half dollar. Issued to commemorate the 200th anniversary of the establishment of Norfolk as a royal borough. Designed by William Marks Simpson and Marjorie Emory Simpson. Obverse: seal of the city of Norfolk, featuring a three-masted ship; reverse: Royal Mace presented by Lieutenant-Governor Dinwiddie in 1753. Quantity issued: 1936, 15,000.

Roanoke Island, N.C. half dollar. Issued to commemorate the 350th anniversary of the founding of the "Lost Colony" on Roanoke Island. Designed by William Marks Simpson. Obverse: bust of Sir Walter Raleigh; reverse: Eleanor Dare holding the infant Virginia Dare, first white child born on what is now American territory. Quantity issued: 1937, 29,030.

Battle of Antietam half dollar. Issued to commemorate the 75th anniversary of the battle of Antietam, fought in 1862 during the Civil War. Designed by William Marks Simpson. Obverse: accolated heads of Generals Robert E. Lee and George B. McClellan; reverse: Burnside Bridge. Quantities issued: 1937, 18,028.

New Rochelle, N.Y. half dollar. Issued to commemorate the 250th anniversary of the founding of New Rochelle by French Huguenots. Designed by Gertrude K. Lathrop. Obverse: John Pell and calf; reverse: fleur-de-lis from New Rochelle's seal. Quantity issued: 1938, 15,266.

Iowa Centennial half dollar. Issued to commemorate the 100th anniversary of the admission of Iowa into the Union. Designed by Adam Pietz. Obverse: Iowa state seal; reverse: first stone capitol at Iowa City. Quantity issued: 1946, 100,057.

Booker T. Washington Birthplace Memorial half dollar. Issued to commemorate the centennial of the birth of Booker T. Washington in 1846.

Designed by Isaac Scott Hathaway. Obverse: bust of Booker T. Washington; reverse: view of Memorial and slave-cabin birthplace. Quantities issued:

1946	1,000,546	1949	6,004
1946 D	200,113	1949 D	6,004
1946 S	500,279	1949 S	6,004
1947	100,017	1950	6,004
1947 D	100,017	1950 D	6,004
1947 S	100,017	1950 S	512,091
1948	8,005	1951	510,082
1948 D	8,005	1951 D	7,004
1948 S	8,005	1951 S	7,004

Both this coin and the following one have been issued in exceptionally large quantities.

Washington-Carver half dollar. Issued in honor of Booker T. Washington and George Washington Carver. Obverse: accolated busts of Washington and Carver; reverse: map of the United States with inscription: "Americanism: Freedom and Opportunity for All." Quantities issued:

1951	110,018	1953	8,003
1951 D	10,004	1953 D	8,003
1951 S	10,004	1953 S	108,020
1952	2,006,292	1954	12,006
1952 D	8,006	1954 D	12,006
1952 S	8,006	1954 S	122,024

GOLD COMMEMORATIVE COINS

Louisiana Purchase Exposition gold dollar. Issued to commemorate the centennial of the Louisiana Purchase of 1803. Designed by Charles E. Barber. Obverse: two types, one with bust of Jefferson and one with bust of President McKinley; reverse: inscription: One Dollar 1803–1903. Quantities issued: 1903 (Jefferson) 17,375; 1903 (McKinley) 17,375.

Lewis and Clark Exposition gold dollar. Issued to commemorate the centennial of the Lewis and Clark Expedition. Designed by Charles E. Barber. Obverse: bust of Meriwether Lewis; reverse, bust of William Clark. Quantities issued: 1904, 9,997; 1905, 10,000.

Panama-Pacific Exposition gold dollar. Issued to commemorate the completion of the construction of the Panama Canal. Designed by Charles Keck. Obverse: bust of Panama Canal laborer; reverse: value encircled by two dolphins. Quantity issued: 1915 S, 25,000.

Panama-Pacific Exposition quarter eagle. Issued to commemorate the completion of the construction of the Panama Canal. Designed by Charles E. Barber and George T. Morgan. Obverse: Columbia with a caduceus, seated on a seahorse; reverse: American eagle with raised wings. Quantity issued: 1915 S, 6,749.

Panama-Pacific Exposition $50. Issued to commemorate the completion of the construction of the Panama Canal. Designed by Robert Aitken. Obverse,: bust of helmeted Minerva; reverse: owl. Quantity issued: 1915 S (round), 483; 1915 S (octagonal), 645. This is by far the most valuable of the whole commemorative series. The designs on both obverse and reverse are derived from ancient coins of Athens. Each one of the eight angles of the octagonal coin contains a dolphin.

Panama-Pacific Exposition gold $50.

McKinley Memorial gold dollar. Issued in connection with the building of a memorial at Niles, Ohio, McKinley's birthplace. Obverse (designed by Charles E. Barber): bust of McKinley; reverse (designed by George T. Morgan): memorial building. Quantities issued: 1916, 9,977; 1917, 10,004.

Grant Memorial gold dollar. Issued to commemorate the centennial of Ulysses S. Grant's birth. Designed by Laura Gardin Fraser. Obverse: bust of Grant; reverse: Grant's boyhood home at Point Pleasant, Ohio. Quantities issued: 1922 (with star in obverse field), 5,000; 1922 (no star in obverse field), 5,000. The no-star variety is worth somewhat more than the star variety.

American Independence Sesquicentennial quarter eagle. Issued to commemorate the 150th anniversary of the signing of the Declaration of Independence. Designed by J. R. Sinnock. Obverse: Liberty with scroll (the Declaration) and Torch of Freedom; reverse: Independence Hall in Philadelphia. Quantity issued: 1926, 46,019.

Commonwealth (1649–60): When Charles I was dethroned and a prisoner in the hands of the Puritans, coins were still struck bearing his effigy and name; after his execution in 1649, however, drastic innovations were made in the coinage. No portrait was graven on the coins (although Cromwell later issued patterns with his own portrait). Latin was eschewed: it was the language of the Papacy! Hence the

Commonwealth crown issued by Oliver Cromwell.

legend was expressed in English (the first and last time that English coins have borne an English inscription). The larger coins bear the motto GOD WITH US on the reverse. The design was austere, and the joined pair of shields on the reverse appeared to the Cavalier wits of the time like a pair of breeches to cover the "Rump" Parliament.

Communion Tokens: In the Scottish Presbyterian Church it was the custom the day before the Communion Service to issue a token, or pass, usually of lead or pewter, to the intending communicants. The custom arose in the days of the Covenanters, to eliminate Government spies. They date officially at least back to 1635. The tokens are usually stamped with the name of the parish. The earliest are square, and bear nothing but the initial of the parish; later ones bear a date and the minister's initials.

Condition of Coins and Paper Money: The condition of a coin is affected considerably by the way it was struck, by the amount of wear it has had in circulation, and by oxidation, etc., from the earth and the atmosphere. The value of a coin is largely governed by its condition. To grade the condition of a coin the following abbreviations are used:
Proof (Pr): a coin with a mirror-like surface, struck with polished dies on a polished blank. Usually sold at a premium by the mints.

Uncirculated (Unc.): in perfect condition, showing no signs of wear or damage but not necessarily brilliant.

Extremely Fine (EF): no definite signs of wear but having a less desirable surface than an uncirculated coin.

Very Fine (VF): showing inconsequential signs of wear but only slightly less desirable than the preceding classification.

Fine (F): perceptible signs of wear but still a desirable piece.

Very Good (VG): definite signs of wear but not altogether unattractive.

Good (G): worn but lettering and design all clear.

Fair (Fr): quite badly worn and usually highly undesirable.

Poor (P): less desirable than "fair," yet the design can usually be distinguished.

The influence of condition on value is seen in this typical catalogue listing for the same coin in different conditions:

G-VG $.60; F $1.00; VF $1.75; EF $2.75; Unc. $4.00; Pr $7.50.

Currency conditions may be summarized as follows:

Uncirculated (Unc.): A crisp note that has never been circulated and that has no creases or pin holes.

Extremely Fine (EF): New and possibly even uncirculated, but with creases, or pin holes from having been spindled or pinned with other notes. These comparatively minor flaws are quite acceptable in the case of scarce pre-1929 notes.

Very Fine (VF): A note that shows signs of brief circulation. This is generally the best condition obtainable in really old notes.

Fine (F): Hardly any crispness left; rather worn and possibly with tears; all lettering firm. Age and rarity of the note may be compensating factors.

Very Good (VG): Note still intact but with frayed edges and some color fading. The previous comment applies here.

Confederate Coinage: On the outbreak of the Civil War in 1861 Confederate forces seized the U.S. mint at New Orleans. More than 2,000,000 1861 O U.S. half dollars were struck from the original dies under Confederate auspices. (See *Half Dollar*.)

In addition, a Confederate die was substituted for the original reverse. So far as is known, only four specimens of this hybrid coin were struck. In later years there were some private restrikes of the new coin.

The Confederate regime authorized the preparation of dies for a cent. Apparently only 12 coins of the lower denomination were struck. In this case too there were later restrikes.

Confederate Currency: See *Paper Money*.

Conjoined: See *Accolated, Jugate.*

Connecticut Tercentenary Commemorative Half Dollar: See *Commemorative Coins (U.S.)*, p. 64.

Consecration Coin: The Romans struck special coins to commemorate the apotheosis (*consecratio*) of an emperor or other member of the imperial family. Such coins bear the word DIVUS, or (in the case of a female) DIVA, signifying a deity. Many of these coins show the actual ceremony of consecration in the Campus Martius; they depict the elaborate funeral pyre of four stories, with an eagle soaring from the peak, symbolical of the deified soul ascending to the gods.

Roman Empire, consecration coin with portrait of Pertinax (193).

Consular Coins: Those coins of the Roman Republic which do not bear the name of a family. Originally so called because believed to have been struck by the authority of the consuls; this supposition is now discredited, but the term remains as a convenient means of distinguishing these earlier coins from the later and more varied class of *Family Coins* (q.v.).

Controller Coins: In American coin collecting, these are the rarest—and hence the most valuable—coins of a given series. Some key dates:

Indian Head cents: 1864 (L on ribbon); 1869–72; 1877; 1908 S; 1909 S; in general, 1866–79.

Lincoln Head cents: 1909 S (VDB); 1909 S; 1910 S; 1911 S; 1912 S; 1914 D; 1914 S; 1921 S; 1923 S; 1924 D; 1924 S; 1926 S; 1931 S; 1933 D. Less rare, but still important: 1913 S; 1915 S; 1922 D; 1932; 1933; 1939 D; 1955 S.

Buffalo nickels: Generally all D and S coins, 1913–28; 1937 D (three-legged buffalo).

Jefferson nickels: 1939 D; 1939 S; 1942 D; 1950 D; 1951 S; 1955.

Winged Head Liberty (Mercury Head) dimes: 1916 D; 1919 D; 1919 S; 1921; 1921 D; 1926 S; 1927 D; 1942 D (over '41). Other short issues: 1930 S; 1931 D; 1931 S.

Roosevelt dimes: 1949; 1949 S; 1950 S; 1951 S; 1952 S. Also secondarily 1955; 1955 D, S.

Standing Liberty quarters: 1916; 1917 D, S (both varieties); 1918 S (over '17); 1919 D, S; 1921; 1923 S; 1926 S; 1927 S. Other short issues: 1926 D; 1927 D; 1929 D, S; 1930 S.

Washington quarters: 1932 D; 1932 S; 1936 D; 1938. Also secondarily 1951 S; 1955 D.

Standing Liberty half dollars: 1916 S; 1917 D, S; 1919; 1919 D, S; 1921; 1921 D; 1938 D. Another short issue: 1916.

Franklin half dollars: 1948; 1949; 1953.

Peace dollars: 1921; 1928; 1934 S.

Convention Money: In medieval Europe, a currency shared by two or more states or cities, somewhat similar to the *alliance coins* of Ancient Greece.

Copper (L. *Cyprium aes*, brass from the Island of Cyprus): An important metal, hard and reddish in color, used pure or in the form of various alloys (bronze, brass, etc.). In England pennies are still referred to as "coppers," although since 1860 they have been struck in bronze.

Copperheads: See *Civil War Tokens.*

Cornucopia (L. *cornu copiae*, horn of plenty): A frequent and apt emblem on coins, especially the Roman series. It is shown as a large horn filled with corn and fruit, fabled never to fail. It is a symbol of fortune, happiness, and prosperity. The Goddess Fortune is always shown bearing a cornucopia.

Coronet Type: See *Cent (U.S.), Double Eagle, Eagle, Half Eagle, Quarter Eagle.*

Corrugated Edge: Same as *Reeded Edge.*

Cos (L. abbreviation for *consul*): On coins of Imperial Rome, this abbreviation indicates that the emperor held the office of Consul in the year that the coin was struck. It is often followed by a number showing the number of times he had been consul. By reference to a list of consuls with dates, such as that given at the end of *Smith's Dictionary of Greek and Roman Biography*, it is usually possible to find the exact year the coin was struck, but complications occur where an emperor was consul for a number of years in succession. A better method of dating Roman coins is by the number given to the tribunitial power (see *Tri. Pot.*).

Counter: The name explains itself; they were small, thin, brass disks placed on a checkered cloth (an *exchequer*) to facilitate counting and the calculation of accounts. As they were made to resemble coins, the word came to mean any form of imitation coin, and, from their frequent use as tokens, the word was often used, in rather a derogatory sense, to mean money itself. Vast quantities of these counters were made in Nuremburg, hence they are often known as *Nuremburg Tokens* (q.v.).

Brass card counters turned out by the sackful in mid-Victorian days are often mistaken for antique coins; such is the brass imitation of a spade guinea of George III, usually inscribed "In memory of the good old times."

(Known in U.S. numismatics as "game counters.")

Counterfeit (O. Fr. *contrefait*, M.L. *contrafactum*): An imitation, especially one made with express intent to deceive. References to the more notorious counterfeits will be found under *Spurious*.

Counterfeit Detectors: Periodicals published during the State Banknote era. They gave information about the financial condition of the banks and listed counterfeits known to be circulating.

Counterfeiting: The story of coinage is largely bound up with a ceaseless struggle against the art and wiles of the counterfeiter. Both ancient Greek and Roman coins were frequently counterfeited, as we know from many specimens extant, as well as from references in literature. For example, in Petronius LVI an amusing comparison is made between the craft of a physician, who must know all about the inside of a man, and the craft of a banker (*numularius*), who must know all about the inside of a coin (*per argentum aes videt*). It was on account of such numerous forgeries that, according to Tacitus, the Germans of the first century A.D. preferred Roman coins that were old and familiar, the serrated and the biga type (*Pecuniam probant veterem et diu notam, serratos bigatosque*).

In England the counterfeiter was at work in the days of the Roman occupation. At Halton Chesters, near a fort on the Roman Wall, the remains of a Roman coiner's den have been discovered; many forged Roman coins were found here, together with a mold for manufacturing them. In the days of the Saxons, Athelstan, King of Wessex (925–35) ordained that the penalty for forgery should be the loss of a hand. In spite of this, matters steadily got worse. In the reign of Henry I it was so rife that the *Anglo-Saxon Chronicle* tells us (A.D. 1125):

"In this year King Henry commanded all the moneyers in England to lose each of them the right hand, *et testiculis infra.* . . . And the Bishop Roger of Salisbury sent over all England, and bade them that they should all come to Winchester at Christmas. When they came thither, they were taken one by one, and deprived each of the right hand, *et testiculis infra*. All this was done within the Twelfth-night."

This Christmas ceremony was somewhat drastic treatment. In China they did things differently. On one occasion we read that after a long and futile struggle between the Government and the counterfeiter, it was decided that the most skilful of the forgers should be rounded up and be offered highly paid jobs at the Imperial Mint.

The forgery of gold or silver coins, as infringing the exclusive prerogative of the Crown, was formerly held by English law to be treason; the penalty as such was transportation or hanging. The striking of copper coins, however, was not regarded as a regal prerogative, and the counterfeiting of these was therefore looked on merely as a misdemeanor. As a consequence, the eighteenth-century forger concentrated his energies on counterfeiting copper coins. This was done to an enormous extent; the forger made his profits proportionately higher by the vast quantities he could more or less safely turn out. In the middle of the eighteenth century more than one-half of the copper coins in circulation was counterfeit; in 1789 things were even worse, as we can see from a letter written in that year by Matthew Boulton, the famous coin manufacturer:

". . . In the course of my journeys I observe that I receive upon an average two thirds counterfeit halfpence for change at tollgates, etc., and I believe the evil is daily increasing as the spurious money is carried into circulation by the lowest class of manufacturers who pay with it the principal part of the wages of the poor people they employ. They purchase from the subterranean coiners thirty-six shillings's worth of copper (in nominal value) for twenty shillings, so that the profit derived from the cheating is very large."

In order to evade the law altogether, the forger would often place a more or less meaningless inscription on his copy (see *Evasions*). (See also *Electrotype*.)

Countermark: A sign or device, such as lettering, numerals, etc., stamped on a coin subsequent to its issue, whereby a fresh or further guarantee is given to the coin, or the value of the coin is changed, or the coin is rendered current in some other country from that in which it was issued. A well-known example is the Spanish dollar countermarked for use in England in the time of George III. (See *Dollars, Countermarked*.)

Great Britain, countermarked Spanish Piece of Eight.

Cowrie (Hind. word): A small, yellowish-white, and glossy sea-shell (*cypraea moneta*), about ½ in. in length, popular as a charm, an ornament and as currency from prehistoric times, and still used as currency in certain parts of the East and of the African Coast. Despite the labor involved in boring, polishing, and threading them, the value is minute; in India, until recent times, more than two hundred would be required to equal the value of one cent.

Cromwell: Coins struck by Cromwell, as Protector, are ranked as "pattern" coins, but the half-crown of 1656 usually shows marks as having been in circulation, and was therefore probably a current coin. Cromwell's crown piece was imitated about 1700 in Holland, and copies of the crown and other of his coins were made in the eighteenth century by Tanner, chief engraver to the Mint. These imitations can be distinguished by slight variations in the lettering, etc. Even these imitations, however, are rather scarce, and consequently fetch good prices.

Cross: There are four principal forms of crosses, namely:

 (I) the Latin Cross (*crux immissa*, or the Cross of the Crucifixion);
 (II) the Greek Cross (the Cross of St. George);
 (III) St. Andrew's Cross (*crux decussata*);
 (IV) St. Anthony's Cross (*Crux commissa*, or *tau* cross).

But many varieties of these crosses occur in numismatic works, among which we may note:

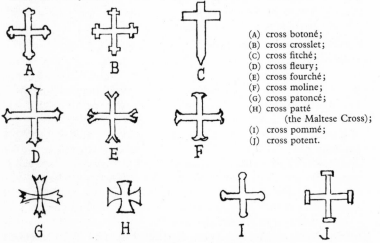

(A) cross botoné;
(B) cross crosslet;
(C) cross fitché;
(D) cross fleury;
(E) cross fourché;
(F) cross moline;
(G) cross patoncé;
(H) cross patté
  (the Maltese Cross);
(I) cross pommé;
(J) cross potent.

(For voided cross, see *Cut Halfpennies and Farthings*.)

Crosslet 4: In dating early American coins, two styles of the numeral "4" were used: crosslet 4 and plain 4. The crosslet 4 has a vertical foot at the end of the horizontal bar (**4**). The plain 4, as the name implies, has no foot (**4**).

Crown: So called because it was an adaptation of the French *écu à la couronne* (*couronne* = crown). It was first issued as a gold coin, in the reign of Henry VIII (see *Crown of the Rose* below), and continued to be struck in gold, together with the double crown and half-crown, until the time of Charles II. The silver crown and half-crown were first struck in the reign of Edward VI (1551). This, by the way, was the first

Crown of Edward VI, 1551.

dated English coin using Arabic numerals (see *Dating Coins*). The silver crown of Edward VI, James I, and Charles I, following Continental types and the device of the Great Seal of England, showed the king on horseback. No crowns were struck by Philip and Mary, nor by William IV. During the latter reign, pattern crowns were struck in 1831 and 1834. They are scarce and accordingly valuable. During the long reign of George III no crown pieces were struck until 1818. In that year the first issue from the new mint on Tower Hill was the famous crown piece designed by Pistrucci, on which St. George and the Dragon made a first appearance on the English crown. In Victoria's reign no crowns were struck from 1847 until 1887. However admirable the crown may be regarded as a work of art, it has never proved popular as an English coin.

In American numismatics the term "crown" is used to refer to any foreign dollar-sized silver coins. Collecting crowns is a recognized specialty, as these coins are attractive, rich in historical significance and generally reasonable in price.

Crown Gold: Gold with 2 carats alloy (i.e., 22 carats fine), so called from the gold crown of 1526 (crown of the double rose), which was struck with this amount of alloy. From the time of Charles I, English gold coins have been of crown gold standard. Previous to the introduction of crown gold, the old standard was practically one of pure gold, and contained only ⅛ carat alloy.

Crown of the Rose: Name given to the first English crown, a gold coin struck under Cardinal Wolsey in 1526. It was modeled after the French *écu au soleil*, and represented the value of 4s. 6d. On the obverse was a shield with a crown over, on the reverse a large rose over a cross. In the same year the **Crown of the Double Rose** was struck, valued at five shillings. This had on the obverse a double Tudor rose with a crown over, on the reverse a shield with a crown over. A crown of the rose is today valued at about $2,200, but a crown of the double rose can be bought for about $22.

Crowns, Roman: The word "crown" applied to the portrait on a Roman coin is really a misnomer. The crown as an emblem of royalty was abhorrent to the mind of a Roman. The so-called "crown" on a Roman bust was a wreath or garland of real or artificial flowers and leaves, and worn as a distinction of honor. The Emperor is frequently represented as garlanded with the triumphal "corona," and sometimes he is shown wearing the *corona radiata*, or radiated crown. This was a distinction of gods or heroes, and was assumed by the Emperor as a symbol of divinity.

Other "crowns" to be seen on Roman coins are as follows:

(1) The Civic Crown: this was of oak leaves, and was bestowed on a soldier who had saved the life of a Roman citizen (*civis*) in battle and had slain the opponent. The legend OB CIVEM SERVATUM, or (in the plural) OB CIVES SERVATOS, occurs on coins of Galba and other emperors.

(2) The Mural Crown: this was a golden crown decorated with turrets or battlements. It was bestowed on the soldier who first scaled the walls of a besieged city, etc., and succeeded in planting the standard there. The design of the crown is familiar to us from the figure of Cybele.

(3) The Rostral Crown—seen on coins of Agrippa—was adorned with a pattern representing the prows of ships (*rostra*). It was awarded to a victorious naval commander.

Crusado, Cruzado (Port. *cruzar*, "to mark with a cross"): A coin of Portugal, originally 400 *reis* in value, and so named from the large cross on the reverse. It bears the motto *in hoc signo vinces* ("by this sign thou shalt conquer"). On the obverse is a coat of arms, crowned, with the ruler's name, the date, and the value indicated in figures, namely 400.

Crux-type Penny: A type of penny of Athelred II (979–1016) with the four letters C R V X (=cross) in the angles of the cross, similar to the *PAX Penny* (q.v.).

Cuarto (Span. a fourth, or quarter): Copper coin of Spain, being one-quarter of the *real* (q.v.). It was first issued under Ferdinand and Isabella (1476–1504), and shows the arms of Castile and Leon in the form of a castle and the figure of a lion. The name is also given (though usually spelled "quarto") to the privately issued but abundant tokens of Gibraltar, struck 1801–2. Pieces of one and two quartos were struck, equivalent to the English halfpenny and penny respectively. In 1842 a British coinage for Gibraltar was issued, consisting of a half quarto, a quarto, and a two-quarto piece.

Cup Coins: See *Scyphate*.

Cupro-nickel: Owing to the inflated price of silver, in 1947 an issue of English coins in cupro-nickel was made almost identical in size, weight, and type to the existing silver coinage. Cupro-nickel consists of 75 per cent copper and 25 per cent nickel. The intrinsic value of a cupro-nickel crown piece is a trifle under 1*d*.

Currency (M. L. *currentia*, a current or stream): Money in its widest sense, including not only metallic coins and tokens but also banknotes and all forms of paper money; in fact, any medium of exchange and value that passes from hand to hand in daily use. Currency assumes strange forms in various ages and among differing races. The early coins of China clung for centuries to the traditional shapes of knives, cloths, shirts, etc., indicative of the original forms of currency in that country (see *Knife Money, Spade Money*). Cattle, wedges of gold and silver, bars of iron, bronze axheads, torques, rings were all popular forms of currency among the early races of the world. In North America beaver skins, wampum (q.v), tobacco (in Virginia), fishhooks, dried cod (Newfoundland), barrels of rum, sugar (West Indies), salt (Abyssinia), and such like were used in commerce until fairly recent times. Today, in Mongolia and Tibet, blocks of compressed tea are popular as currency, and cowrie shells (q.v.) are in use over a wide-spread area in Africa. Rum was the principal currency of Australia in the early days of the settlement. What the inhabitants (mostly trans-ported convicts) could not spend, they could at least consume.

Currency Bars: A peculiar form of currency, frequently found in early stages of civilization, in the form of "spits" or sword-shaped bars of iron.

In Sparta "iron money" seems to have been in use up to the end of the third century B.C. That this "iron money," and in fact the early currency of all Greece, consisted of currency bars we learn from Plutarch, who in his *Life of Lysander* tells us:

"This money was of iron, dipped in vinegar, while it was red hot, to make it brittle and unmalleable, so that it might not be applied to any other use. . . . Perhaps all the ancient money was of this kind, and consisted either of pieces of iron or bronze, which from their form were called *obeliskoi* whence we have still a quantity of small money called *oboli*, six of which make a *drachma* or 'handful', that being as much as the hand can contain." (Langhorne's translation.)

(See *Iron Currency, Obel, Drachma*.)

The *Aes rude* of the Romans apparently included currency bars. Stamped bars of cast copper were said to have been introduced by the sixth king of Rome, Servius Tullius.

Currency bars of the Ancient Britons have been unearthed at many places in the West of England. They vary from 20 to 30 in. in length, and weigh from 13 to 18 oz. Caesar, in his Commentaries, *De Bello Gallico*, V. 12, speaking of the inhabitants of Britain, seems to allude to these currency bars:

"They use either gold coins or iron bars regulated by weight for money."

The appearance they give of some sort of embryo sword seems to suggest they were fabricated by actual swordsmiths.

A form of currency bars is employed today by the Kissi tribe of Western Africa.

Cut Halfpennies and Farthings: Before the small round halfpennies and farthings were officially issued in the reign of Edward I, the silver penny was split along the inside of the voided cross (q.v.) on the reverse,

Cut pennies of Edward the Confessor.

thus giving a literal "half-penny" and a "fourthing" (or "farthing"). These forms of small change are frequently found in various hoards, and were apparently issued as such by the moneyers. Several early Saxon coins are divided, either by the design of the ornamentation or by the inscription, into three parts, for the purpose of splitting off a third of a penny, this denomination being mentioned in legal documents of the Saxon period. (See also *Voided Cross, Halfpenny, Farthing*.)

Cut Money: In the eighteenth century the Spanish dollar, sometimes countermarked "G.R." (Georgius Rex), circulated freely in the West Indies, but there was still the pressing need for small change. In the Island of St. Lucia the dollar was cut into three portions, each stamped with the name of the island, and thus one coin was made into three. Other countries cut up the dollar in various ways, or stamped out small portions of a peculiar shape, until they are hardly recognizable as coins. Cut money was last used in the Virgin Islands in 1892. (Also referred to as "sharp money.")

D

D. (Denarius): Abbreviation for "Penny." (See *L.s.d.*)

D.N. (L. *Dominus noster*, Our Lord): These initials first appear on coins of Diocletian and Maximian Hercules, after their abdication, afterwards appearing on coins of Licinius, father and son. The successors of Constantine used the title on their coins in place of *Imperator*.

Daler (Ger. *taler*, a dollar): The Swedish dollar. Originally Scandinavian money of account. The early Norse currency consisted of large copper slabs, weighing several pounds, stamped with a value in dalers. The world's largest coin is a ten-daler piece, struck in Sweden in 1644. It weighs nearly twenty pounds. In the seventeenth century the daler became common in Sweden as an unwieldy round copper coin.

Danegeld: A land tax originally levied on the English people for the purpose of buying off the Danish invaders at the end of the tenth century. The type of penny illustrated was struck by Aethelred II in enormous quantities. These coins, however, are found mostly in Scandinavia, a fact which seems to indicate that Danegeld was paid mainly with this type of penny.

Coins of Athelred II used for Danegeld.

Daric (Gr. *Dareikos*, probably from Persian *Dara*, a king—cf. *Sovereign*): The standard gold coin of the Persian Empire. It was struck in almost pure gold, and weighed a little more than the English sovereign. The usual type was a bearded king with spear and bow on the obverse; the reverse was a rough incuse square. It bore no inscription. The *Daric* and *Siglos* (q.v.) formed the principal currency of Asia under Persian dominion, for many centuries, until the time of Alexander the Great.

Both Daric and Siglos bore this type of the royal bowman,* in fact the coins were popularly known as "archers." This gave point to the pun of Agesilaus; when recalled to Sparta he complained he "was driven out of Asia by ten thousand of the king's archers"; for, as Plutarch tells us: "the orators of Athens and Thebes, having been bribed with so many pieces of money, had excited their countrymen to take up arms against Sparta."

Dating Coins: For the dating of Greek and Roman coins see references under *Cos, L, Tri. Pot.*†

The dates of the earliest English coins can be found only by laborious study of the various types, mint marks (q.v.), lettering, symbols, etc. James V of Scotland issued a forty-shilling gold piece bearing the date 1539 (a ducat or bonnet piece), but the first English coin to bear a date is the shilling of Edward VI, which is inscribed in Roman figures MDXLVIII (1548). Later in this reign dates in Arabic figures appear. Dates are frequent on coins from the time of Elizabeth, but it was not till 1662 that all English coins were permanently dated, and the system of dating coins by mint marks (or privy-marks, as they are sometimes called) died out.

A curiosity of dating English coins appears on the sixpence of George V, 4th last issue (1927–36) where the letters A.D. appear!

(See *Mohammedan Dates, Gun Money*.)

Debasement: To reduce to a lower value, to adulterate coin by the addition of something of less value: a lowering of purity and quality, and consequently of the value.

Greek coins, before Hellenistic times, were rarely debased, but Roman coins were frequently debased, especially from the times of Caracalla, when the *antoninianus* (q.v.) of base silver was introduced.

In medieval Europe, Philip the Fair of France was one of the first who deliberately debased his coinage; to meet the expenses of his Flemish campaign in 1302 he debased the coinage to one third of its value (see Dante's *Paradiso*, XIX, 118).

English silver, from earliest times until the reign of Henry VIII, was kept of the same fineness. The weight of the coins tended to lessen, but there was no attempt to force money to bear a fictitious value. The first official debasement of English coinage took place in 1526 under Henry VIII, when, to enrich his coffers and provide for his lavish expenditure, the gold crown and half-crown were reduced to *crown gold* (q.v.); later

---

* The bow was the national weapon of Persia.

† A curious and unique example of a Roman coin bearing a date in figures is a first brass of Hadrian inscribed ANN. DCCCLXXIIII. NAT. URB. P. CIR. CON., i.e., 874 years from the foundation of Rome. It was struck A.D. 121.

in the same reign the gold was further reduced to 20 carats. Silver coins were struck in one-third alloy, then (1544) half, and finally (1545) the silver content was reduced to only one third. The copper content of these so-called "silver" coins was so obvious that in the later years of his reign the king himself was nicknamed "Old Copper-nose." Edward VI struck coins of debased silver with the portrait and title of his father, Henry VIII. At the accession of Elizabeth the base testoons of Edward were countermarked with a portcullis or a greyhound, reducing the values to $4\frac{1}{2}d$. and $2\frac{1}{4}d$. respectively. In 1920, for financial reasons, British silver coins were debased by 50 per cent, and in 1947 silver was totally eliminated from the coinage, which became purely a token coinage.

United States coins still have a high silver content; the intrinsic value of the coins, however, is exceeded by their face value. (See also *Scottish Coinage, Depreciation of Currency.*)

Decimalization of Money: Any system of coinage based on multiples of 100. Proposals have been made at various times that English currency should be put on a decimal basis. The introduction of the florin (q.v.) was an actual step towards this, the coin, as stated in the inscription, being "one tenth of a pound." The system would adopt the formula:

    10 mils = 1 cent
    100 mils = 10 cents = 1 florin
    1,000 mils = 100 cents = 10 florins = £1

France adopted decimal coinage during the Revolution, and the U.S.A. in 1792. By the Latin Monetary Union (q.v.) of 1865, a number of European countries followed suit. The system was adopted by India from April 1957, with the rupee as the standard coin.

Declaration Type: Type of coins of Charles I, bearing across the field the motto, though abbreviated: RELIGIO PROTESTANTIUM, LEGES ANGLIAE, LIBERTAS PARLIAMENTI (the Protestant religion, the laws of England, the liberty of Parliament).

Oxford sixpence of Charles I
(Declaration Type).

In 1642 Charles declared war against Parliament; he made a declaration to preserve the Protestant religion, the liberty of Parliament, and the English laws. The terms of this declaration were introduced on the coins struck by Charles at Shrewsbury in 1642. The legend was afterwards placed on the Oxford coins (1643–46), the mint having been transferred there after the Battle of Edgehill. It was also placed on later coins struck at Bristol, Weymouth, Chester, and Exeter.

Decus et Tutamen: See *Mottoes on Coins.*

Dei Gratia (L. by the Grace of God): This title appears at different times on European medieval coins from the ninth century. Edward I introduced it on English coins, 1279. It figures on all the great seals since the time of William the Conqueror, but it was not till Edward I introduced it on his groat that it became a feature of the legend on English coinage. It appeared continuously until the silver florin of 1849 was struck. (See *Godless Florin.*)

Dekadrachm, also **Decadrachm** (Gr. *deka*, ten, *drachme*, a drachm): A ten-drachma piece, a large silver coin of the ancient Greeks, weighing about 660 grains. They were issued only rarely, on special occasions such as a military victory, and are more in the nature of a medallion than an actual coin. The most famous are the dekadrachms of Syracuse.

One of the famous dekadrachms of Syracuse.
Left: obverse.
Right: reverse.

Delaware Tercentenary Commemorative Half Dollar: See *Commemorative Coins (U.S.),* p. 67.

Denarius (L. containing ten, *sc. nummus,* a coin of ten *asses*): The principal silver coin of the Romans in Republican and Imperial times, superseding the *quodrigatus* and the *victoriatus.* It was probably first minted at Rome in the second century B.C. On the obverse was the helmeted head of ROMA, the genius of Rome, and on the reverse were the *Dioscuri* (q.v.) charging on horseback, the legend ROMA in exergue. Later the reverse bore the device first of Diana in a biga, with the legend ROMA in the exergue, and then the figure of Victory in a biga (probably commemorative of the victorious termination of the Second Punic War 201 B.C.).

Roman Empire, denarius of Augustus.

The earlier denarii bore the mark X, signifying the coin was a ten-*as* piece, but during the Second Punic War (218–201 B.C.), when the *as* was reduced to 1 oz. the sign was changed to)⟨ signifying the value was sixteen *asses*. During succeeding centuries a great variety of types were struck, some mythological, some historical, many relating to the semi-legendary history of the great families of Rome (see *Family Coins*). During the Imperial period, the denarii, of course, bore the head and titles of the reigning Emperor. In course of time the denarius became more and more debased, until it became merely a bronze coin, and was superseded by the *antoninianus*. It was revived as a silver coin under Diocletian, A.D. 296, as the *argenteus*, which itself continued to be struck in small numbers until the time of Julian II (A.D. 360–63).

The so-called "penny" of the Authorized Version of the New Testament is the silver denarius. The value at that time was about $8\frac{1}{2}d$., the wages of a laborer for a day's work (St. Matt. xx). (See *Tribute Penny*.)

The divisions of the denarius were its half, the *quinarius* of five *asses*, and its quarter, the *sestertius*, of two and a half *asses*.

The denarius naturally had a great influence in shaping the later coinage of Europe and even that of the Orient. Hence the *denier*, *dinar*, etc.

A gold denarius was struck, of the same weight as the silver coin. This was valued at 25 silver denarii, and was known as an *aureus* (q.v.). (See also *Consular Coins, Family Coins*.)

Denier (L. *denarius*, see above): The *novus denarius* (new denarius) or silver "penny" (weighing 24 grains), was first struck by Pepin, and introduced into Europe by Charlemagne in the eighth century. Charlemagne divided the silver pound (the *libra*, or *livra*) into twenty *sols* (*solidi*) of twelve deniers each. Two hundred and forty deniers were therefore struck from 1 lb. of fine silver. The denier was further divided into two *oboles* each weighing 12 grains. It rapidly became the standard current silver coin of Western Europe, though, of course, there were many variations of type and legend. In fact, until the middle of the thirteenth century it was the only coin issued in Europe in any abundance.

King Offa of Mercia (757–94) established the type in Saxon England,

and the long series of English medieval silver pennies is a variety of the denier. In France the denier suffered depreciation in the course of time. During the reign of Philip I, in 1103, one-third of copper was mixed with the silver of the denier. In the time of Louis-le-Gros (1108–1137) the denier was half silver and half copper. It eventually became a minute copper coin, until the time of Louis XVI, when it ceased to be struck.

The Anglo-Gallic penny, issued in France by English sovereigns, was also known as a *denier*. (See also *Obole, Sol, Tournois*.)

Depreciation of Currency (L. *de*, down, *pretio*, price): A lowering of value. Currency depreciates in value either from natural causes, such as wars, increase of the ratio of imports over exports, or, as was often the case in the past, through the direct intervention of the ruler of a country endeavoring to increase his personal wealth. This was effected either by debasing the current coin or issuing coin in an inferior metal. An instance of this in early history is mentioned by Aristotle (Oecon. ii. 21); he tells us that Dionysus of Syracuse, in order to cope with his vast expenditure, issued tin coins in place of silver. These coins were made to pass for four-drachma pieces; their actual worth was one drachma.

After two disastrous world wars, the coinage of all European countries has been greatly depreciated and debased.

When a government is troubled by an excess of its country's imports over its exports, it may seek to remedy the situation by *devaluing* its currency in relation to foreign currencies. This has a twofold effect: it encourages purchases by foreign buyers (thus increasing exports); and it discourages its own people from buying foreign products (thus decreasing imports). (See *Debasement*.)

Device (Fr. *dévise*, a division, an emblem): An emblematic design; the figure or pattern of a coin or medal used in an heraldic sense. Thus we speak of a coin bearing the device of a bird, a flower, etc. The earliest devices on coins probably originated from the impression of a signet ring, this being the earliest way of "signing" a document and so making it official.

Diademed (Gr. *diadêma*, a band, fillet): A bust or head on a coin may be described as bare, diademed, or radiate. A diademed head is one surmounted by a headband, fillet, or crown, as an emblem of royalty or supreme authority.

Didrachm, Didrachma, Didrachmon (Gr.): A two-drachma piece. (See *Drachma*.)

Die: A piece of hard metal, engraved with the design of the obverse or the reverse of a coin or medal, so that the design can be stamped on to the *flan* (q.v.). The lower die is known as the standard, staple, or *pile* (q.v.);

the upper die is the *trussel* (q.v.) or puncheon. In the early days of hand-struck coins the upper die wore out sooner than the lower; moreover, it tended to split as it received the direct force of the blow when a coin was hammered; it was therefore customary to supply two trussels to every pile, and an official "die" consisted of one standard and two trussels.

Medieval dies were not engraved; the design was struck on soft metal (afterwards hardened), and this was effected by a small set of punches of simple geometrical patterns. A few straight lines and some curves gave all the letters of the alphabet, and the portrait could be made up from about six sorts of these geometrical patterns.

Dime: Authorized by the Acts of April 2, 1792 and October 1794, the issue of this silver coin started in 1796 and has continued to date. The following types have appeared:

> Bust (Liberty Head) 1796–1807
> Turban Head 1809–37
> Liberty Seated 1837–91
> Liberty Head (Barber) 1892–1916
> Winged Head Liberty ("Winged Mercury") 1916–1954
> Roosevelt 1946–

The designs of the dimes are very similar to those on the half dimes for the corresponding years. The bust type (Liberty facing right) was discontinued after 1807, no dimes being issued in 1808.

In 1809 the coinage of dimes was resumed with the Turban Head type (Liberty facing left). The motto E PLURIBUS UNUM appears in a ribbon over the eagle on the reverse. Up to 1829 these coins had no indication of value.

With the introduction of the Liberty Seated type in 1837, the slight reduction in weight and fineness was indicated in the same manner as

Left: Dime, Bust Type (1828). *Right:* Dime, Liberty Seated Type (1837).

on the half dimes—through changes in the drapery of the seated figure, and the addition of stars to the obverse. From 1838 through 1860, there are quite a few dates with the "O" mint mark from New Orleans. The first San Francisco coins were struck in 1856 and continued there-after. From 1871 through 1878 dimes were struck at Carson City, Nevada ("CC" mint mark). The 1871–74 Carson City dimes were issued in fairly small quantities and are all valuable. The mint marks for the

Liberty Seated type are located on the reverse, under the wreath or within it.

As in the case of the half dimes, arrows were placed on each side of the date on the 1853–55 dimes to indicate a slight reduction. In 1859, again as in the case of the half dime, the obverse of 1859 and the reverse of 1860 are used, so that the legend UNITED STATES OF AMERICA does not appear on the coin. On the 1860 dimes and thereafter, the legend replaces the stars on the obverse.

On the 1873 and 1874 dimes arrows at the date indicate another change—this time a slight increase in weight. In 1891 the New Orleans mint resumed coinage operations, so that the "O" mint mark reappears on succeeding issues of the dime.

The Liberty Head dimes (1892–1916) were designed by Charles E. Barber, Chief Engraver. His initial ("B") appears at the truncation of the neck. The mint mark for coins struck at San Francisco, New Orleans and Denver (starting in 1906) is under the wreath on the reverse. The 1894 S dime, of which only 24 pieces were struck, is one of the outstanding rarities of United States coinage.

The design of the Winged Head Liberty dime—popularly known as the "Mercury" dime—is explained under *Roman Influence on U.S.*

Dime. *Left:* Liberty Head type. *Right:* Winged Head Liberty type.

Coinage. The initials "AW" (for A. A. Weinman, the designer) are found in back of the neck. The "S" and "D" mint marks appear to the left of the fasces on the reverse. The inscription LIBERTY appears along the upper curve on the obverse; the motto IN GOD WE TRUST is on the obverse under the chin; E PLURIBUS UNUM appears on the reverse to the right of the fasces. No proofs were issued during 1916–39 and 1943–45.

On the succeeding type, the Roosevelt dime, these inscriptions appear in the same relative positions. The obverse carries the bust of President Franklin Delano Roosevelt; on the reverse the torch of liberty is placed between sprigs of laurel and oak. The initials "JS" (for John R. Sinnock, the designer) appear at the truncation of the neck.

The Roosevelt dime has appeared from 1946 to date. However, no proofs were issued during 1946–49. See *Controller Coins*.

Dinar (Arab. from L.·*denarius,* a silver coin): An Arabian gold coin, originally struck by the Caliph of Damascus, in A.D. 696. In this year the Arabian coinage was reformed by Abd-al-Malik, the fifth Ommiad Caliph. Hitherto the Arabian coins had copied Byzantine types in gold and copper, and the Sassanian Persian coins in silver, though the old name *dinar* survived, derived from the *denarius aureus* of Byzantium. In accordance with the dictates of the Mohammedan faith, on this new type of dinar and dirhem no imagery of any living thing appeared. Texts from the Koran and other pious inscriptions took the place of imagery. The art of the coins was calligraphic rather than pictorial; it was an art of arabesques and florid geometrical patterns. The various conquerors and foreign rulers of the Arabian Empire, such as the Turks and the Mongols, made few alterations in the general types of the dinar and dirhem, though naturally the size, weight, and legends varied in the course of ages. Whatever varieties were introduced in later times, however, the names of dinar and dirhem continued to be the generic name for all gold and silver coins of Mohammedan countries.

Dioscuri (Gr. *Dios kouroi*, Sons of Zeus): Castor and Pollux, the Heavenly Twins. They are depicted on the earliest type of *denarius* (q.v.), lances in hand, charging on their white steeds, their sacred stars shining over their heads (the constellation of *Gemini*), as they had appeared in a vision fighting for Rome at the Battle of Lake Regillus (494 B.C.).

Rome, silver denarius, Castor and Pollux.

Dirhem (Arab. from Gr. *drachma*, a silver coin): An Arabian silver coin. (See *Dinar*.) Apart from the difference in the metal and weight and legend, it conforms closely to the type of the dinar.

Doit (Dutch *duit*): A small copper coin current in the Netherlands and the Dutch provinces from the latter part of the sixteenth century to the early nineteenth century. The usual type of the obverse was heraldic, representing the province where it was current.

Dollar (Dutch *daler*, Ger. *taler*): A gold and silver coin, the standard of currency in the U.S.A., Canada, Mexico, most of the South American States (where it is known as the *Peso*); it is also current in China, and a special form of British silver dollar and half dollar is current in the Malay Straits, Hong Kong, etc. The early form of dollar is bound up in the history of the *taler* (q.v.). It is a form of metric currency, one hundred cents (or an equivalent coin) making the dollar.

DOLLAR

(See also *Bank of England Dollar*, *Maria Theresa Dollars*, *Peso*, *Ring-dollar*.)

Dollar, Canadian Silver: These coins have been struck from 1935 to date, though none were issued during 1940–44. The first one was struck to commemorate the twenty-fifth year of George V's reign. The canoemen reverse became the standard design of the reverse on the succeeding regular issues.

There have been several other commemorative dollars: one in 1939 to commemorate the royal visit (reverse with Parliament buildings at Ottawa); the Newfoundland commemorative in 1949 (reverse with John Cabot's ship); and the British Columbia centennial commemorative in 1958 (reverse with totem pole).

Dollar Sign: There are various theories as to the origin of the sign $ signifying American and other dollars. The most reasonable explanation is that it is a variant of the ancient Spanish contraction for peso or piece of eight, which consisted of the figure eight between two sloping lines, thus: /8/.

Dollar, U.S. Gold: The introduction of the gold dollar, authorized by the Act of March 3, 1849, was a consequence of the discovery of gold in California. The coinage of the gold dollar extended from 1849 through 1889 and embraced the following generally recognized types:

Type I	1849–54
Type II	1854–56
Type III	1856–89

Liberty Head Type   Indian-Head-dress Type   Larger Indian-Headdress Type

Aside from the Philadelphia coinage, some coins were struck at San Francisco, Charlotte (North Carolina) and Dahlonega (Georgia). The branch coinage was consistently smaller than at Philadelphia, and the mint-marked dollars are with few exceptions the most valuable. The mint marks appear below the wreath on the reverse.

Type I is the smallest coin of the series. It is variously known as the small-size type, Liberty Head type, Coronet Head type. It has two types of reverses—the open wreath and closed wreath. There is only one known 1849 C open wreath dollar. It sold for $6000 in 1956.

In 1854 the dollar was redesigned with a larger diameter and thinned out to keep the weight unchanged. Liberty received a feathered crown, so this second type is known as the Feathered Headdress or large-size type.

In 1856 the head was slightly enlarged, giving rise to Type III. This design continued until the end of the coinage in 1889. The most valuable dollar of this group is the 1861 D coin, which was struck under Confederate auspices after seizure of the Dahlonega mint.

Dollar, U.S. Silver: This coin, a direct descendant of the Spanish Milled Dollar (see *Peso*) was authorized by the Act of April 2, 1792 and first issued in 1794. The following types were issued:

Bust	1794–1804
Liberty Seated	1840–1873
Liberty Head (Morgan)	1878–1921
Peace	1921–35
Trade	1873–85

The early dollars were struck in many varieties and generally in small quantities. They are all valuable, the rarest being the 1804 date which has brought as high as $12,500 in auction sales. The Bust dollars, like the lower silver denominations, featured Liberty (facing right) on the obverse, and an eagle on the reverse. These coins showed no value on the face, but they had lettered edges reading HUNDRED CENTS, ONE DOLLAR OR UNIT.

The 1804 coin is the great puzzle of the series. Though the mint records claim an issue of 19,570 1804 dollars, the coins with this date are exceedingly rare. On the evidence of certain technical details some authorities believe these 1804 coins were actually struck in 1836 or later. The motto E PLURIBUS UNUM first appears on 1798 dollars, set in a ribbon on the reverse above the eagle.

Left: Dollar, Bust Type (1796). *Right:* Dollar, Liberty Seated Type (1840).

During 1805–39 no silver dollars were issued, but from 1836 to

DOLLAR

1839 Christian Gobrecht, the assistant to the Mint Engraver, executed a series of beautiful pattern dollars which are rare and valuable. For his obverse Gobrecht used the Liberty Seated design which became the standard obverse on the silver coins of the period. For his reverse Gobrecht designed the graceful flying eagle which was later adapted for the reverse of the small cents but which was inexplicably dropped from the reverse of all the Liberty Seated silver coins.

The Liberty Seated dollars were struck from 1840 through 1873. The lettered edge was dropped and replaced by a reeded edge, the value (ONE DOLLAR) being shown at the bottom of the reverse. The flying eagle on the reverse was discarded in favor of an eagle grasping an olive branch and arrows.

The first "O" mint mark appeared in 1846, the first "S" mint mark in 1859. The mint mark can be found under the eagle on the reverse. In 1866 the motto IN GOD WE TRUST was added to the reverse, set in a ribbon above the eagle. The first dollar with the "CC" mint mark was issued in 1870. All the "CC" coins are valuable, but the 1870 S dollar is even rarer.

During the years 1874–77 no standard silver dollars were issued, but under the provisions of the Bland-Allison Act of 1878 silver-dollar coinage was resumed with the striking of the Liberty Head dollar. The initial "M" (for George T. Morgan, the designer) appears at the truncation of the neck on the obverse and also on the left-hand loop of the ribbon on the reverse. The "S," "O" and "CC" mint marks all appear on the reverse under the eagle. On the early Morgan dollars the eagle had eight tail feathers. This was subsequently reduced to seven. The motto E PLURIBUS UNUM is found inside the upper curve on the obverse, and IN GOD WE TRUST appears above the eagle on the reverse.

Dollar, Liberty Head (Morgan) Type

On the Liberty Head dollars Liberty faces left, whereas on the lesser denominations she faces right. The Liberty Head dollars were discontinued after 1904, but there was one final issue in 1921 under authority of the Pittman Act of 1921.

The Peace dollar issued during the period 1921–35 was struck to commemorate the victorious conclusion of World War I. It is perhaps the most Roman of our coins (see *Roman Influence on U.S. Coinage*). The radiate head of Peace is reminiscent of the old Roman imperial coins. IN GOD WE TRUST appears on the obverse, and E PLURIBUS UNUM on the reverse. The initials of the designer, Anthony de Francisci, are located under the neck on the obverse.

The eagle on the reverse likewise seems to have been modeled on ancient Greek and Roman devices. The rays on the reverse repeat the radiate pattern of the obverse. The mint mark appears on the reverse above the eagle's tail feathers. The coinage of silver dollars came to an end in 1935 with the discontinuance of the Peace type.

The Trade dollars of 1873–85 are in a class by themselves During the Civil War American merchants fell behind in trade with the Orient. To help them compete in the Chinese and Japanese markets, the government issued the Trade Dollar. This was a silver coin which contained 420 grains instead of the standard 412½ found in the regular dollar. The metal weight and fineness are specified on the reverse under the eagle.

The coin is a very handsome one, with a figure of Liberty seated on the obverse—not the same figure found on the standard dollars of the period. The inscription E PLURIBUS UNUM appears in a ribbon over the eagle on the reverse, and the value is stated at the bottom of the reverse as TRADE DOLLAR. The "S" and "CC" mint marks appear on the reverse under the eagle.

Originally the law authorizing this coin established Trade dollars as legal tender in the United States up to $5.00. Subsequently, however, the price of silver declined; Congress therefore removed the legal-tender provision in 1876 and stipulated that future coinage of Trade dollars should be geared to demand in the Far East.

The hope of competing with the Mexican peso was not realized. From 1879 through 1885 only proofs were issued, apparently for collectors. As a matter of fact, there are no official records of any proofs issued in 1884 and 1885, and these coins did not become known to most collectors until 1908. It is believed that 10 proofs were struck in 1884 and 5 in 1885; these rarities are naturally extremely valuable. In the opinion of some authorities these proofs must have been struck illegally by mint employees.

Dollars, Countermarked: Owing to the scarcity of silver at the end of the eighteenth century, Spanish dollars and half-dollars were made legal tender in Great Britain in 1797. They were countermarked with the stamp of the Goldsmith's Company—a small *oval* stamp with the king's head. The value of this token dollar was 4*s*. 9*d*. Both the dollar and the countermark were considerably forged, and so in 1804 an *octagonal* countermark was used. The same year an official issue of Bank of England dollars was made (see *Bank of England Dollars*).

Double (i.e., a double denier): An old French silver coin, a two-denier piece, equal to one-sixth of a *sol* (or sou), current from the fourteenth century. In its later form it became a small copper coin, Obv/Bust of king, Rev/DOUBLE TOURNOIS, with date; in the field, three fleurs-de-lis.

In the Anglo-Gallic series (q.v.) the double signified the *double gros*.

Double Eagle: This $20.00 gold coin was authorized by the Act of March 3, 1849 and was first issued that year, thanks to a heavy influx of gold from California. The following types were struck:

Coronet	1849–1907
Liberty Standing	1907–33

There is only one 1849 double eagle known—it is in the official mint collection. The 1861 reverse and 1861 S reverse (both designed by A. C. Paquet) are also notable rarities. On this type the value appears on the reverse as TWENTY D. The mint mark appears on the reverse under the eagle. Beginning with the 1866 issue IN GOD WE TRUST was placed in a ribbon above the eagle.

Double Eagle, Coronet
Type without motto

The Liberty Standing double eagle, designed by Augustus Saint-Gaudens, is universally acknowledged as the artistic gem of American coinage. The 1907 coin and some 1908 coins do not carry the motto IN GOD WE TRUST, which, however, appears in subsequent issues (see *Eagle*).

The 1907 double eagle comes in quite a few varieties. There is just one specimen of the coin in high relief with a flat edge. The high-relief double eagle with Roman numerals was struck on 16 coins. One of these sold in 1956 for $9,250. Another variety has the date in Roman numerals; some of these come with a wire edge, others with a flat edge. There is still another 1907 style with the date in Arabic numerals. On only one of these coins (a proof) the lettering on the edge is large. All the other coins of this group have small lettering.

On both obverse and reverse, rays highlight the handsome figures on the designs. Liberty, holding a torch in her right hand and a sprig of leaves in her left, appears on the obverse. On the reverse is a flying eagle even more graceful than Gobrecht's flying eagle reverse. The mint mark is above the date on the reverse.

Double-struck: When the old hammered coins were struck, often a first blow of the hammer would not be effective; if a second blow was given to the die the coin was liable to shift, causing double lines to appear. Such a coin is said to be double-struck.

Doubloon (Fr. *doublon*, Span. *doblon*, a large double): A double *Escudo*; gold coin of Spain and Spanish America, first struck in the fourteenth century. The original type was a three-turreted castle on the obverse, but in the time of Ferdinand and Isabella (1475–1516) this was changed to the royal portrait type.

In 1849 Spain adopted the metric system, and the doubloon was then made equal to ten *escudos*, or 100 *reales*, equivalent to about $5.

Drachma (Gr. *dragma*, a handful): The basic silver coin of Ancient Greece, also a weight. The coinage of Greece was mainly based on fractions and multiples of the drachma, in much the same way as the modern Latin Monetary Union was based on the franc.

The origin of the drachma goes back to the days when the Greeks, like the later Celts, used iron *currency bars* (q.v.). The drachma was literally a "handful" (for purposes of reckoning standardized at half a dozen) of *obeliskoi*. (See *Obel*.)

In later times the drachma was equated to the value of two denarii.

The drachma is still the monetary unit of modern Greece; under the Latin Monetary Union the drachma of 100 lepta was made equal to the value of the franc.

Draped Bust Type: See *Cent (U.S.)*; *Half Cent*.

Ducat (L. *ducatus*, a duchy): A gold or silver coin (usually gold) current in many forms in various parts of Europe over an extensive period. The first ducat in silver is supposed to have been minted by Roger II of Sicily for his Duchy of Apulia, about the middle of the twelfth century. It bore the motto:

SIT. T. XTE. D.Q. T.V. REG. ISTE. DUCAT.

Sit tibi, Christe, datus,

Quem Tu regis, iste Ducatus

("Unto Thee, O Christ, be dedicated this Duchy which Thou rulest.") From the last word—"Ducatus"—is derived the name of the coin.

About 1280 the gold ducat, afterwards called a *zecchino*, was struck in Venice. On the obverse is a figure of Christ standing in glory, and on the reverse the Doge receiving the gonfalone, or sacred banner, from St. Mark, the Patron Saint of Venice.

The gold ducat was extensively imitated all over Europe, though with much variation of type, and the term is somewhat loosely applied to European gold coins which have little or nothing in common with the original ducat. (See also *Zecchino*.)

Ducaton, or **Ducatoon** (It. *ducatone*, a large ducat): A large silver coin, the dollar of the Low Countries in the seventeenth and eighteenth centuries.

Duodecimal System (L. *duodecim*, twelve): A system of reckoning weights, measures, coins, etc., by dozens. Originating in the arithmetical notation of Ancient Rome, it is still largely the basis of the modern English weights, measures, and coinage. (See *As, Pound*.)

Dupondius (L. *duo*, two, *pondus*, weight): The *two-as* piece of Ancient Rome, struck (or rather cast) for the cities of southern Italy (see *As*.). Obv/Minerva, Rev/Prow of galley, and mark of value "II." In the reconstruction of the coinage under Augustus, the dupondius was struck in brass, or orichalcium, whereas the *as* was copper. In later times, to distinguish further the dupondius from the *as*, the bust of the Emperor bore a radiate crown.

The dupondius is usually known to numismatists as "second brass," represented by the abbreviation Ae. II.

E

E : The letter E beneath the bust on silver coins of Queen Anne (from 1707 to 1709) indicates that the coins were struck at the Edinburgh mint. (See *Scottish Coinage*.)

E.I.C.: Some of the gold coins of the earlier part of the reign of George II are stamped with the letters E.I.C. beneath the bust; this indicates that the gold was furnished by the East India Company.

Eagle: This $10.00 gold coin, authorized by the Act of April 2, 1792, was first issued in 1795 and ended with the 1933 coinage. The following types were struck:

Liberty Cap	1795–1804
Coronet	1838–1907
Indian Head	1907–33

The Liberty Cap style (Liberty facing right) had two reverses. The earliest was the small eagle also used on the reverse of the first half eagles. This was replaced by the large heraldic eagle with shield. The outstanding rarity of this type is the 1798 overstrike on the 1797 eagle,

Eagle. *Left:* Liberty Cap type. *Right:* Coronet type.

with 7 stars on the left and 6 on the right. The motto E PLURIBUS UNUM appears on a ribbon over the heraldic eagle. None of the coins of the Liberty Cap type had a stated value.

During the period 1805–37 no eagles were issued, apparently because of the steady drain on gold for export. In 1838 the first coins of the Coronet type (Liberty facing left) were issued. Throughout, the value appears on the reverse as TEN D. The mint mark is below the eagle on the reverse.

The outstanding Coronet eagle is the 1858 date. The motto E PLURIBUS UNUM was never used on these coins, but IN GOD WE TRUST appears in a ribbon over the eagle from 1866 on.

The Indian Head type, designed by the famous sculptor Augustus Saint-Gaudens and first issued in 1907, is one of the most beautiful examples of American coinage. The 1907 issues have several kinds of edges. On the 1907–11 edges there are 46 stars, while beginning with 1912 the number is increased to 48. The mint mark is to the left of the eagle's claw on the reverse.

Eagle, Indian Head (Saint-Gaudens) type.

Both mottoes (E PLURIBUS UNUM and IN GOD WE TRUST) appear on all the coins from 1908 on. The latter motto is missing from the 1907 and some 1908 coins as President Theodore Roosevelt considered the use of this motto on a coin blasphemous. The following year, however, Congress passed a law restoring the motto to the coin. On the reverse of these coins the value is always spelled out in full: TEN DOLLARS.

Ecclesiastical Mints: In the early days of the Saxons, archbishops, certain bishops, and abbots were permitted to issue coins, by privilege of the king, of their own design, and inscribed with their own names. In fact, the archbishops were allowed their own portraits. The earliest extant are the coins of Archbishop Ecgberht (734–66), Jaenberht, Archbishop of Canterbury, minted from 766 to 790. At the Council of Greatley, A.D. 928, it was decreed by Athelstan that there should be one kind of money throughout the realm; henceforth, though coins from the ecclesiastical mints were issued (principally at Canterbury, York, Durham, and London), they resembled those from the Royal Mint. The name of the ecclesiastic was omitted, but there is some significant letter, mint mark, or symbol to distinguish them from the regal issue. No gold coins were permitted to be struck, and in fact the ecclesiastical mints confined themselves practically to the penny. The right for ecclesiastics to issue coins was abolished by Henry VIII, the last of these mints being that of Thomas Cranmer, of Canterbury (1533–56). (See *Wolsey's Groat*.)

Ecu (Fr. a shield, from L. *scutum*, a shield): For a long period the "crown" or "dollar" of France; it corresponds to the *scudo* of Italy, the *escudo* of Spain, the *schild* of Holland, etc. For over two and a half centuries it was of gold, and assumed a bewildering variety of types and titles. The *écu d'or* (golden crown) was first struck by Philip VI (1328–50). It showed the king beneath a canopy, with the motto VINCIT XPS REGNAT XPS IMPERAT (Christ conquers, Christ reigns, Christ commands). On the reverse was a shield with a crown. This type was imitated in the Anglo-Gallic series of Edward III. In 1422 a new type was struck by Charles VI; in place of the king there is a large shield on the obverse, bearing the fleurs-de-lis of France. The *écu à la couronne* ("écu with the crown") was struck by Charles VII (1422–61). The obverse now has a large crown added over the shield. The *écu au soleil* (crown of the sun) was struck by Louis XI (1461–83). Over the shield and crown on the obverse is a small sun. The reverse of this coin was imitated by Henry VIII in his *Crown of the Rose* (q.v.).

During the seventeenth and eighteenth centuries the écu was a large silver coin—the *écu d'argent*, or *écu blanc*, and as such was first issued by Louis XIII in 1641. It was reckoned at a value of three *livres* (sixty *sols*). (See also *Crown*.)

Edward VIII: On the death of George V (January 20, 1936), the Prince of Wales automatically became king of Great Britain, as Edward VIII. He was, however, never crowned, and abdicated the throne after a period of little more than ten months. On the following December 10 dies were prepared for the expected new reign, but the English coins were never issued. For a few of the British colonies, however, some coins were struck with the name of Edward VIII, though they do not bear his portrait. These coins are as follows: New Guinea, bronze penny; Fiji, nickel penny; East Africa, bronze five and ten cents; West Africa, nickel tenth-penny, halfpenny, and one penny. English coins of 1936, though bearing the head of George V, are strictly speaking, coins of Edward VIII.

Egypt, Coins of: For literally thousands of years Ancient Egypt got on very well without any coins at all. It was largely a self-supporting community, with very insignificant international commerce. Barter sufficed for the small transactions of everyday life, while for bigger finance, as we see from numerous paintings on the walls of temples and tombs, the merchants weighed out rings of gold (see *Ring Money*). Such rings were about 5 in. in diameter, and the weights varied. It was not until the time of the Ptolemies that a proper currency was established in Egypt. This was superseded in the period of the Roman conquest by Egypto-Roman types of coins minted at *Alexandria* (q.v.).

Electrotype: A replica of a coin or medal made by a process somewhat resembling silver-plating. This process gives a faithful copy of the original, though a slight variation in size is discernible, and the weight will differ from the original. As the obverse and reverse are made separately, an inspection of the edge of an electrotype will reveal the join, though of course this can be plated over.

Electrum (Gr. *elektron*, amber, hence any amber-colored metal): The electrum of the Ancient Greeks was a natural blend of about three parts gold and one part silver, copper, etc. It usually was dug up from the river sands of Asia Minor. The earliest coins (*c.* 700 B.C.) were of Electrum (see *Lydia*). The word is also applied to an artificial alloy of gold and silver, such as were struck in the *Merovingian* series.

Elephant and Castle (Before 1675, an elephant only): As a symbol on English coins, both gold and silver, it signifies that the metal came from Guinea, in Africa (hence the term *Guinea*). It appears on coins of Charles II, James II, William and Mary, William III, Anne, and George I.

Elephant Coin: In 1694 the "Elephant" piece was struck for the British possessions in North America, New England, and Carolina.

Elephant coin issued in British Colonies.

The obverse is an elephant, without inscription. This obverse was taken from the same die as a halfpenny pattern or London token of William and Mary, struck the same year in London. Two tokens were struck, one with reverse "God Preserve New England, 1694," the other with reverse "God Preserve Carolina and the Lords Proprietors 1694."

Elgin, Ill. Centennial Commemorative Half Dollar: See *Commemorative Coins (U.S.)*, p. 66.

Encased Postage Stamps: The shortage of coins during the Civil War led the Federal government to authorize the use of postage stamps as a medium of exchange; that is, as money. Such use of stamps had many disadvantages; they soiled and tore quickly, the adhesive made them hard to handle.

John Gault of Boston hit on an ingenious way to preserve these stamps by designing a brass case that displayed a stamp and yet preserved it from damage. In 1862 he patented his idea. The stamp was placed on a round brass disk, covered with a round, transparent piece of mica and then both parts were fastened together in a brass frame. Merchants and business organizations issued these cases in sizeable quantities, placing slogans and mottoes on the back of the cases to advertise their products.

Encased postage stamp currency.
Left: Thomas Jefferson.
Right: George Washington.

The government issued the following denominations for use as encased postage: 1, 3, 5, 10, 12, 24, 30 and 90 cents. After several months, however, a better solution made its appearance: the fractional currency notes. Soon the further manufacture of the cases came to an end. See *Civil War Tokens, Fractional Currency Notes, Postage Currency Notes.*

English Coinage: The earliest English coin was the silver *penny*, with its fractions. The *groat*, introduced in the reign of Edward I, became popular in the time of Edward III. The *Florin* and *Noble* of Edward III begin the great series of English gold coins, followed by the *Ryal* and *Angel* of Edward IV. Realistic portraiture begins with the Renaissance coins of Henry VII. The greatest variety of denominations occurs in the reign of Elizabeth I. In this reign the process of *milling* coins began, though only experimentally. Copper coins were late in appearing, and were issued by Charles II to replace the swarm of unofficial tokens struck by private firms and individuals for small change.

Engrailed: A coin is said to be engrailed when its edge, in place of the usual straight reeding, is a succession of dots or curved indentations (as on some Spanish milled dollars, popularly known as "Pieces of 8").

Engraver: In the early days of English coinage the processes of designing a coin, engraving the dies, and striking were the work of one artisan. Later, these processes became specialized, but even today the term "engraver" is often applied to the "designer" of a coin. Undoubtedly the finest coin artists cut their own dies, as they did with their medals.

The Italians of the Renaissance had raised the engraving of medals to a fine art, and it was then that the genius of such great artists as Leonardo da Vinci and Benvenuto Cellini endeavored to raise the engraving of coins to a supreme art, as it had been in the days of the Ancient Greeks. Great medalists and coin engravers were also to be found in Germany. It was from this country that Henry VII invited Alexander of Brugsal to remodel the English coinage. The medievalism of the coins was not swept away, but became transformed into something simpler, more realistic, where harmony and perfection of form were blended with florid grace. For the first time since the days of the Romans, the portrait became realistic—slightly idealized, perhaps—but clear and discernible.

In the time of Elizabeth (1561) Eloye Mestrell from the Paris Mint introduced the mill and screw press (see *Milled Money, Screw Press*) a greatly improved process of minting coins. The work of the engraver was simplified, for coins could now be produced on a circular and symmetrical flan, and with even pressure. Unfortunately Mestrell turned out to be a rogue, and in the end was hanged for counterfeiting. The newfangled process was looked at somewhat askance, and was abandoned for over half a century.

Nicholas Briot then reintroduced the process. He was also from the Paris Mint, but a far greater man and artist than his predecessor. He worked at the Tower Mint for Charles I, and later cut dies for the Scottish Mint, before returning to France. Many of his coins bear a privy mark "B," or a small flower. During the time of the Civil War, during the seventeenth century, although employed officially by the Parliamentary Party at the Tower, he struck coins for the King at York and at Oxford. Another fine engraver of this period was Thomas Rawlins, whose most noted piece is the pattern *Oxford Crown* (q.v.).

The rivalry of two great artists, Thomas Simon and John Roettier, resulted in some masterpieces of engraving, more particularly on the medallic side. Of the two, Simon was the finer artist, but the austerity of the Puritan Commonwealth under which his principal coins were struck bridled the genius of his numismatic art, nor would he be looked on with favor at the Court of the Restoration. Roettier of Antwerp was more of a personal friend to Charles II, and that king favored friendship rather than fine art. The famous *Petition Crown* (q.v.) of Simon was the artist's final and greatest appeal for recognition, but the prize of office went to his rival. Simon retired in 1664, and in the following year died.

Engravers of varying degrees of merit worked at the Mint in succeeding reigns—Croker (chief engraver from 1704–41), Tanner (1741–73), Pingo (assistant engraver in the early years of the reign of George III)—but the next engraver of note is an Italian, Benedetto Pistrucci. He initiated St. George and the Dragon of the popular type on the English coinage.

The last of the great English engravers came from the Wyon family, of German origin, and as numerous in the ramifications of medallic art as the Bach family in the world of music. From the time of George III to the end of the reign of Queen Victoria, the Wyon family held the field for fine engraving, both of coins and medals.

In the field of American coinage, the best-known engravers and designers are:

Jean Pierre Droz, a Swiss. He is believed to have cut the dies for the first official American coin, the Chain cent of 1793. This style was quickly discontinued, as the chain or link on the reverse was considered a bad omen for Liberty (pictured on the obverse).

Christian Gobrecht. Noted for the Seated Liberty dollar, half dollar, quarter, dime and half dime first struck in 1837. The Gobrecht dollar and half dime were issued through 1873, the other coins through 1891. Gobrecht was also the designer of the Liberty Head quarter eagle, half eagle and eagle.

James B. Longacre. Best known for his design of the Indian Head cent, on which his initial, "L," appears on a ribbon of the headdress from 1864 on. Longacre also designed the two-cent piece, three-cent silver, three-cent nickel, shield nickel, gold dollar, three-dollar gold piece, and the Liberty Head double eagle.

George T. Morgan. Originally a pupil of Wyon at the Royal Mint in London, Morgan was the designer of the silver dollar of 1878-1921. This coin is usually referred to as a "Morgan dollar"—also "Liberty Head dollar." Morgan also designed the coiled-hair obverse for the "Stella" patterns (q.v.).

Charles E. Barber. Designer of the Liberty nickel (1883–1912), and the dime, quarter and half dollar of 1892–1916; also the "Stella" pattern (q.v.) with flowing-hair obverse.

Augustus Saint-Gaudens. Designer of the Indian Head eagle and of the double eagle, 1907–1933. These are generally considered the most beautiful and artistic examples of American coinage.

Victor D. Brenner. Designer of the Lincoln cent (1909 to date).

A. A. Weinman. Designer of the Winged Head Liberty ("Mercury") dime of 1916–1945, and also of the Liberty Walking half dollar (1916–1947).

As for current American coinage, the new Lincoln Memorial reverse was designed by Frank Gasparro; the Jefferson nickel by Felix Schlag; the Roosevelt dime and the Franklin half dollar by John R. Sinnock; and the Washington quarter by John Flanagan.

Errors: In the early days of hand-struck coins, with a multitude of moneyers at work in various parts of England equipped with crude dies, and copying words and designs which were often unintelligible to them, it is easy to understand why so many errors and blundered inscriptions abound, more especially in the spelling of names of towns and people. Even so late as the time of the Georges, the official coins of the realm have errors; for instance, on a halfpenny of George II (1730) we find the king's name spelt GEOGIVS, and on a halfpenny of George III (1772), GEORIVS.

The abundant forged copper coins of the Georges often present amusing errors; some appear to have been made deliberately, so that the counterfeiter, if caught, could conveniently plead he was merely making an imitation, and not purposely copying coins of the realm (see *Evasions*).

Actual errors in design are rare; such an error, however, appears on the Kruger coins of the South African Republic, where the wagon on the arms of the Republic has double in place of single shafts. This curious error appeared later on the postage stamps of the Republic.

See also *Mint Errors (Freaks), Three-Error Large Cent.*

Escudo (Sp. a shield, L. *scutum*): The Spanish crown, equivalent to the Italian *scudo* and the French *écu*. It was struck in both silver and gold. Today it is current in Portugal, and also in Chile, where it is a gold coin of the value of five pesos. From 1864 to 1868, the silver escudo of ten reales was the official Spanish monetary basis.

Essay: A trial piece. (See *Experimental Pieces, Pattern Coins, Transitional Pattern, Trial Pieces.*)

European Coinage: The Roman Empire as a body collapsed in the surge of barbarian hordes in the fifth century A.D.—Goths, Vandals, and

Huns—who split up the imperial unity into a number of petty king-doms; but the spirit of Rome lived on, a great unifying force. The Catholic faith she had adopted and spread over the world, her civiliza-tion, her learning, her laws, conquered her conquerors in the course of time. Merged in her long and potent traditions, the barbarians settled down and built up a new civilization founded on ancient Rome. They took over her laws, they imitated her coinage. They were but crude copies of an already debased coinage that they struck, but the · Christiano-Roman types were predominant. The unifying spirit of Rome was still potent, and when Pepin (752–68) struck the *novus denarius* (see *Denier*), it was not so much a new coin as the old Roman denarius in a new dress; it was destined to become the pattern and standard coin for all Europe for more than five centuries.

It was not until the thirteenth century that any appreciable change came about in the coinage of Europe. Increase of wealth and expansion of trade, especially trade with the Orient, necessitated a gold currency. The gold coinage of Rome had been limited in its circulation, and since the time of the Merovingians, the very types had been forgotten. Entirely new designs came into being, principally the *fiorino d'oro* (the florin) and the *zecchino*. At the same time, a larger silver coin than the denier became necessary, and the *gros* of France became the pattern type for the *grosso, groschen, groat*, etc.

Coinage is essentially conservative in values and types, and the greater the extent of circulation, the less welcome is any innovation or even deviation from the accepted type. Similarly, a group of countries, such as Europe, closely connected by politics and trade, will tend to assimilate coin types and values. Thus England copied the Continental *denier*, and smaller nations, in turn, such as Flanders, Luxembourg, many northern German States, copied the popular English penny. At the same time, coinage, until quite recent times, was largely inter-national. Even in England official decrees authorized the circulation of many foreign coins. This helped to eke out the scarcity of the national mint. Numerous brass coin weights are extant, as well as the actual balances, for checking the values of these monetary strangers.

At the end of the fifteenth century the coinage of Europe completely changed. The new method of striking coins by machinery in place of the slow and laborious process of hammering out by hand enabled coins of better shape and more detail to be produced. Large, imposing pieces of silver, with elaborate portraits and florid heraldic devices on the reverse, began to predominate. The growth of international trade called for a vastly increased output of currency. This was brought about by the opening up of the large silver mines of Bohemia and Tyrol (see *Taler*), and the influx of *pesos* (q.v.) from Spanish America in the sixteenth century.

In the eighteenth century the *crown* or *dollar* had become the standard coin of the Continent. It was a convenient method of reckoning, as it was established on a decimal basis. England, however, was more insular in her coinage. From the Tudor age onwards, though the florin and crown were struck, they did not fall in easily with the duodecimal system on which the rest of her coin was based; hence a number of coins distinct from the Continental series were produced by the English mints.

Evasions (Lit. an artful or dishonorable means of escape, a subterfuge: L. *evado*, to escape): Imitations of regal copper coins, fabricated in the reigns of George I, II, and III. They were made to resemble as closely as possible the official issues of the realm, but at the same time not close enough to warrant the charge of forgery—hence the counterfeiter *evaded* the law. Though some sort of likeness of the king was on the obverse, and the figure of Britannia or something resembling Britannia was on the reverse, the inscriptions were often nonsensical, and the name of the king was ludicrously perverted or misspelled. To the illiterate masses the inscription conveyed no meaning, but it evaded the law. Halfpennies were usually imitated, though copies of the farthings are fairly plentiful, but there are no penny "evasions," as the first Georgian penny was not struck until 1797. The light weight of these imitation coins showed a handsome profit to the fabricator, the wholesale dealer, and the private trader. The dealer purchased them in bulk at about half the ostensible value, and an unscrupulous trader could buy from the dealer thirty-shillings' worth of value for a guinea. (See *Counterfeiting*.)

Exchequer (O. Fr. *eschekier*, M.L., *scaccarium*, a chessboard, a cloth or table with squares): The Court of the Exchequer was established by the Norman kings and it dealt with everything pertaining to the royal finance, the Crown revenues, etc. The Court was held twice yearly, at first at Winchester, and afterwards at Westminster. The complicated accounts were worked out in a simple manner by counters on a checkered tablecloth (see *Counter*). In the nineteenth century the Court ceased to function as the royal tribunal, and in 1875 became a part of the High Court of Justice.

Today the word is applied to that department of the British Government which deals with all questions relating to public finance and revenue. It is presided over by the Chancellor of the Exchequer.

Exergue (Gr. *eks* out of, beside, *ergon*, the [main] work): The bottom part of a coin or medal, that small space which gives the date, value, country, etc. It is usually separated from the field of the coin by a line.

Experimental Pieces: These involve a departure from accepted coinage practice. In some cases the innovation is based on a new metal (see *Stella*); in others a change of shape may be proposed, as the 1884 nickel with an octagonal hole in the planchet.

F

F.: Abbreviation on Roman Republican coins for *Filius*, son (of). On the later imperial coins it is an abbreviation for *Felix* (blessed by Fortune).

Face Value: The denomination of a coin, as contrasted with its *market value* or *premium value*.

Falu (L. *follis*, q.v.): Originally an early Arabian copper coin, derived from the Byzantine *follis*. Later it became a general term for any *copper* coinage, as distinguished from gold or silver. Today the very common cast copper coins of Morocco, bearing the Seal of Solomon and a Mohammedan date, are known as Falus. One- to ten-falu pieces have been minted.

Family Coins, Roman: Denarii of the Roman Republic which bear the symbol or name of a moneyer. Three moneyers were usually appointed annually by the Senate, the *Tres viri aere argento auro flando feriundo* (triumvirs for the casting and striking of bronze, silver, and gold). They were young senators, and, more often than not, they struck coins with types glorifying some noted ancestor of their family who had achieved some great work in the building up of the Empire. Often under this glorification of the past, allusion was made to contemporary happenings. Thus Brutus in his famous denarii commemorates his famous ancestors, L. Junius Brutus, the first Consul of Rome, who expelled the hated Tarquin kings from Rome, and C. Servilius Ahala, the tyrannicide. Such coins, however, were struck not so much to glorify the past as rather to challenge the impending tyranny of Caesar. (See also *Consular Coins*.)

Farthing (A.S. *feorthling*, a "fourthling," or fourth part): In early times the silver penny was cut into two or four parts, along the lines of the voided cross on the reverse, thus giving halfpennies and farthings respectively. The round silver farthing was first struck, along with the round halfpenny and the groat, by Edward I, in 1279. Such a minute coin as this was never popular, and consequently ceased to be issued after the time of Edward VI. In 1684 Charles II issued tin farthings with a square plug of copper in the center. Round the edge they bore the somewhat apologetic inscription NUMMORUM FAMULUS (the Knave

Pattern farthing of Charles II (1665).

of Coins). In 1672 the first copper farthing was struck, similar in type to the halfpenny (q.v.). Half-farthings, third-farthings, and quarter-farthings have also been struck. (See under the respective headings. See also *Queen Anne Farthing*.)

Farthing, Biblical: In the Authorized Version of the New Testament "farthing" is the rather inaccurate translation of two different Greek words: *Assarion* (Matt. x. 29, Luke xii. 6), and *kodrantes* (Matt. v. 26, Mark xii. 42). The former was worth about half a cent, and the latter an eighth of a cent. (See *Assarion, Quadrans*.)

Fasces: A bundle of rods around an ax; carried by the lictors in ancient Rome as a symbol of consular authority. The fasces appears on our Winged Head Liberty ("Mercury") *dime* of 1916–1945; also on several Italian coins of the Mussolini period (from which is derived the word "fascism").

Feathered Crown: The head of Liberty with a feathered headdress in the shape of a crown as it appears on the large-size ("Indian Head") gold dollars of 1854–1889 and the three-dollar gold pieces of the same period.

Feuchtwanger Composition: Dr. Lewis Feuchtwanger produced a copper-nickel alloy which he proposed to Congress for use in minor American coinage. In 1837 he made some trial cents and three-cent pieces. As these tokens were produced in relatively large quantities they are often encountered and are interesting additions to a collection.

Fiddler's Money: Small silver pieces, such as were given to a minstrel by those attending country wakes and other festivals.

Fidei Defensor (L. Defender of the Faith): This is an early title of royalty, and occurs occasionally in medieval documents. In 1521 Pope Leo X formally conferred the title on Henry VIII for his book written against Luther, *Defense of the Seven Sacraments*, when it appeared on the royal seal. It did not appear on his coins, however, though the quarter-angel of Elizabeth (struck 1566–1602) bears the words REGINA FIDEI, and F.D. appears on a crown and half-crown of Charles II struck in Ireland. It was not until the time of George I that it was placed permanently on English coins. It was no doubt then intended as a

Protestant counterblast to the Jacobite party. Sometimes the title is written in full, but it is more often abbreviated to FID. DEF., or to the bare initials, F.D.

Field: All that part of a coin which is not occupied by the device or the exergue. This space may be completely void, or may bear a letter, numeral, or symbol.

Fifty Cents Silver (Canadian): Issued from 1870 to date. For years of regal types see *Cent (Canadian)*. The reverse design is the same through 1936 as on the five-cent piece, and the mint mark is located in the same position.

This denomination was issued in smaller quantities than the lesser denominations; premium values therefore run higher. This is especially true of the following dates: 1890 H, 1894, 1904. Most of the fifty-cent coins of 1921 were melted down because of lack of demand and less than 50 are known. This is the outstanding rarity of Canadian coinage. A crowned shield appears on the reverse for the first time on the 1937 coinage. The most valuable Canadian coin of recent times is the 1947 Maple Leaf variety with a curved 7 pointing to the right. Starting with the 1959 issue the Canadian coat of arms replaced the crowned shield on the reverse.

Five-Cent Nickel: See *Nickel Five-Cent Piece*.

Five Cents (Canadian): Issued as a silver coin up to 1921 and from then on in nickel—with changes to be noted below. For years of regal types see *Cent (Canadian)*. Through 1936 the reverse design is similar to that of the cent. On the five-cent piece the wreath is crowned and there is no circle around the value and date. During the period 1870–1903 there are some coins with the H mint mark. It appears below the center of the ribbon tying the wreath on the reverse.

About 2,500,000 five-cent silver pieces had been struck in 1921 when the mint decided to replace them with a larger nickel coin. The silver coins were melted down, but a few silver coins went to collectors who had visited the mint or who had ordered complete sets. About 50 silver 1921 coins are known, and they are of course quite valuable. The change in the reverse design introduced two maple leaves similar to the new design on the cent. The attractive beaver reverse appeared for the first time in 1937.

During World War II and subsequently, the five-cent coin underwent numerous transformations. The pressing wartime need for nickel resulted in a 1942 five-cent piece of tombac brass, an alloy containing 88 per cent copper and 12 per cent zinc. To avoid confusing this coin with the bronze cent, the new coin was struck in a twelve-sided shape.

In 1943 tombac was used again, but this time with a new reverse: a torch and a V for victory. Around the border there appeared the inscription, "We win when we work willingly" in Morse code.

The new design was retained in 1944 and 1945, with chromium-steel replacing the tombac. In 1946 the mint reverted to nickel and the original beaver design but retained the twelve-sided shape. In 1951 a commemorative five-cent piece (still twelve-sided) was issued to commemorate the 200th anniversary of the discovery of nickel. The regular beaver design was continued in steel (1951–54) and later on in nickel again.

Five-Guinea Piece, Five-Pound Piece: Five-guinea pieces and two-guinea pieces were minted by Charles II, James II, William and Mary, Anne, George I, and George II, but not by George III, probably owing to the shortage of gold caused by the Napoleonic Wars. George IV struck a double sovereign in 1823. Victoria in 1887 and in 1893 struck a five-pound piece together with a two-pound piece; these two denominations were also struck by Edward VII and George V in 1902 and 1911 respectively and later by George VI and Elizabeth II, but such coins were more in the nature of souvenirs or commemorative medallions than for use as currency.

Flan (Fr. originally a flat cake or pie): A blank; metal cut to the shape of a coin, but as yet unstamped.

Fleur de Coin (Fr.): A numismatic term (usually abbreviated to **F.D.C.**), denoting the condition of a coin or medal to be as fine as when it came from the mint. The word *coin*, however, has not the same meaning as our English word, but is really a French word meaning *die*; the expression *fleur de coin* may therefore be translated as "bearing the bloom of the mint."

Florin (It. *fiorino*, a little flower, in allusion to the lily on the reverse): European gold coinage began in the second half of the thirteenth century with the gold coins of Florence. In 1252 the *fiorino d'oro*, or gold florin (value 3s.) was struck. It showed the figure of St. John the Baptist, and on the reverse the lily, or fleur-de-lis, which was the badge of Florence, with the legend FLORENTIA (i.e., Florence). This coin, together with the gold *Ducat*, struck in 1280 at Venice, became extremely popular, and was imitated over most of Europe. In England, in 1344, Edward III struck a gold *florin*, value six shillings, showing the king seated beneath a canopy, with the legend IHS TRANSIENS PER MEDIVM IBAT (see *Mottoes on Coins*). Half and quarter florins were also issued (see *Helm, Leopard*).

The English silver florin originated in 1849 in the demand for the

Florence, gold florin (*c.* 1450).

currency to be placed on a decimal basis, the coin being one-tenth of a sovereign. It was intended to supersede the half-crown. This latter coin was consequently not struck between 1852 and 1874. The first florin to be struck was the *Godless Florin* (q.v.).

A double florin, or four-shilling piece, was minted from 1887 to 1890, but this was never a popular coin. (See also *Gothic Florin.*)

Flying Eagle Type: See *Cent (U.S.)*.

Follis (L. a money-bag): Originally a large leather purse, or money-bag, especially one in which the army pay-money was kept; it was then used as a term for money of account; afterwards, in the time of Diocletian's reform of the coinage (A.D. 296), it was applied to an actual coin, which was intended to function as a double-denarius piece. A common type of the follis was that of the Genius of the Roman people crowned with a *modius* (corn measure) and holding a cornucopia: Legend, GENIO ROMANI POPULI ("to the Genius of the Roman people"). The coin was a broad but thin piece of copper, washed with silver. Originally larger than the *antoninianus*, it rapidly dwindled in size in succeeding reigns, and the value depreciated accordingly. It was revived as a large copper coin in the Eastern Empire, under the Byzantine emperor Anastasius. It bore on the reverse a large letter M, the Greek numeral signifying 40, i.e., 40 *nummi*.

Forgery (Fr. *forgerie*, the working of metal): Originally this word had quite an innocent meaning, signifying to work anything, such as a metal, with a forge:

> . . . the forgery
> Of brazen shield and spear.
> (Milton, *Samson Agon.* 1,131),

but later the word became synonymous with *counterfeit* (q.v.).

Fort Vancouver Centennial Commemorative Half Dollar: See *Commemorative Coins (U.S.)*, p. 62.

Four-Dollar Gold: See *Stella*.

Fractional Currency Notes: A collective term applied to five issues of diminutive United States paper money to relieve the Civil War shortage of coins. All the notes were less than a dollar in value.

Two of the issues actually appeared after the end of the war, the last one occurring as late as 1876. In all, some $40,000,000 worth of these notes was issued. A high amount, in the neighborhood of $2,000,000, was never redeemed at the Treasury.

The first issue (August 1862) carried reproductions of current stamp designs and even had perforated edges; but the notes were ungummed. The size of the notes was approximately 2¾ by 3⅜ inches and they were printed on durable banknote paper. The denominations (5, 10, 25 and 50 cents) were obviously issued with a view to replacing the scarce half dimes, dimes, quarters and half dollars. Portraits of Washington and Jefferson were featured on this issue, the 25-cent note bearing five reproductions of the 5-cent stamp, while the 50-cent stamp had five reproductions of the 10-cent stamp. See *Civil War Tokens, Encased Postage, Postage Currency Notes.*

Fractional Currency, First Issue, 25 cents value with portrait of Thomas Jefferson.

The second issue appeared during October 1863 and February 1867. All four denominations (5, 10, 25, 50 cents) carried portraits of Washington. Each reverse had a different color.

The third issue (December 1864 to August 1869) had these denominations: 3, 5, 10, 25, 50 cents (two designs). A great hue and cry went up when it was discovered that the 5-cent note carried a portrait of Spencer M. Clark, Superintendent of the National Currency Bureau. The public outcry became so strong that Congress passed a law forbidding the use of the portrait of any living person on the coins, currency and postage of the United States. One reason why the reaction was so strong was that two other officeholders were pictured on notes of the third issue—F. E. Spinner, United States Treasurer, and William P. Fessenden, Secretary of the Treasury. (The solution that "there ought to be a law" is not always effective: witness the portraits of Senators Joseph Robinson and Carter Glass and President Calvin Coolidge on commemorative coins issued during their lifetime.)

A 15-cent note intended for the fourth issue used the portraits of Generals Grant and Sheridan. However, it was issued only in essay form, as its regular issue might have started a fresh storm of indignation, despite the fact that these generals were wartime heroes. The providential appearance of the new 5-cent nickel in 1866 helped the 5-cent Clark note on its way to oblivion.

The fourth issue (July 1869 to February 1875) comprised these denominations: 10, 15, 25, 50 cents (three designs).

Fractional Currency, Fourth Issue, portrait of Columbia.

The fifth and last issue (February 1874 to February 1876) was made up of a 10-cent, 25-cent and 50-cent note. Interestingly enough, the top denomination carried a portrait of a Southerner, William H. Crawford, who, however, had died long before the outbreak of the Civil War. See *Encased Postage* and *Postage Stamp Currency*.

Fractional Currency Shield: Specimen fractional-currency notes printed by the U.S. government and mounted on a cardboard shield. These were made available to banks and other interested parties so that questionable notes could be compared with known genuine specimens as an aid in detecting counterfeits.

Franc (Fr. probably derived from the original legend on the coin *Francorum Rex*, King of the Franks, i.e., France): A French coin, first struck in the fourteenth century in gold, and worth about $2.50; in the sixteenth century it was struck in silver and then worth about 85 cents. Although it ceased to be struck after 1641, it was still used in reckoning as money of account.

In the reorganization of the currency at the time of the French Revolution (1795) the name was transferred to a silver coin (now aluminum), which was adopted as the unit of the currency. One hundred centimes constituted a franc. The metric system of currency was later adopted by Switzerland, Belgium, Italy, Greece, and Serbia (see *Latin Monetary Union*). The value of this modern franc, pre-1914, was about 23 cents.

France, Coinage of: The story of French coinage goes back to the Merovingians and more especially to the Carolingians, but the Kingdom of the Franks was Teutonic, and included Germany as well as France. As an independent kingdom France comes into being with the accession of Hugh Capet in 987. Apart from a few extraneous coins such as the gold *byzant*, the *denier* or *novus denarius* was then the sole current coin, as it was throughout practically the whole of Europe. Unlike the English penny, this small and insignificant coin was struck from numerous private mints; the striking of money was farmed out to princes, barons, dukes, counts, lords, and a swarm of ecclesiastics. This led to a bewildering variety of weights and values.

It was not until the time of Louis IX (1226–70) that a proper standard of currency was fixed for the whole country. He was the first European monarch to strike an extensive gold currency, the principal coin of which was the *denier d'or*. The gros was introduced from Italy, and the famous *gros tournois*, or four-denier piece, was destined to become a standard coin throughout the whole of Europe (see *Groat*).

France, silver gros tournois of Louis IX (1226–70).

The modern coinage of France may be said to date from the reign of Louis XII (1498–1515), when the first realistic portraits take the place of the conventional medieval type of head.

The milling process (see *Milled Money*) is said to have been invented by Antoine Brucher, and coins were produced by this process from the time of Henry II of France (1553) until the time of Henry III of France (1585). It was then discontinued for a period of fifty years, when Louis XIV reintroduced it permanently into the coinage.

From 1792 to 1795, the copper coins in France mark the progress of the Revolution, and are often made the medium of revolutionary propaganda. The bust of Louis XVI was retained on the obverse of the coins up to the time of his execution, but on the reverse appears the revolutionary symbol of the fasces surmounted by the Cap of Liberty; around is the legend LA NATION, LA LOI, LE ROI. The bust of the king becomes very crudely engraved, and after his execution, in 1793, the bust of Liberty takes the place of the head of "Louis Capet." On all these coins of the Revolution appear the years of the new calendar; *l'an un de la Liberté* (year one of Liberty) was reckoned from midnight of September 21-22, 1792. This calendar lasted until December 1805.

In 1795 a thorough reconstruction of the coinage was effected. In place of the fluctuating gold *Louis* and the silver *écu*, the decimal system was introduced, based on the silver *franc* as the monetary standard. Native French inscriptions took the place of the old Latin legends.

References to French coins will be found under: *Châtel Tournois, Ecu, European Coinage, Franc, Gros, Liard, Louis d'Or, Sol, Sou.*

Franklin Type: See *Half Dollar.*

French Revolutionary Calendar: This will be useful in dating copper coins of the Revolutionary period:

Year	Began	Year	Began
I	September 22, 1792	IX	September 23, 1800
II	September 22, 1793	X	September 23, 1801
III	September 22, 1794	XI	September 23, 1802
IV	September 23, 1795	XII	September 24, 1803
V	September 22, 1796	XIII	September 23, 1804
VI	September 22, 1797	XIV	September 23, 1805
VII	September 22, 1798	XV	September 23, 1806
VIII	September 23, 1799		

Friedberg Numbers: Collectors of United States currency attribute their notes according to listings in *Paper Money of the United States*, by Robert Friedberg.

Fugio Cent (From the obverse legend FUGIO, "I fly," accompanying the device of a sun dial): On the reverse are 13 links in a chain, symbolic of the original 13 states. This coin, dated 1787, was the first to be issued by the United States. The motto in the exergue, MIND YOUR BUSINESS, was a characteristic saying of "Poor Richard" (Benjamin Franklin), and was used in the sense of "tend your business diligently."

Fugio Cent.

G

Garble (O. Fr. *grabeller*, to sift, as spices; Ar. *ghirbal*, a sieve): To garble coins is to sort good coins from the bad; this can be done officially, as by a bank when it returns worn and lightweight coins to the Mint, or illegally, when good coins are remelted, or sent abroad and inferior ones are passed into circulation as opportunity arises.

Gateway: Often known as a Praetorian Gateway (i.e., gateway of the camp or barracks), this is a very common type of reverse on Roman coins of the fourth century A.D. In conjunction with such legends as SPES ROMANORUM (Hope of the Romans), PROVIDENTIA CAESARUM (Providence of the rulers), VIRTUS MILITUM (Valor of the soldiers), etc., the type appears to symbolize the power of the emperor and his armies to withstand the barbarian hordes that were then threatening the existence of the Empire. The type was copied in England on a coin of Edward the Elder, and was imitated on the later Saxon Burg-type pennies. (See *Architecture*.)

Gaul, Coins of: Massilia, the ancient Marseilles, was a colony founded by the Greeks. The staters of Philip II (see *Philippus*) circulated freely long after the death of Philip. They became the most popular coin of Gaul, and were frequently imitated by the natives. The Gallic imitations were, in their turn, imitated by the southeast tribes of Britain.

It is easy, however, to overemphasize the imitative aspect and to regard them as mere distortions of Greek art. In many cases, especially with the British Celtic coins, Philip's gold stater was but the starting-point of a highly original and often richly imaginative coinage. The somewhat pedestrian coin of Macedonia and Marseilles was turned into "something rich and strange." The placid Greek Apollo becomes the fiery sun-god Ogma (or whatever name we choose to call him); the stud horses of Philip are metamorphized into the sun-steed of Heaven, a galaxy of mystic solar symbols clustered round him. (See *Britons, Coins of the Ancient*.)

Gazzetta (It. diminutive of *Gazet*, a small Venetian coin): A small Venetian copper coin, dating from the sixteenth century, and worth two *soldi* (somewhat less than a cent). This is the coin which gave its name to the earliest form of European newspaper, the *gazette*, perhaps because this was the price charged to hear the newspaper publicly read.

George Noble: English gold coin of the reign of Henry VIII, and worth at the time 6*s*. 8*d*. On the reverse was St. George slaying the dragon,

George noble of Henry VIII.

on the obverse a ship with Tudor rose and large cross and above, the initials H.K. (Henry and Katherine of Aragon). The coin is extremely rare; of the half-George noble only one specimen is known.

Germany: The native coinage of Germany begins with the coins of the Ostrogoths. Odoacer struck bronze coins 476–90. The early history of German numismatics is bound up with the history of the Franks, a Teutonic race, but as this race covered France as well as the greater part of modern Germany, we must look to the *Merovingian* and *Carlovingian* coins (see under these names) for the early coinage of Germany. An important and magnificent series of coins was issued for some centuries under the Holy Roman Empire, but strictly speaking, this is outside the province of Germany proper. As in practically the whole of Europe, the *novus denarius* was the standard coin of the early Middle Ages in Germany. In fact, it was almost the only coin at that period in Germany. Though derived from the *denier* of the Carlovingians, owing to the number and variety of mints of the different German cities and states, the novus denarius showed a greater complication of types than anywhere else.

For small payments, the *bracteates* (q.v.), issued between the twelfth and fourteenth centuries, were the popular coins of the small trader. Gold coins were late in appearing. Louis IV of Bavaria (1328–47) made copies of the Florentine fiorini, and of the French *écu* (q.v.). About 1470 the discovery of large silver-mines led to the striking of the large *taler* (q.v.). The coins of Germany that have influenced European coinage most are the *pfennig* and the *taler*.

Gettysburg Commemorative Half Dollar: See *Commemorative Coins (U.S.)*, p. 67.

Ghost Penny, Ghosting: English pennies of the first issue of George V (struck 1911–27) are popularly known as "ghost" pennies. They were of such poor workmanship that the obverse usually showed through on the reverse. Such phenomenon is known as "ghosting."

Gilbert Numbers: Specialists in collecting half cents refer to die varieties and attribute their coins according to listings in *United States Half Cents*, by Ebenezer Gilbert.

Glass: Glass tesserae of the first to fourth centuries A.D. have been found in Egypt. It seems probable they were used as coins. It is believed certain glass weights found in Arabia were used as small currency tokens.

Godless, or **Graceless, Florin:** The first English *silver* florin, struck in 1849. So called from the fact that the obverse bore the bare title "Victoria Regina, 1849," omitting the customary "Dei Gratia, F.D." It

Great Britain, silver ("Godless") florin, Victoria (1849).

was designed, like the Gothic crown, in the Victorian gothic style, though the inscription was in plain lettering. The innovation in the legend led to a great popular outcry. The outbreak of cholera that year was even attributed to an outraged Deity. The offensive florin was immediately called in: the Master of the Mint, a Roman Catholic, had to shoulder most of the blame; he was promptly dismissed from his post.

Gold (Numismatic abbreviation AU or AV = L. *aurum*, gold): Gold is an ideal medium for coins of value, being highly ductile and malleable, rustless, and untarnishable by water and acids. Native gold is an alloy of gold and silver (see *Electrum*). Pure gold is too soft for the rough usage to which coins are subject, and therefore is alloyed, usually with copper. English coins have eleven parts of gold to one of copper. Other countries have adopted a standard of nine parts of gold to one of copper.

Gold Coins: The earliest Greek coins, struck in Asia Minor, were of electrum, and the device they bore was rather a guarantee of quality than an indication of a definite weight. The first issue of gold coins is attributed to Croesus, King of Lydia (561–546 B.C.) (see *Lydia*). For centuries, however, Greece produced very few gold coins. The Persian *daric* sufficed for transactions involving gold. It was not until the time of Philip II of Macedon that Greek gold coins appear in any abundance. Philip obtained vast supplies of gold from his mines at Philippi in Thrace. Henceforth, for a long period, coins were struck of fine gold, namely 23 carats, 3 grains fine to one grain of alloy. The few gold coins that Greece proper produced in the course of her history are disappointing; the finest numismatic art was lavished on her silver coinage.

In Ancient Rome gold coins were more abundant, even up to the fall of the Empire. The *bezant* (q.v.) was issued at Byzantium, and this became the standard gold coin of early medieval Europe. The Merovingian dynasty in their *Tremissis* imitated the *Triens* of Rome, and the Merovingian coin has been found as far afield as England. The *Tremissis* was in turn copied by the Anglo-Saxons, though specimens are of great rarity. These Anglo-Saxon coins are known as *Thrymsas*.

117

GOLD

Florence and Venice in the thirteenth century produced a gold coinage, and the popularity of the Florentine coin—the *Florin*—led to a somewhat premature attempt by Henry III to introduce a gold coin into English coinage. In 1257 he struck a gold penny, of the value of twenty silver pennies. This was not a mere copy of the popular European coin, for it had the original device of the king sitting on a throne. It was 24-carat pure gold. Very few of these coins were struck, and it was not until the reign of Edward III that a regular gold coinage began in England. Early in his reign gold coins had been struck in the Anglo-Gallic series, and, in 1344, he struck the gold florin of the value of six shillings, which was double the value of the Florentine coin. U.S. gold coins include the *dollar, quarter eagle, three-dollar gold piece, four-dollar gold piece, half eagle, eagle* and *double eagle* (q.v.). There are also some gold *commemorative coins.* (See also *Britons, Coins of the Ancient, Gold Standard.*)

Canada struck several gold coins: five dollars gold 1912–14; ten dollars gold 1912–14; sovereigns 1908–11, 1913–14, 1916–19. The 1913 C and 1916 C issues are particularly valuable.

Gold Order: On March 16, 1933 a Presidential Order issued by Franklin Delano Roosevelt discontinued all further U.S. gold coinage. The order also removed gold coins from circulation; made it compulsory to turn over all such coins to the Treasury; prohibited private hoarding of gold; discontinued free domestic gold markets. The order further prohibited banks from paying out gold or gold certificates without permission from the Treasury, so that all gold currency could be kept for reserve purposes. To assure the same objective, the order provided that all gold imports and newly mined domestic gold must be sold to the Treasury.

There are a few exceptions, chiefly for coin collectors and industrial users of gold. The order specifically allows coin collectors and the coin trade to continue buying, selling and exchanging gold coins.

Gold Standard: Before the year 1816 the English currency was bimetallic, but in that year the gold standard was adopted by Great Britain. It was enacted that gold only should be legal tender for any amount, and that silver coins, regarded merely as representative coins, should be legal tender for sums not exceeding two guineas. In 1931, owing to the financial postwar complications, it was found necessary to abandon the gold standard. (See also *Latin Monetary Union, Silver Standard.*)

Gothic Crown: Silver coin of Queen Victoria, designed by William Wyon, in the mid-Victorian pseudo-gothic taste, and with the inscription in the Early English style of lettering. It showed the Queen in a

Great Britain, silver ("Gothic") crown, Victoria (1847).

dress of highly ornate pattern, with a crown on her head. It was struck in 1847, and reissued in 1853. It appears to have been more of a commemorative coin (celebrating the tenth anniversary of the accession to the throne) than a medium of currency; in fact, the 1853 reissue was released only in complete proof sets.

Gothic Florin: The second type of silver florin (following the *Godless Florin*, q.v.), issued 1851–87. The bust and reverse were similar to those of the Gothic Crown.

Grant Memorial Commemorative Coins: See *Commemorative Coins (U.S.)*, pp. 61, 69.

Greece: The story of our modern coinage begins with the coins of Ancient Greece. It was the Greek genius that first devised the idea of coins as a symbol and guarantee of value. The coin of today is fundamentally the same as the coin that was struck in Greece in the eighth century B.C. It is still today, as then, something portable, flat, and round, an accepted standard of size and weight, and of precious metal to give it value; it still has a portrait on one side, and something of a symbol or heraldic device on the other.

Greek coinage had its beginnings in the electrum coins of Asia Minor in the eighth century B.C. Croesus of Lydia (561–546) triumphantly discarded electrum, along with the old iron currency bars of indeterminate weight and value, and established a bi-metallic system of pure gold and silver.

There is still much controversy among experts as to whether the earliest Greek types were religious, heraldic, or merely commercial. The most likely solution seems to be that it was a union of all three types. In any case, heraldic types are often religious in origin, and in a sane and healthy community commerce is not something extraneous to religion. The gods were honored on the earliest coins, and it was many centuries before the portrait of a man usurped the figures of the gods. The story of Greek coinage roughly divides itself into two periods:

(1) what we may call the civic period, when cities and city-states struck coins with their own peculiar types and badges, and (2) the regal, or imperial period, the period of the Macedonian princes, when the main feature of the coins becomes an advertising portrait.

The distinctive feature of Greek coinage was its reliance on silver. Just as a person in Victorian days spoke of money in a general way as "gold," so the Ancient Greeks spoke of money as *argurion*, i.e., "silver."

For further references to the coins of the Ancient Greeks, see *Aegina, Architecture, Art, Classification, Incuse, Lydia, Pheidon, Portraits on Coins, Religion, Gold Coins*, etc.

Greek Equivalents of Roman Terms:

ΑΡΧΙΕΡΕΥΣ	Pontifex Maximus (High Priest)
ΑΥΤΟΚΡΑΤΩΡ	Imperator (Military Commander)
ΒΑΣΙΛΕΥΣ	Rex (King)
ΘΕΟΣ	Deus (Divine, a God)
ΚΑΙΣΑΡ	Caesar
ΣΕΒΑΣΤΟΣ	Augustus (Emperor)
ΥΠΑΤΟΣ	Consul

Greek Imperial Series: For a period of nearly three centuries, from the beginning of the Christian era to the reign of Gallienus, the Greek cities in the Eastern part of the Empire were permitted by the Romans to strike bronze money for local use. Usually the bust of the Roman Emperor appears on the obverse, and the reverses show an amazing variety of types, many of them relating to obscure local rites.

Gresham's Law (from Gresham, a former English Master of the Mint, and not, as is often supposed, from Sir Thomas Gresham): An axiom in economics that inferior money tends to drive superior money out of circulation, or in other words, "Bad money drives out good."

Groat (Low Ger. *grote*, lit. the "great" coin; Low L. *grossus*, great; cf. Fr. *gros*, big): Name given in the Middle Ages to all thick silver coins, as distinguished from thin coins such as *deniers* and *bracteates*. The name is a translation of *denarii grossi* (large denarii), and in England was applied specifically to the fourpenny-piece, introduced in 1279 in the time of Edward I. This coin was copied from the continental *gros tournois* (see *Gros*). In type it was not unlike the penny, though more ornate and of finer workmanship. Very few were struck in this reign, but in the reign of Edward III it became a popular coin. Groats were issued in various types, in later times as a minute silver coin. They were current until 1662, and even after that date were still struck as *maundy money* (q.v.).

Groat of Edward III.

In the last two years of William IV (1836–37), a small silver groat, known as the BRITANNIA GROAT, was struck at the instance of Joseph Hume, the economist and politician (see *Nicknames*). This had a figure of Britannia on the reverse, as on the copper coins. These groats were common in Victorian days, and continued to be issued until 1855.*

The name was also applied to various small continental coins, hence the proverbial saying "not worth a groat."

Gros (for derivation see above, *Groat*): During the latter part of the thirteenth century bracteates and other inferior, debased silver coins known as denarii were current in Europe. These sufficed for the limited commerce of the times, but as trade increased in volume, a coin of larger size and enhanced value became necessary. A large form of denier, the *nummi grossi* or *grossi denarii* (i.e., thick coins or pennies), were first struck in Bohemia about 1300. The coin at once became popular all over Europe, and soon assumed a bewildering variety of types. From this were derived the German *Groschen*, the English *Groat*, the *Gros* of France, the Italian *Grosso*, etc.

Of all these types, the French *Gros Tournois* was the most important and the most influential. This was a billon piece of four deniers, struck originally at the Abbey of St. Martin at Tours by Louis IX, in the middle of the thirteenth century. In England it became the *groat* (q.v.). On the obverse was the famous *châtel tournois* (q.v.) and the reverse bore the well-known motto BNDICTV. SIT NOME. DNI. NRI. IHV. XPI. (see *Mottoes on Coins*). The coin quickly became popular, and was extensively copied by other European countries. The English groat was suggested by, and partly modeled on, this coin, although it bore the king's head in place of the *châtel tournois*.

Guinea (Originally *Guinea-pound*, so-called from the coin being struck from gold brought over from the Guinea Coast in West Africa†): An

---

* An issue, with "Jubilee Head" was struck in 1888 for colonial use.

† The coins struck from guinea-gold bore the mark of an elephant, or of an elephant and castle (1675) beneath the bust. The name was later given to gold coins of this type, whether the gold came from Guinea or not.

English gold coin, struck 1663–1799, with a belated issue in 1813.*
The guinea was originally the ordinary sovereign, or twenty-shilling
piece, and was legal tender for this amount until 1717, though the actual
value varied. The gold being of such fine quality, the coin soon commanded a premium; in 1694 it was actually worth 30 shillings; under
the recoinage of 1696–97 it was reduced in value to 21s. 6d., but was
fixed at 21 shillings in the reign of George I (1717). Until nearly the end
of the reign of George III (1813) the guinea was current in place of
the gold sovereign. In this year the last guinea was coined, and its place
as the standard gold coin was taken by the sovereign, first minted in
1817. The guinea, however, is still a popular money of account;
professional fees, for instance, are usually reckoned in "guineas." (See
also *Spade Guinea*.)

Between the reigns of Charles II to George III inclusive, five-guinea
(from Charles I to George II), two-guinea, half-guinea, third-guinea
(1797), and quarter-guinea (1718 and 1762) pieces were also struck.

Gulden (Ger. *Gulden Pfennig*, the golden penny): Originally a gold
coin, the florin of Germany, Austria, and Hungary, and known as the
guilder in the Netherlands, current from the fourteenth to the seventeenth century. The name was later applied to a silver coin, equivalent
to the *Taler*, though afterwards it was reduced in size and value.

Gun Money: A coinage, consisting of crowns, half-crowns, shillings, and
sixpences, struck as emergency money, or money of necessity, in 1689
and 1690, in Ireland, by James II, after he had been driven off the

Gun Money of James II.

English throne. It was so called because it was cast from scrap metal,
such as old cannons, bells, kitchen utensils, etc. James landed in
Ireland in 1689, and set up his mints in Dublin and Limerick. At first
the issue consisted of sixpences, shillings, and half-crowns. Later,
crowns were issued, showing the king on horseback, and these were
usually restruck on the large half-crowns. Often parts of the older coin
can be seen through the restrike, creating a blundered impression. A

---

* The so-called "Military" guinea, struck mainly for payment of the troops in the Peninsular
War.

curiosity of this coinage is that on all the coins, except the crowns, the actual month of minting is indicated, in addition to the year; there is no doubt James intended redeeming the coins month by month had his cause achieved success. On the accession of William and Mary, however, the coinage was reduced to its mere metal value, and it was decreed:

"The large half-crown of copper money, together with the crown pieces, of like metal and weight, lately stamp'd, shall pass at one penny sterling. The small half-crown shall pass at 3 farthings. The large copper shilling and sixpence, shall pass each at one farthing."

The result of this disastrous decree was that coins representing a value of £22,500 were bought back for £640.

The dating of the gun-money coins followed this chronological order:

July, 1689	February, 1689
August, 1689	March, 1689
September, 1689	March, 1690
October, 1689	April, 1690
November, 1689	May, 1690
December, 1689	June, 1690
January, 1689	

At first sight there seems to be no rhyme or reason to this sequence. But in those days the Old Style calendar was in use, and the new year started on March 25 (not January 1). Consequently the coins dated March, 1690 must have been struck only a few days after those dated March, 1689. Similarly, January 1, 1689 was the day after December 31, 1689.

H

H on Victorian bronze coins: On many Victorian English bronze coins (1874–76 and 1881–82) will be found a small letter H beneath the date. This denotes the coins were minted by Ralph Heaton & Sons, at the Birmingham Mint, at a time when the Royal Mint was unable to supply the great demand for bronze coins. One hundred tons of bronze coins were minted at Birmingham in 1874.

Half Cent: Authorized by the Act of April 2, 1792, this coin had the lowest face value of any issued by the United States. The series was struck from 1793 through 1857, in the following types:

Liberty Cap	1793–97
Draped Bust	1800–08
Turban Head	1809–36
Braided Hair	1840–57

Alexander Hamilton was one of the initial supporters of the half-cent value. He felt it would aid the poor since there would be many small items priced at ½ cent which would otherwise cost a penny if no such coin existed. But even in those days of low prices there was little demand for the coin; in fact, it was one of the most unpopular ever issued in this country. The coins were not legal tender and in consequence they were often refused in business transactions. This in turn led to great variations in the number of half cents struck annually; and with so many of the coins failing to get into circulation, there was an unusually large number of restrikes.

At first the Liberty Cap half cents had a lettered edge, but from 1795 on, some coins had plain edges. On the 1793 half cents Liberty faces left; on all the remaining issues of this type, she faces right. Some of the 1795 half cents have a "punctuated date" (see *Punctuated Date*). Another variation in design is that on some of the half cents of this type the Liberty Cap is supported by a pole; on other coins there is no pole. The most valuable Liberty Cap half cent is the 1796 issue with plain edge and no pole.

No half cents were struck in 1798–99. In 1800 the Draped Bust type (facing right, and without Liberty Cap), first appeared and continued through 1808. There are some interesting varieties of this type—see *Crosslet 4* and *Stemless Wreath*. A flawed die gave rise to the "Spiked Chin" variety of 1804.

Liberty Cap   Draped Bust   Turban Head   Braided Hair

Half Cent types.

The Turban Head type (with Liberty facing left) is officially listed as having been issued during 1809–36, but actually no half cents were struck in 1812–24. In 1811 all the banks of the country refused to accept half cents, leading the government to discontinue this coinage until the beginning of 1825. Some authorities believe that the spurned half cents were melted down to furnish the alloy content of gold and silver coins of the period. The outstanding Turban Head rarity is the 1811 restrike with the 1802 reverse. These restrikes were made not by the mint, but by J. J. Mickley, a Philadelphia collector who had obtained the dies.

The last half-cent type (Braided Hair, with Liberty facing left), presents a confused picture because the issues of the 1840–57 period contain a great many restrikes; even some of the proofs were restrikes. In quite a few cases it is impossible to determine the quantity issued annually. Many years are rare and valuable.

Because of the unpopularity of the half cents, some individuals and banks tended to accumulate sizeable quantities; and over the years a number of hoards of half cents have been discovered.

Half-crown, Silver: This coin has been struck in every reign from the time of Edward VI, with the exception of the reign of Philip and Mary.

Half Dime: Authorized by Congress on April 2, 1792, this silver coin was issued from 1794 through 1805, and from 1829 through 1873. The series was struck in these types:

Bust (or Liberty Head)	1794–1805
Turban Head	1829–37
Liberty Seated	1837–73

Half Dime. *Left:* Bust type. *Right:* Liberty Seated type.

During 1794–1805 a bust of Liberty (facing right) appeared on the obverse, and the reverse featured an eagle with outspread wings. A peculiarity of these coins was that the denomination was not indicated. The two rarest and most valuable items of this series are the 1802 half dime and the 1796 overstrike on 1795.

Die breaks during this period give us the inscription LIKERTY on some 1796 half dimes and LIBEKTY on some 1800 coins.

In 1829 the coinage of half dimes was resumed, the obverse being changed to a Liberty Head facing left and wearing a turban. The denomination, 5¢, now appears under the eagle on the reverse. There are no rarities in this series.

In 1837 the Act of January 18 established a new design and a slight reduction in the weight and silver content. Now Liberty Seated appears on the obverse, and on the reverse the eagle is replaced by the value in a wreath. A ribbon above the eagle carries the motto E PLURIBUS UNUM. The 1837 change in weight and fineness is indicated by changes in the obverse: the early issues have no stars and no drapery from the elbow on the obverse, while beginning with 1840 the coins have stars and drapery from the elbow.

The Act of February 21, 1853 authorized another slight reduction in the weight of the half dime. This is indicated on the 1853–55 issues by arrows at each side of the date.

In 1859 and 1860 the inscription UNITED STATES OF AMERICA was shifted from the reverse to the obverse. During this transitional period some coins were issued which did not carry the inscription at all. These half dimes (see *Transitional Pattern*) are the most valuable of the series. Beginning with the regular coinage of 1860 the inscription replaces the stars on the obverse.

From 1838 through 1860 half dimes were issued with the O mint mark. The S mint mark appears on 1864–1873 issues. On half dimes the mint mark appears under the wreath, or within it, on the reverse.

Half Dollar: Authorized by the Act of April 2, 1792, these silver coins were first struck in 1794 and are still being issued. The following types have been issued:

Bust	1794–1807
Turban Head	1807–39
Liberty Seated	1839–91
Liberty Head (Barber)	1892–1915
Liberty Walking	1916–47
Franklin	1948–

The value ("50 CENTS") did not appear on the half dollars until the 1836 issue. Instead, there was a lettered edge on these early coins with the inscription FIFTY CENTS or HALF A DOLLAR. On the 1836 and subsequent half dollars the lettering and the motto disappeared and a reeded edge was substituted.

The Bust type (Liberty facing right) was succeeded in 1807 by the Turban Head type (Liberty facing left). The motto E PLURIBUS UNUM appears on the reverse in a ribbon over the eagle. The early half dollars have some curious varieties. Some 1807 half dollars, for example, were struck with a 20 C value (which did not exist at the time) and then overstruck with 50 C. (What appears as 20 C is caused by an error on the part of the die sinker who inverted the 5 and then corrected his error.) One variety of the 1811 coins has a punctuated date (18.11). The 1806–40 half dollars were struck in fairly large quantities to make up for the silver dollars which were not struck during this period.

The first half dollar struck at the New Orleans mint appeared in 1838 and is extremely valuable. It seems that only 20 pieces were struck. The 1838 O and 1839 O mint marks appear on the obverse. Thereafter, with several exceptions to be noted later on, the half-dollar mint marks always appeared on the reverse.

The Liberty Seated half dollars were struck from 1839 through 1891. Though the eagle was retained on the reverse, the motto continued to be omitted. The value was changed to HALF DOL. Slight changes in the

Left: Half Dollar, Bust Type (1803). *Right:* Half Dollar, Liberty Seated Type (1840).

weight of the half dollar in 1839, 1853 and 1873 led to familiar alterations in the design. To indicate the first change, some of the 1839 half dollars were struck with drapery from the elbow on the figure of Liberty. This became a standard feature, although as late as 1845 some coins were struck with no drapery.

The 1853 weight change was indicated by placing arrows on the date on the obverse and rays above the eagle on the reverse on the 1853 half dollars. On the 1854–55 half dollars the arrows were retained, but the rays disappeared. Beginning with the 1856 coins the arrows were dropped.

Unlike the half dimes and dimes, the half dollars underwent no changes in 1859. The pattern of stars on the obverse which appeared on the first issue of Liberty Seated half dollars was retained throughout the "lifetime" of this coin.

On the Liberty Seated half dollars the "O," "S" and "CC" mint marks appear under the eagle on the reverse. The 1853 O without arrows is a great rarity, only two specimens being known. The 1861 O had a curious history. It was issued under three different authorities— first for the United States government; then, after seizure of the mint by the Confederate regime, more coins were issued for Louisiana and later for the Confederacy. However, since all the 1861 O half dollars were struck from the same official U.S. government dies, there is no way of telling under whose authority any one of these coins was minted.

The rarest of the Liberty Seated half dollars is the 1866 date (without motto), only one specimen (a proof) being known. On some of the 1873 and all the 1874 half dollars arrows appeared at the date to call attention to a change in weight. The arrows were dropped beginning with the 1875 issue. Although according to mint records 5000 1873 S half dollars were issued without arrows, not a single one of these coins is known to be in any present collection. The motto IN GOD WE TRUST was placed on the half dollars in a ribbon on the reverse over the eagle, beginning with the 1866 coins.

HALF DOLLAR

The Liberty Head (Barber) half dollar was struck from 1892 through 1915. The designer's initial "B" appears at the base of the neck on the obverse. The "S," "O" and "D" mint marks can be found on the reverse under the eagle. The last of the "O" mint marks appears in 1909, the first of the "D" mint marks in 1906. The E PLURIBUS UNUM motto is used throughout on the reverse, and IN GOD WE TRUST likewise appears in every issue on the obverse. This is the first type to have the full name of the coin spelled out.

The designs for the Liberty Walking half dollar (1916–1947) reflect the prewar atmosphere in which they first appeared. The Director described the new half dollar in these words: "The design of the half dollar bears a full-length figure of Liberty, the folds of the stars and stripes flying to the breeze as a background, progressing in full stride toward the dawn of a new day, carrying branches of laurel and oak, symbolic of civil and military glory. The hand of the figure is outstretched in bestowal of the spirit of Liberty. The reverse of the half dollar shows an eagle perched high upon a mountain crag, his wings unfolded, fearless in spirit and conscious of his power. Springing from a rift in the rock is a sapling of mountain pine symbolical of America."

Half Dollar. *Left:* Liberty Head (Barber) type. *Right:* Liberty Walking type.

The initials "AW" for A. A. Weinman (the designer) appear on the reverse under the tip of the wing feathers. The "S" and "D" mint marks appear on the obverse in the case of the 1916 coins. They also appear on the obverse of some of the 1917 coins; on other 1917 half dollars the mint mark is found on the reverse, to the left of HALF DOLLAR (the fully spelled-out value). Thereafter the mint mark always appears in the latter position. As usual, IN GOD WE TRUST is found on the obverse, and E PLURIBUS UNUM on the reverse.

No half dollars were issued in 1922, 1924–26 and 1930–32. No proofs were struck in 1916–35 and in 1943–47. In uncirculated condition the Liberty Walking half dollar has more rare issues than any other modern coin. This includes 1917 S (mint mark on obverse), 1919 S and D, 1920 S and D, 1921, 1921 S and D, 1923 S and 1936 proof.

The Franklin-Liberty Bell half dollar, the current type, was first issued in 1948. The initials of the designer, John R. Sinnock, appear under the shoulder. The "S" and "D" mint marks are found above the bell beam on the reverse. The familiar motto IN GOD WE TRUST appears on the obverse and E PLURIBUS UNUM on the reverse. Proofs of this type have been struck regularly from 1950 on. See *Commemorative Coins (U.S.), Controller Coins.*

Half Eagle: This $5.00 gold coin, authorized by the Act of April 2, 1792, was first issued in 1795 and ended with the 1929 coinage. The following types were struck:

Liberty Cap	1795–1807
Turban Head (Round Cap)	1807–34
Ribbon	1834–39
Coronet	1839–1908
Indian Head	1908–29

On the 1795–98 issues of the Liberty Cap type (Liberty facing right) the reverses come in two styles—with a small eagle or a large (heraldic) eagle with shield. Most of the coins are quite valuable, the outstanding rarity being the 1798 half eagle with small eagle on the reverse. None of the coins carries a stated value.

In 1807 the Turban Head (Round Cap) type made its appearance, with Liberty facing left. The value (5D.) was added to the bottom of the reverse, and a ribbon containing the motto E PLURIBUS UNUM was placed above the eagle. On this type the heraldic eagle is used throughout—reduced in size, however, to make room for the new material on the reverse. The 1822 half eagle is the most valuable rarity in U.S. coinage, but there are many other notable rarities in the period 1815–30.

Half Eagle. *Left:* Liberty Cap type. *Right:* Turban Head type.

The Ribbon type was introduced in 1834, with a reduction in the size of the coin. The 1838 half eagles struck at Charlotte and Dahlonega have mint marks above the date on the obverse.

The Coronet type was issued from 1839 through 1908. In 1866 the motto IN GOD WE TRUST was artfully set on a ribbon above the eagle without resulting in any appreciable overcrowding. Throughout, the value appears as FIVE D. The mint mark is below the eagle on the reverse. The outstanding rarity is the 1854 S half eagle.

The Indian Head type (1908–1929) was the last half eagle issued. Like the quarter eagle of the same period, it is an incuse coin designed by Bela Lyons Pratt and has both mottoes (E PLURIBUS UNUM and IN GOD WE TRUST) on the reverse. The mint mark is below the date on the obverse.

Half Eagle. *Left:* Coronet type. *Right:* Indian Head (Incuse) type.

Half-farthing: Struck in the reigns of George IV, William IV, and Victoria (last issue 1868). They were used for the convenience of small change in Ceylon. In 1842 they were proclaimed as current English coin, but they were regarded more as curiosities than as actual coins.

Halfpenny: Apart from a few round halfpennies struck by the ninth-century Viking invaders and the later Saxon kings, the earliest form of ha'penny was literally a "half-penny," for it was the half of a silver penny which had been cut into two parts. The lines of the cross on the reverse enabled this to be done with ease. Round silver halfpennies, similar to the penny, but smaller, were struck by Edward I in 1280. It was not, however, until the time of Charles II (in 1672) that copper halfpennies, bearing the figure of Britannia, as on our modern half-pennies, were struck, together with copper farthings. Tin halfpennies were struck during the reigns of Charles II and William and Mary. These, like the corresponding farthings, were plugged with copper. In 1860 the copper halfpenny was changed to bronze, along with the penny and the farthing.

The modern halfpenny is exactly 1 in. in diameter. (See *Cut Half-pennies.*)

Hammered Coins: Until 1662, when the milling process of coining was made permanent, the usual method of producing coins was by "hammering," i.e., the roughly sheared coin blank was held between two dies by a long pair of tongs, and a heavy blow was given with a mallet. The last hammered coins to be struck in England were the small penny, twopenny, threepenny, and fourpenny silver pieces of 1662.

Hammered coins ceased to be legal tender in 1697, in the reign of William III.

Hand of Providence: A symbol found on the Anglo-Saxon coins of

Edward the Elder and Athelred II; it represents a hand descending from the clouds, in the act of blessing. It is sometimes shown between A and Ω (Alpha and Omega). The symbol is probably of Byzantine origin.

Hardhead (O. Fr. *hardit*): A billon coin of Scotland, known also as a *Lion*, from the lion rampant, crowned, on the reverse. First struck (1555–58) under Mary, Queen of Scots. It was intended to serve for small change, its value being reckoned at $1\frac{1}{2}d$., though reckoned at a value of twopence in the reign of James II, as indicated by two pellets on the reverse. Motto, VICIT VERITAS ("Truth has prevailed") on the hardhead of Mary; VINCIT VERITAS ("Truth prevails") on that of James.

Hard Times Tokens: A series of political tokens issued in the United States during the period 1832–44. As they were of the same size as the large cents they were pressed into service to alleviate the shortage of small change that prevailed at this time, particularly after the Panic of 1837. The tokens must have circulated widely, for the majority of them encountered nowadays are quite worn. Most of the designs allude to Andrew Jackson's presidential campaigns and the bitter controversy over the rechartering of the Bank of the United States. Many of these coins are imitations of the then current cent, but with a satirical device and legend on the reverse.

Harp or **Harper:** Irish coin, current in the sixteenth and seventeenth centuries, bearing a large harp on the reverse. The name applies in particular to the groat and half-groat struck by Henry VIII for Ireland.

Hawaiian Sesquicentennial Commemorative Half Dollar: See *Commemorative Coins (U.S.)*, p. 63.

Heller (from *Hall*, a town in Wurtemburg, where the coin was first issued): A small silver (later copper) coin, current in Germany from the thirteenth century. The heller is still current in Austria today, being the hundredth part of the *Kreutzer*.

Helm: Name given to the quarter-florin, a small gold coin, struck by Edward III in 1344. On the obverse was a helmet, surmounted by a lion. (See *Florin, Leopard*.)

Hiberniae Rex (L. King of Ireland): The title DOMINUS HIBERNIAE (Lord of Ireland) appeared, in abbreviated form, on English coins from the time of Edward I. After Henry VIII in 1542 had quelled a rebellion in Ireland he altered his title to HIBERNIAE REX on the coins of 1544.

Hiberno-Danish: Name given to a series of silver pennies, the earliest coins to be struck in Ireland. They were originally struck by the Danish invaders, the Vikings. The earliest of these with a decipherable inscription is attributed to Sihtric III (989–1029); the issue continued for about a century and a half. The types show rough imitations of contemporary English pennies, copies of the types of Athelred II being especially common. A frequent symbol on the reverse is a figure representing what could be either a hand (the "Hand of Providence" of the Anglo-Saxon coins) or a branch of a tree. More often than not, the inscriptions are a mere jumble of strokes and scratches, which, to us at any rate, are meaningless.

Hittites: A great and extremely ancient nation of Asia Minor, whose history is as yet but little known. The empire had dissolved long before the invention of coins, although the early type of Lydian coins showing the heads of lions and bulls is a typical Hittite device. On Hittite sculptures the type of the double-headed eagle can often be seen. This heraldic device, taken up by the Turkoman princes, was later adopted by the Crusaders in the fourteenth century. The device figures on coins of the German emperors and on the more modern coins of Russia and Austria.

Hoards: Ancient coins are rarely found singly; where one coin has been unearthed, others usually make their appearance. Occasionally, by mere accident, a chest, a pot, or other vessel has been brought to the surface, and found to contain hundreds, or even thousands, of coins. Such a discovery will often considerably affect the market price of a certain type of coin; a coin that was previously rare may become common, and a careful study of the variations in the types will often result in added knowledge to the type. Some noteworthy hoards often referred to in the study of numismatics are the following:

In 1878 at Carrawburgh, near Hadrian's Wall, on the site of a well dedicated to the Ancient British water-goddess Coventina, more than 16,000 coins were found, dating from A.D. 100 to 300, in addition to pottery and jewelry. More than 300 of these Roman coins were of the "Britannia" type. (See *Britannia*.)

In 1840, at Cuerdale Hall Farm, on the banks of the River Ribble, in Lancaster, after the river had overflooded its banks, a hoard of over 7,000 coins was uncovered, together with 1,000 ounces of silver ingots and broken jewelry. The treasure had originally been enclosed in a leaden chest. The hoard was claimed by the Crown as treasure trove. Our knowledge of the late ninth-century Viking coinage is largely based on the study of this hoard. It seems to date from the reign of Edward the Elder (900–25), and may possibly be the booty of the Danes defeated by Edward in Northumbria in 911. It probably consisted originally of over 10,000 coins. Most of the Alfred and Canute coins of our collections today originated from this great hoard.

In 1833, at Beaworth, in Hampshire, a lead chest containing 8,000–

9,000 silver pennies of William I and II was unearthed. The coins had been originally carefully packed in rolls, and appeared to be entirely uncirculated. The majority of the coins were PAXS pennies of William I; as a result, this type, hitherto rare, became the most common.

Probably the largest single find of coins in England was in 1831, near Tutbury (Staffordshire), where some 200,000 pennies of Edward I and II were unearthed by laborers engaged in deepening the River Dove. (See also *Treasure Trove.*)

Hog Money: Copper money of the Bermudas (*2d.*, *3d.*, *6d.*, and *1s.*), struck in the early seventeenth century. The coins bear the inscription SOMMER ISLANDS. This was the name then given to the Bermudas. Obv/a hog; Rev/a three-masted ship; value in Roman figures. These coins are extremely rare.

In 1609 the vessel of Sir George Somers was cast ashore at the Bermudas. The islands were found to be uninhabited, but swarms of pigs abounded, the descendants of animals brought ashore by ships that had previously touched in at the islands.

Hudson, N.Y. Sesquicentennial Commemorative Half Dollar: See *Commemorative Coins (U.S.)*, p. 64.

Huguenot-Walloon Tercentenary Commemorative Half Dollar: See *Commemorative Coins (U.S.)*, p. 61.

I

I: Greek numeral letter, signifying ten, and found on the quarter-follis, or ten-nummi piece of Byzantium—a denomination introduced by Anastasius in his reform of the coinage in A.D. 498. (See *Follis.*)

Also, the Roman numeral letter signifying one.

Iconographic (Gr. *eikon*, an image, *grapein*, to inscribe): An adjective signifying something that represents an object or an idea by means of some visual form, such as a picture, a symbol, or an image. The noun, ICONOGRAPHY, signifies the science or art of achieving this.

Imperator (L. *imperare*, to command): Originally the term was applied by the Romans to one having *imperium*, or authority, that is to say, a general-in-chief, one holding supreme authority in time of war. Thus on a coin struck by Casca we see the portrait of his colleague Brutus in a laurel wreath, with the inscription *Brutus Imp.* This does not mean he was *emperor*; but in imperial times it became the customary official title of the emperor, as he was always Commander-in-Chief of the Army.

The title IND. IMP. (Emperor of India) appeared on English coins from 1893 to 1949. As India is now a republic, the title is defunct.

Inchiquin Money: Money of necessity, struck in 1643 by Lord Inchiquin the Vice-President of Munster for Charles I. The plate for making these coins was loaned by the Irish supporters of Charles, under the auspices of Murrough O'Brien, 6th Baron of Inchiquin. The series consists of a half-crown, shilling, ninepence, sixpence, groat, and threepenny piece, all in silver. The shape of these coins is polygonal.

Incuse (L. *incudere*, to strike with a hammer, to forge): When the design is impressed on a coin so that the pattern sinks into the flan, the coin is said to be *incuse*; if the pattern is raised, instead of being sunk into the coin, the coin is said to be in *relief*. The earliest Greek coins are incuse, so that the design is in intaglio on one side, and the same design appears in relief on the reverse. The staters of Sybaris (*c.* 550 B.C.) are finely wrought specimens of incuse coins. A later development in Greek coins was to have a small design in relief inside an incuse square. On many

Thebes, silver stater, incuse style (about 450 B.C.).

early Greek coins we find the ordinary obverse in relief, but on the reverse is a rough incuse square, often showing the marks where it was held in position on the anvil. Sometimes these anvil marks are arranged in a rough decorative pattern, thus marking an intermediate stage between the incuse square and the reverse proper. (See *Punch Marks.*)

There is a curious series of Greek coins of Magna Graecia of the sixth century B.C. The reverse is repeated (with minor differences) in the obverse, but the former is incuse. These coins were produced by the Pythagorean Brotherhood, a hierarchy of philosopher-statesmen and mystics. It would seem they bear some esoteric allusion to the mystical etheric "double."

American coinage includes two interesting incuse examples, the familiar Indian Head quarter eagle and half eagle of 1908-1929.

India, Coinage of: The story of the Indian coinage is long, intricate, and often obscure. Of its origins and early history little is known. The earliest coins of which there is any abundance are the small square or oblong pieces, cut from a thin sheet of silver or copper, hand-stamped by a punch with a number of intricate symbolic designs. These apparently date from the fourth century B.C., and circulated, at least in southern India, as late as Roman imperial times.

In the course of its varied history India was subject to many invaders, whose coins circulated freely in the country, but left no influence on the native production of the various States. It was different, however, with the coming of the Greeks. The conquests of Alexander the Great opened India to an active commerce with the Western world. Not only did the actual Greek coins circulate freely, but the native coins were greatly influenced in their style and art by Hellenic types. Particularly was this the case with the Bactrian coins (q.v.) of the second century B.C., with their Indo-Greek types and bilingual inscriptions.

Gradually, however, the Hellenic gods and the Greek legends were replaced by native deities and legends. The later invasions of the Kushans, the Guptas, the Huns, and others, all left their mark on the coinage, but a great new era in the coinage of India begins in 1193, with the coming of the Mohammedans. The copper coins in use by the common people in small everyday transactions retained their local and native characteristics, but the invaders introduced a more orthodox type of Mohammedan gold and silver coin, namely, the *tankah*. The tankah was a gold and a silver coin, of equal weight in either metal, and under the succeeding Moguls, in the sixteenth century, it developed into the *rupee*, the standard silver coin of India, and the *mohur*, the standard gold coin.

These types were taken up by the East India Companies of France and England in the eighteenth and early nineteenth centuries, and stamped with their appropriate commercial emblems (e.g., the familiar scales, bale mark, heraldic arms). In 1858 the last Mogul emperor was deposed, and the Government of India transferred to the English sovereignty. The coins were still based on the rupee and the mohur as the standard of coinage, but bore the head of the British ruler.

In May 1957 the currency of India was reorganized on a decimal basis, much, it would seem, to the confusion of the native population. (See *Anna, Mohammedan Coins, Mohur, Pagoda, Rupee.*)

Indian Head Type: See *Cent (U.S.), Eagle, Half Eagle, Nickel Five-Cent Piece (U.S.); Quarter Eagle.*

Ingot (M.E. *ingot*, a mold): Originally signifying a mold, this word is now used to denote any mass of metal turned out from a mold. Ingots vary in size and shape, according to the use they are to be put to.

Inscription: Any word, or combination of words, appearing on the *field* of a coin (cf. *Legend*). The term also includes any abbreviation of a word, such as the ATHE on coins of Athens, but, strictly speaking, it does not include a single letter, or group of single letters, which are usually symbols.

The earliest known inscribed coin is the unique electrum stater, ascribed to Halicarnassus, now in the British Museum. It dates from somewhere between 700 and 545 B.C. On the obverse is a browsing stag (the Ephesian badge of Diana), and it bears the inscription in archaic Greek: "I am the sign of Phanes." Who Phanes was, and where he minted this coin, are quite unknown. As the word "Phanes" means "bright," we can, of course, read this inscription as "I am the sign of the Bright One" (i.e., the moon goddess, or Diana).

Occasionally we find obsolete spellings and letters preserved in coin inscriptions, such as the letter Ϙ (*Koppa*) on coins of Corinth. It is curious to note, too, that the letter E of ATHE referred to above, is not the long form of E (*Eta*), which the Greeks would have written at the time the coin was struck.

Every coin collector knows the exasperating experience of *nearly* being able to decipher a worn inscription, but not quite. The inscription can be made *temporarily* more legible if the coin is placed on a red-hot poker. The words appear in a greenish tinge, which fades away as the heat passes off.

Intaglio (It. *intagliare*, to cut into): Hollowed out, not raised as in relief. If the whole pattern of a coin is in intaglio, it is said to be *incuse* (q.v.).

Intrinsic Value (L. *intrinsecus*, inside, inward): The actual metallic value, as opposed to mere *token* (or face) value.

Iowa Centennial Commemorative Half Dollar: See *Commemorative Coins (U.S.)*, p. 67.

Ireland: The story of a regular coinage in Ireland comes late in history. The two main reasons for this are that first, unlike England, the civilizing influence of Rome was lacking; there were no Roman coins for her to imitate or motivate an original coinage; and, secondly, there was no centralized government, nor any centers of trade and commerce. Gold rings, useful both as ornaments and a standard of wealth, were apparently abundant, judging from the number found in Ireland, for Ireland was in early days one of the principal gold-producing countries of Europe. When the Vikings settled in Ireland, they struck a crude silver currency (from *c.* A.D. 1000 to 1150, see *Hiberno-Danish*). They were mainly rough imitations of English pennies of the time, especially those of Athelred II (979–1016), the "voided cross" type.

The first organized Irish currency—the Anglo-Irish—begins with the English settlement of 1177, when Prince John was made Lord of Ireland by his father, Henry II. From 1177 to 1199 halfpennies were struck bearing a full-faced head traditionally supposed to be that of St. John the Baptist. Farthings, halfpennies and pennies were struck by John as King of England and Overlord of Ireland in later days. The type was the king's head within a triangle; on the reverse were a crescent moon, a star, and a solar emblem. Silver coins were struck for Ireland also by Henry III, the three Edwards, Henry VI (pennies, groats, and possibly a copper half-farthing, or Patrick), Edward IV (double groats, groats, half-groats, etc.), Richard III, and Henry VII. Henry VIII, who claimed to be supreme monarch of Ireland, coined groats with a harp on the reverse—the heraldic device of Ireland. On his Irish coins he placed his own initial ("H") and the initials of some of his many wives. Silver or billon coins were struck for Ireland by all the following kings up to the time of Charles II. After this, the Anglo-Irish coins were of copper or pewter, with an issue of Bank of Ireland tokens in the reign of George III. No gold coins were ever struck for Ireland,* nor any of the higher denominations until the time of Charles II. In 1828 the Anglo-Irish coinage came to an end.

In 1928 the Republic of Eire commenced striking its own coins; the types were a complete breakaway from the English tradition, and show highly original designs.

For special issues of Irish coins, see *Gun Money*, *Harp*, *Inchiquin Money*, *Kilkenny Money*, *Limerick Money*, *Ormonde Money*, *Saint Patrick's Money*, *Voce Populi*, *Wood's Irish Halfpence*.

Iron Currency: As a medium for coins, iron is heavy to carry, it is of small intrinsic value, it is brittle, and it is liable to rust. Iron coins have, however, been struck on occasion in China, Byzantium, and in the regions round the Euxine Sea. According to Julius Caesar, the Ancient Britons used iron *currency bars* (q.v.). The most celebrated iron coinage is that of Sparta. The great lawgiver and founder of the Spartan State, Lycurgus (ninth century B.C.), according to Plutarch:

"stopped the currency of the gold and silver coin, and ordered that they should make use of iron money only; then, to a great quantity and weight of this he assigned but a very small value; so that to lay up ten *minae* (about $120), a whole room was required, and to remove it, nothing less than a yoke of oxen." (Translated by Langhorne)

Plutarch goes on to say that this effectually prevented theft and bribery, and the purchase of luxury goods from abroad as well as at home. It is doubtful, however, whether this currency was in the form of actual coins.

Coming to modern times, iron coins, chemically treated against the action of rust, were used in Germany in 1915 (five- and ten-pfennig pieces). Some iron coins were struck in Sweden after the Second World War, also in Finland, where they are still being struck.

The abbreviation for iron is Fe (L. *ferrum*).

Isabella Commemorative Quarter: See *Commemorative Coins* (*U.S.*), p. 60.

---

* For the only exception see *Inchiquin Money*.

ISRAEL

Israel: Apart from the very great interest of Scriptural allusion, the coinage of the ancient Hebrews is appealing mainly to specialists in the field. The Jews for the most part used coins of other nations. As with other Semitic peoples in early times, rings and wedges of gold and silver, weighed in the balance, were in use. There are several references to these in the Old Testament.

The *shekel*, like the *talent*, was in those days merely a weight and not a coin (see *Shekel, Talent*). It is not until post-exilic times that we find in the Scriptures any mention of coins as such. It was then that the *daric* and *siglos* (q.v.) of the sprawling Persian Empire became current in Israel. Coins from the borderland of Phoenicia were also used. With the conquests of Alexander and the sovereignty of his successors, the Egyptian Ptolemies and the Seleucids, the Persian coins were superseded by Greek. Then, after the revolt against Hellenism, the first Jewish national coins were struck by Simon Maccabaeus (141–135 B.C.), John Hyrcanus (135–104 B.C.), and Alexander Jannaeus (103–76 B.C.). In Macc. xv. 6 we are told how Antiochus VII granted the right of coining to the Jews, *c.* 139 B.C.:

"I give thee leave also to coin money for thy country with thine own stamp."

The types chosen were simple and unpretentious; no image of divinity, no face or figure of man or beast. We find such devices as a sheaf of twigs between two citrons (referring to the Feast of Tabernacles), Rev/a chalice, a poppy head between two cornucopiae, an anchor or a wheel. In 37 B.C. Judea became a Roman province; Roman gold and silver were in common use, but local bronze pieces were minted by the Herodians, who were in power for the whole of the first century A.D. The legends were in Greek, in place of Hebrew lettering, with the image of a Roman emperor or the Jewish ruler occasionally appearing. Thus Herod Agrippa (A.D. 37–44) struck a coin with his own bust, and on the reverse the typically pagan figure of Fortune. The inscription reads BASILEUS MEGAS AGRIPPAS PHILOKAISAR (King Agrippa the great Lover of Caesar).

From *c.* A.D. 6 to A.D. 58 Roman governors (procurators) were set over Judea, the best-known being Pontius Pilate. While the inscriptions on their coins (also in Greek lettering) assert Judea's dependence on Rome, the types shown were not so obnoxious to the Jews. Bronze coins only were struck. Years A.D. 66–70 were years of revolt against Rome. Once again national Jewish coins were struck by the High Priest and Sanhedrin in both silver and bronze. The well-known shekel (often reproduced) bears a chalice on the obverse and a triple lily (the so-called "Rod of Aaron") on the reverse. These and other types on the smaller

Palestine, First Revolt (A.D. 67–70).

bronze coins are reminiscent of the Maccabaean period. The Hebrew legends on the coins are DELIVERANCE OF ZION and THE REDEMPTION OF ZION. The second revolt in the time of Hadrian, A.D. 132–35, under the pseudo-Messiah Simon Bar Cochba ("Son of a Star"), is signalized by a shekel showing a star above the screen of the Tabernacle with the Ark of the Covenant. (See also *Mite; Penny, New Testament; Shekel; Talent.*)

J

Jacobus: See *Broad.*

Janus: The old Roman god of beginnings, probably a solar deity or god of day (Dianus) in origin. He is represented with two joined heads, to symbolize the god that looks before and after. The Romans appropriately represented his double head (*Janus bifrons*) on the *as* (q.v.), as this was the standard unit, the "one" of the old system of coinage. Our first month of the year, January, is named for Janus. A favorite present of the Romans on their New Year's Day was an *as* bearing the head of Janus. The gates of the Temple (or rather shrine) of Janus were closed only when the whole (Roman) world was at peace. So rare was this event that it is commemorated on certain coins (Augustus, Nero).

Rome, didrachm with portrait of Janus (about 220 B.C.).

Janus-headed, Janiform (see above): A head with two faces, one looking right, the other left, as on certain satirical medalets of the seventeenth century.

Jefferson Type: See *Nickel Five-Cent Piece* (*U.S.*).

Jeton, or Jetton (Fr. *jeton*, a counter, medalet, *jeter*, to throw): So called because they were quickly thrown about on the counting board of checkered cloth used in medieval accountancy, *Exchequer*. A comprehensive word, including counters such as *Nuremburg tokens*, card counters, political medalets, and small commemorative pieces, in fact, almost any small base metal piece resembling a coin but not intended for currency. (See *Canadian Tokens, Counter, Nuremburg Tokens*.)

Jewish Coins: See *Israel*.

Johannes (Port. *João*, John): Gold coin of Portugal, first struck in the eighteenth century by John V; an eight-escudo piece. As we can see from existing coin weights (see *Weights*), this coin circulated in England, and was reckoned at a value of £3 12s.; it also circulated in America together with various Spanish coins. Often referred to as a "Joe" or "Half Joe."

Jubilee Coinage, Queen Victoria: A series of English coins, first struck in 1887, to celebrate the Golden Jubilee of the Queen. The coins were designed by J. E. Boehm. The type continued to be struck until 1893. A new and elderly portrait of the Queen was devised for these coins. The portrait, though dignified, was adversely criticized, principally on account of the one-arched crown of state of midget size perched on top of the head. A long veil is draped from the crown to the shoulders.

The coinage consisted of a five-pound piece, a double sovereign, sovereign, half-sovereign, crown, double-florin, half-crown, florin, shilling, sixpence, and threepenny-piece. The five-pound piece and double sovereign were principally treasured as souvenirs rather than circulated as coins. The five-pound piece, double sovereign, sovereign, and crown bore the famous device designed by Pistrucci of St. George and the Dragon on the reverse. The double-florin was an innovation in the coinage, but proved unpopular as currency. Both double-florin and florin were designed from the reverses of the gold coins of Charles II and James II issued by Simon, the famous medalist (cross of four shields with scepters in the angles). The half-crown, shilling, and sixpence have various shields on the reverses. The sixpence was quickly withdrawn, as it was found it could be easily mistaken for a half-sovereign if gilded, and it then reverted to the earlier type of value in wreath. The threepenny-piece, like the Maundy threepence, has the value "3" surmounted by a crown.

Jugate (L. *jugatus*, yoked): Two or more heads joined together, or overlapping (as on the coins of William III and Mary). Cf. *Vis-à-vis*. (See also *Accolated*.)

K

K: Greek numeral letter signifying twenty, and found on the half-follis, or twenty-nummi piece of Byzantium, introduced by Anastasius in his reform of the coinage in A.D. 498. (See *Follis*.)

Kilkenny Money: Money of necessity, issued during the wars in Ireland,

Holy Roman Empire, silver taler (1590). See "Jugate," page 140.

by the "Confederated Catholics," in 1642. A copper halfpenny and farthing were struck.

Klippe (Swedish *klippa*, to cut or clip): A general name for any square or lozenge-shaped coin.

Knife Money: Knives are still a popular form of currency in certain parts of Africa. The Chinese "Knife money" (*tao*), introduced in the seventh century B.C., was something intermediate between barter (in which tools and weapons formed a convenient standard of exchange) and actual coins. The so-called "knife" money was really a miniature model of a bill-hook, and represented the value of that tool. It was about 7 in. long, with a slightly curved blade, and a ring as a handle. It was inscribed on one side with the weight or value, and on the other with the place of issue. Round coins were struck in place of knife and spade money from the time of the Emperor Shih Huang Ti (221–210 B.C.), but unofficial issues of knife money were still popular in obscure parts of China.

The usurper Wang Mang (A.D. 9–22), in his zeal to restore the "good old days," restored the issue of knife money. The shape, however, was modified; it was made thicker, and only about half as long, with a straight back. In place of the ring at the end, the handle was a disk with a square hole in the center. The rims of the disk and of the central hole were formed into a ridge, thus giving the handle very much the appearance of the *cash* (q.v.). It is sometimes stated that the *cash* originated from the handle of the knife money, but the typical round Chinese coins, with square holes and raised rims, are known as early as the fourth century B.C.

Late forms of jade knife money are extant; these represented higher values, possibly varying with the quality of the jade.

Kopeck or **Copeck** (Russ. *kopiejka*, from *kopati*, to cut, engrave):

Originally a small silver coin of Russia, bearing the device of a horseman armed with spear; under the reorganization of the coinage under Peter the Great in 1704, it became a copper coin valued at one-hundredth part of the *rouble*.

Kreutzer or **Kreuzer** (Ger. *kreuz*, a cross): Originally an old German coin in silver and copper, bearing the common medieval device of a cross; now a modern Austrian copper coin, usually with the double eagle on the obverse, and reckoned at one-hundredth part of the florin.

Krone, pl. **Kroner** (Dan. a crown): The standard silver coin of Scandinavia, value 100 *ore*.

L

L.: An abbreviation commonly found on the Romano-Egyptian series of Alexandrian coins, and signifying "year." Greek numerals are denoted by letters of the alphabet, and the "L" is not in this case a letter, but a conventional sign that the letters following it are to be read as numerals. The origin of the sign is disputed, some numismatists regarding it as an Egyptian hieroglyphic or the relic of such, but a more probable theory is that it is to be read as a shorthand form of the Greek "E," the initial letter of *etous* (year). The numerals following give the years of the reign in which the coin was struck, an example of the early dating of coins.

"L" is also the Roman numeral letter for fifty.

L. s. d.: Abbreviations introduced by the Lombards for *librae*, *solidi*, *denarii*, these being the Latin words they used to represent pounds, shillings, and pence. The stroke through the "L" (£) is a medieval sign indicating a contraction. The English "pounds, shillings, and pence" were based on the medieval French "*livre, sol*, and *denier*," which in their turn, represented the "*librae, solidi*, and *denarii*" of the Romans.

The above explains why "d" is used as an abbreviation for "pence."

Labarum (Gr.): A late form of the Roman military standard, richly bejeweled, and bearing the effigy of the emperor. It is usually applied to the Christian form, as established by Constantine after his conversion, bearing the cross and the sacred monogram of Christ. In later times the word signified the *Chi-ro Monogram*: ☧, in which the Greek х (Chi) of the initials Chr. becomes a cross. It is frequent on coins of the early Christian emperors.

Large Cents: See *Cent (U.S.)* and *Cent (Canadian)*.

Latin Monetary Union: In the middle of the nineteenth century the great Californian gold rush began, and the Australian goldfields were opened out. As a consequence, the value of silver was considerably depreciated. A convention was formed in 1865 by France, Belgium,

Switzerland, and Italy (afterwards joined by Greece in 1868), which formulated a standard system of currency, based on the decimal system of the French franc. A gold standard was adopted in place of the previous bimetallic system. Each country agreed to accept the coins of all the other countries of the Union.

Laureate (L. *laureatus*, crowned with laurel): A bust is said to be laureate when it bears a wreath of laurel. On the coins of the Romans this represents the *corona triumphalis*, i.e., a wreath of laurel leaves without the berries, or an imitation of such wrought in gold. (See *Crowns, Roman*.)

Holy Roman Empire, gold aureus with laureated bust of Frederick II (1228).

Laurel: The *Unite* of the third coinage of James I (1619–25) is known as a Laurel, from the bust of the king bearing the classical laurel wreath in place of the usual crown. Half-laurels and quarter-laurels were also struck. (See *Broad*.)

Lead Coins: Although there are many literary references to coins in this metal, not many specimens have survived as lead is a soft and impermanent metal. Among the earliest known specimens are those of the Ardhras of central and southern India (third century B.C. to first century A.D.) and certain Bactrian coins. In the early Christian era we have coins of Egypt and Numidia, and a few specimens from Roman Gaul. Japan issued a comparatively prolific currency in lead for some five centuries, from the ninth century A.D., and in the eighteenth century *duits* (see *Doit*) were struck by the Dutch for use in their colonies of Ceylon and Java. Lead coins were struck abundantly in Siam in the mid-nineteenth century.

Leather Money: The so-called leather money of the Ancients was probably some sort of barter currency of dried skins, or strips of skin, bearing a certain form of official stamp of value. According to Aeschines, the Carthaginians wrapped a substance, the size of a four-drachma piece, in a small piece of leather. Nobody except the maker knew what this substance was. It was then sealed and issued for circulation as currency.

In time of war certain leather tokens are known to have been issued at various periods as money of necessity. The nearest approach to an actual currency of leather is that of certain primitive Russian coins.

They probably took the place of strips of leather used as barter currency, although they were of circular shape. The word *rouble* is derived from a word meaning to cut off, and the Russian coin *pul* is derived from a word meaning leather. Leather tokens circulated in England in the time of Elizabeth.

Legal Tender: Currency or other money which by law may be offered in payment of money debts and may not be refused by creditors.

European currency in the Middle Ages was a mixed affair; coins from one country circulated freely in another. Thus the *bezant* of Constantinople was, until the fourteenth century, the sole gold coin which circulated all over Europe. Any gold or silver coin could be put in the balance, and, according to the weight of the precious metal, it would pass anywhere as coin. With the coming of nationalism, however, each country provided its own coin, and became more jealous of any coin encroaching from outside. Laws were made defining what was to be legal tender, although up to the time of George III specified foreign denominations were allowed in times of national emergency (see *Weights*). With increased production of coins it became necessary also to limit the amounts of any one sort that could be paid, and by the Coinage Act of 1870, Bank of England notes were made legal tender for any sum above five pounds; gold was legal tender for any amount, but silver was limited to forty shillings, and bronze to one shilling.

In the opinion of Leland Howard, Acting Director of the Mint, the question of what constitutes legal tender in the United States "appears ultimately to be one for determination by the courts."

The Act of February 12, 1873 established one-cent and five-cent coins as legal tender for amounts not exceeding twenty-five cents. The Act of June 9, 1879 provided that all denominations of less than $1 should be legal tender for amounts not exceeding $10.

However, the Act of May 12, 1933 and the Joint Congressional Resolution of June 5, 1933 provide that "All coins and currencies of the United States (including Federal Reserve notes and circulating notes of Federal Reserve Banks and national banking associations) heretofore or hereafter coined or issued, shall be legal tender for all debts, public or private, public charges, taxes, duties, and dues. . . ."

The later legislation thus seems to eliminate the limits imposed by the earlier legislation. The apparent conflict has never been submitted to judicial determination.

Legend (L. *legenda*, things to be read): The words on the edge or rim of a coin or medal. The word is often used synonymously with *inscription* (q.v.). It is always in Latin in the case of English coins, the one exception being in the time of the Commonwealth, when coins bore the legend: "The Commonwealth of England" and, on the reverse, "God with us." The exact position of a legend is often indicated in numismatic works by the relative position of the hours on the dial of a clock; thus: "Legend commences at eleven o'clock."

Legionary Coins: Roman coins bearing the name and number of some special legion. They are nearly always of silver, though usually base. A few gold ones are known. They were probably used for paying the troops. They were first issued by Mark Antony in his struggle against Octavius, and were minted by him in enormous quantities. The common obverse is a praetorian galley, and on the reverse is the legionary eagle flanked by two standards, with the number of the legion. A few other emperors issued legionary coins, though in lesser quantities, including Carausius (A.D. 188–89), the usurper emperor in Britain.

Leopard: The gold half-florin, struck along with the florin and quarter-florin (or "*helm*") by Edward III in 1344. The obverse shows a leopard (see below) bearing a banner with the arms of England and France.

Leopard, Heraldic: The so-called "leopard" of heraldry was originally a lion passant guardant. The heraldic distinction is this: if the beast looks to left or right it is known as a lion; if the head is turned so that it faces towards us it is a leopard. The lion is usually shown rampant, the leopard passant. The three "lions" on the royal English shield are therefore really "leopards" (heraldically speaking).

Lepton pl. **Lepta** (Gr. *leptos*, tiny, i.e., coin): A somewhat vague term used by the Ancient Greeks to designate any very small copper coin. In the Greek New Testament we are told two *lepta* make a kodrantes (or as our English version puts it: "two mites, which make a farthing" (Mark xii. 42) (see *Mite, Widow's*). In Ancient Athens the lepton was the seventh part of the chalcus. In modern Greece the lepton is a copper coin representing the centime of the decimal currency; 100 lepta equal one drachma.

Lettered Edge: To discourage the *clipping* of coins, some early United States coins bore a legend on their edges. On *half cents* of 1793–1797 there appears TWO HUNDRED FOR A DOLLAR; on *large cents* of 1793–1796, ONE HUNDRED FOR A DOLLAR; on *half dollars* of 1794–1836, FIFTY CENTS OR HALF A DOLLAR; on silver *dollars* of 1794–1804, HUNDRED CENTS, ONE DOLLAR OR UNIT.

Lettering: The lettering of the inscriptions on the older English coins, until the middle of Edward III's reign, was Lombardic, i.e., full of curved forms. This form of lettering was derived from the Roman cursive script. Most Italian manuscripts up to the thirteenth century are written in this script. By 1370 black-letter forms had come into use, where instead of curved forms, every letter is formed of straight strokes. The *ryal* of Elizabeth was the last English coin to bear Lombardic lettering.

Levant Dollar: See *Maria Theresa Dollars.*

Lewis and Clark Exposition Commemorative Gold Dollar: See *Commemorative Coins (U.S.),* p. 68.

Lexington-Concord Sesquicentennial Commemorative Half Dollar: See *Commemorative Coins (U.S.),* p. 61.

Liard (Fr. derivation uncertain): A French coin, originally a piece of base silver, first struck in the fifteenth century, in value three *deniers,* but from the time of Louis XIV (1650) it was struck in copper, and represented the fourth part of a *sol.* It was current until 1793.

Liberty Cap Type: See *Cent (U.S.), Eagle, Half Cent, Half Eagle, Quarter Eagle.*

Liberty Head Type: See *Dime; Dollar, U.S. Silver; Half Dime; Half Dollar; Nickel Five-Cent Piece (U.S.); Quarter Dollar.*

Liberty Seated Type: See *Dime; Dollar, U.S. Silver; Half Dime; Half Dollar; Quarter Dollar.*

Liberty Standing Type: See *Double Eagle, Quarter Dollar.*

Liberty Walking Type: See *Half Dollar.*

Libra: The Ancient Roman weight representing 1 lb. or 12 oz. The word is also given to the *as* (q.v.). In early medieval Europe the libra was money of account, representing 240 deniers.

Lima Coinage: Admiral Anson, after his famous three-year voyage round the world, reached the Port of London in 1744, bringing with him specie to the value of £500,000, a treasure so vast that it filled 32 wagons. This treasure came from Lima in Peru, and in particular from a large Spanish treasure galleon Anson had captured. Many of the gold and silver coins of George II dated 1745 and 1746 bore the word LIMA beneath the king's bust, commemorating the fact that they were struck from this captured bullion.

Limerick Money: Halfpennies and farthings in brass, dated 1691, with the bust of James II, and Hibernia with harp seated on the reverse. They were issued at Limerick to serve as currency during the famous siege of that year, and were restruck over "gun-money" shillings.

Lion: (i) Silver denier of the Anglo-Gallic series, bearing the arms of Aquitaine, namely a lion passant guardant, first struck by Prince Edward (afterwards Edward I) in the time of Henry III. A demi-lion was also issued. (ii) Scottish gold coin, first struck by Robert III (1390–1406), and issued up to 1589, when it was known as the *lion noble.* Half-lions were also struck. The modern "Scottish" shilling adopted on the reverse the device of the lion noble, namely a lion sejant crowned, holding sword and scepter. (iii) The *Hardhead* (q.v.).

Lion Shilling and Sixpence: A type of silver coin, issued by George IV in 1825–29, with (reverse) crowned lion standing on crown. This device was repeated on the shillings of Edward VII and various other recent coins.

Great Britain "lion" shilling of George IV (1825–29).

Lira pl. **Lire** (L. *libra*, a pound): As the derivation suggests, this was originally money of account, in use principally in Venice and other Italian states. Not until about the fifteenth century did it become an actual silver coin. Under the Latin Monetary Union (q.v.) the lira was equated with the *franc*, and became the standard unit consisting of one hundred centesimi. It is now struck in aluminum.

Livre (L. *libra*, the Roman lb. of 12 oz., cf. Italian *lira*): Like the "pound" in English numismatics, the *livre* in France was originally merely a money of account, but the name was later applied to an actual coin, at first of gold, but later of silver and sometimes of copper. At the time of the Revolution (1795) the livre became merged in the *franc* (q.v.) of modern France. It was divided into twenty sols, each of twelve deniers. The livre varied slightly in value, the *livre parisis* (livre of Paris) was worth nearly a quarter more than the *livre tournois* (livre of Tournai). (See *Solidus, Denier*.)

London Mint: First established by Carausius (A.D. 287–93). It was closed about A.D. 330, though it was probably reopened for a brief period, under the mint name of Augusta, in the reign of the usurper Magnus Maximus (383–88).

From the time of Henry III, the London Mint was at Westminster. Coins were struck in the Pyx Chapel there. In 1300 an extensive building was erected in the Tower of London, and here most of the English coins were struck until the opening of the Royal Mint on Tower Hill in 1810. (See *Tower Mint*.)

Long-cross Penny: Originally the English silver penny had only a small voided cross on the reverse, extending merely to the inner circle; this left a conveniently wide rim for coin-clippers to shear off bits of silver. To prevent this, in the reign of Henry III (1247), the cross was extended to the edge of the coin. Pennies ceased to be legal tender if more than one end of the arms of the cross were missing. From the time of Edward I the cross was no longer voided. (See *Clipping*, *Cut Halfpennies and Farthings*, *Short-cross Penny*, *Voided Cross*.)

London penny of Edward I.

Long Island Tercentenary Commemorative Half Dollar: See *Commemorative Coins* (*U.S.*), p. 65.

Lord Baltimore Coins: The plantation of Maryland in America in 1632 was ceded to Cecil, Lord Baltimore. Under his direction coins were struck in England for circulation in this plantation. They are dated 1659, and consisted of a shilling, a sixpence, and a groat in silver, and a penny (now very rare) in copper. The silver bears the inscription *Caecilius Dns Terrae Mariae &ct* (Cecil, Lord of Maryland, etc.). The obverse shows the bust of Lord Baltimore, on the reverse are his arms, with the motto *Crescite et multiplicamini* (Increase and multiply— Gen. I. 28).

Louis d'Or: A gold coin of France, first struck in 1640 by Louis XIII, when the coinage was reformed, and worth at that time about 17*s*. 6*d*. The issue ceased at the time of the Revolution, in 1789, and in 1805 it was replaced by the *Napoleon* (q.v.). In the seventeenth century its value fluctuated between ten and fourteen livres; in the eighteenth century it was rated at anything from 15 to 36 livres, though eventually it became stabilized at 24 livres. These coins were popularly known as *Pistoles*.

Louisiana Purchase Exposition Commemorative Gold Dollar: See *Commemorative Coins* (*U.S.*), p. 68.

Love Tokens: A coin was often given in the olden days as a love token. To preserve its amuletic properties, and to prevent its being basely used for purposes of trade, it was often bent.

We frequently find halfpennies, etc., usually about 1760–1800, which have been rubbed down and then re-engraved with some fanciful design, such as hearts thrust through with arrows, true-love knots, etc. In the United States during the latter half of the nineteenth century it was a common custom to engrave fanciful monograms on the reverse of American silver coins.

Lydia: A district and empire of Asia Minor, and the most powerful state of that part of the world in the seventh and sixth centuries B.C. Electrum coins were first struck here in the time of Gyges, the first King of Lydia (seventh century B.C.). They were merely rough oval pieces of native electrum, with a few rough scratches on the face. They may perhaps be considered as the world's earliest coins, though some numismatists would place Chinese coins at a still earlier date. Croesus (561–546 B.C.), the last King of Lydia, is supposed to have struck the first gold coins. Herodotus tells us (Book I, c. 94), that the Lydians were "the first of all nations we know of that introduced the art of coining gold and silver." The coins that are attributed to Croesus are those bearing the type of the foreparts of a lion and a bull facing each other. Lydian coins are the earliest coins of which specimens are extant. The weights of the coins were based on the Babylonian system.

Lynchburg, Va. Sesquicentennial Commemorative Half Dollar: See *Commemorative Coins* (*U.S.*), p. 66.

M

M: On large Byzantine copper coins, from the time of Anastasius (A.D. 491–518), the letter M is the Greek numeral sign for forty, showing the coin to be of the value of forty nummi. Smaller coins were struck with the numeral K (= 20) and I (= 10) respectively.

"M" is the Roman numeral letter for one thousand.

Maille, Mail (L. *metallum*, metal): (*a*) An obole, or half a denier, a small base silver coin, current in France and Flanders from the thirteenth to the fifteenth century. (*b*) Used in a loose sense for money in general, especially when paid at a specified time and rate, such as rent, tribute, or tax. *Blackmail* was originally the tribute paid by the Scottish Border farmers to parties of freebooters to secure exemption from raids.

Maine Centennial Commemorative Half Dollar: See *Commemorative Coins* (*U.S.*), p. 60.

Man, Isle of: This island has a small but interesting coinage, consisting entirely of copper, though silver patterns and proofs exist. While the island was in the hands of the Earl of Derby and the Duke of Athol the currency consisted of legalized tokens. Most of these bear the Stanley crest of the eagle and the child, and the motto beneath the triskelion (see *Triquetra*) QUOCUNQUE GESSERIS STABIT (Wherever you bear it, it will stand). Although the island kept, and still keeps, its own laws and government, it was purchased for the English Crown in 1765. In 1786 regal coins were issued for the island, namely, a penny and halfpenny; Obv/Bust of George III laureate; Rev/The triskelion and the legend QUOCUNQUE IECERIS STABIT (Wherever you throw it, it will stand).

A further issue of these coins was made in 1798 and 1813. In Victorian times a penny, halfpenny, and farthing were struck in 1839; reverse as above, but in 1840 all coins and tokens other than English regal coinage were suppressed.

The interest of the triskelion on the tokens and coins is that it commemorates the solar disk of Manannan, son of Ler (Shakespeare's King Lear!) the eponymous Gaelic God who favored this island.

Maravedis (Murabitin, name of a Moorish dynasty): Gold coin struck in Spain by the Moors in the eleventh and twelfth centuries; later, the name given to a very small copper coin in use in Spain from the sixteenth to the nineteenth century. It was the standard copper coin; 34 maravedi (plural of *maravedis*) were equal to one *real*.

Maria Theresa Dollars: Dollars dated 1780, but which are really modern copies of the old Austrian taler (dollar). They bear the head of Maria Theresa. They are minted even today in the London Mint and

in various Continental mints, for the use of certain countries, mostly in the Levant and the regions bordering on the Red Sea. The natives of these countries will not tolerate debased modern coinage, and, accustomed as they have been for the last 150 years to the pure silver and fine design of the eighteenth-century dollar, prefer these to any other coins. Formerly they were issued by the Austrian mint for anybody who took the silver there. Even today the dollars are 83½ per cent pure silver. These dollars are also known as Levant Dollars.

Mark (A.S., *marc*, a weight, also a coin): Originally a standard weight of precious metal, and more frequently used of money of account than of any actual coin. In 1103 Philip I of France instituted the weight of one mark as two-thirds of the pound as established by Charlemagne, or 3,840 grains. From 1524 the Cologne mark was accepted in central Europe. In England it never appeared as a coin, but figures prominently as money of account, and is first heard of in the Treaty drawn up between Alfred and Guthram the Dane. It then represented 100 silver pennies, but from the twelfth century it was reckoned at a value of 13s. 4d. As late as 1703, we hear of Daniel Defoe being fined the sum of 200 marks. In northern Germany and Scandinavia it was an actual coin from the sixteenth century, and today it is the standard coin of Germany, where it was introduced in 1871 as a unit representing 100 pfennigs.

For the Scottish mark, see under *Merk*.

Market Value: The price at which a collector can buy a coin.

Maryland Tercentenary Commemorative Half Dollar: See *Commemorative Coins (U.S.)*, p. 63.

Mascle (O. Fr. *mascle*, L. *macula*, a spot): A voided lozenge, often found as mint mark, etc.

Mascle.

Master of the Mint: Formerly the officer in charge of the mint. In the days of the Romans the *triumviri monetales* (q.v.) held this office. In early medieval days, when the mint was small and localized, the moneyer did the actual striking of the coins, and was held directly responsible to the Crown. Later the moneyer no longer struck coins with his own hand, but he was held responsible for, and had supervision over, the men that did the actual striking. It was not, however, until the centralization of the various mints into one London Mint that the master moneyer was recognized as Mint Master.*

In the reign of Edward I (1279), William de Turnemire, of Marseilles, was appointed Master Moneyer of England, and he may be regarded as the first official Master of the English Mint. The office of Master of the Mint was held under direct indenture from the king, and was of importance only as long as the mint was regarded as the royal prerogative.

Several well-known persons have held the office, the most famous being Sir Isaac Newton (1692-1727) and Sir John Herschel (1850-55).

In 1870 the office was abolished and the duties of office incorporated with those of the Chancellor of the Exchequer. The practical side of the office was then taken over by a Deputy Master and Comptroller, and it is these officials that have charge of the British mint today.

Matrix (L.L. a womb): A mold, and in particular the intaglio of a steel plate from which punches for making dies are formed.

Maundy Money (L. *Mandatum*, a commandment, referring to the "new

---

* By the time of Edward I the moneyer's name was no longer put on the coin.

commandment" of John xii. 34): A series of four small silver coins, consisting of one penny, twopence, threepence, and fourpence, and first struck in the reign of Charles II. The earliest so-called "Maundy Money" up to the time of George II was merely the ordinary current coin of the realm. In certain years no Maundy money was struck, and occasionally the set was issued incomplete. The Maundy Money of today, in reality a relic of obsolete currency, is now specially struck for the Royal Bounty given to poor persons on Maundy Thursday (the Thursday before Easter). The Bounty is given to as many men as the monarch has years, and to as many women, and in each bounty (or bag) the number of pence is the same as the monarch's age. The ceremony usually takes place in Westminster Abbey, but in 1957 took place at St. Alban's Abbey.

Great Britain, fourpence, threepence, twopence, penny. Maundy money of Edward VII (1902).

McKinley Memorial Commemorative Gold Dollar: See *Commemorative Coins (U.S.)*, p. 69.

Medal (Fr. *Medaille*, It. *medaglia*, L. *metallum*, a piece of metal): A piece of metal, struck to the shape of a coin, not intended for currency, but to commemorate a person, an event, institution, etc.

Mercury Head Type: See *Dime*.

Merk (Scottish form of *mark*, q.v.): A silver coin, first struck by James VI of Scotland in 1580. From the thistle on the reverse it was known as the thistle half-dollar. A thistle dollar, or double merk, was also struck. At the Union of England and Scotland, when James VI became James I of England, the Scottish merk was ordered to be current in England for thirteenpence-halfpenny, though ostensibly in Scotland it was worth two-thirds of the Scottish pound, i.e., 13s. 4d.

Charles II struck half-merk, merk, two-merk, and four-merk pieces, though these coins were assimilated to the English coins. They bear a thistle as mint mark, and the value in Roman numerals in the center of the reverse.

Merovingian Dynasty (from Merovaeus, Latinized form of Merwig, a fifth-century chieftain of the Salian Franks): The grandson of Merovaeus, Clovis, made himself supreme ruler of all the Franks (481–511), thus founding the Merovingian or first Dynasty of the Franks.

This dynasty lasted until Pepin in 751 deposed Childeric III and founded the *Carolingian Dynasty* (q.v.).

The early coins of the Merovingian Dynasty, struck at numerous mints, were small golden coins (see *Tremissis*), crude imitations of Roman types, but with the Christian cross on the reverse. In course of time, as gold became scarcer, the coins became electrum, and in the succeeding Carolingian Dynasty they were nearly all struck in silver.

Miliarensis (L. containing a thousand): A small silver coin, introduced by Constantine I, so called from being one-thousandth part of a pound of gold, i.e., a double *siliqua*, or one-twelfth of the *solidus*.

Milled Edge: A coin rim which has been raised in relation to the surface of the coin. This is done to make the coin more durable and to discourage clipping. See *Clipping, Reeded Edge, Wire Edge*.

Milled Money (so called either from the water mills or horse mills which supplied power for the machinery, or from the actual mills used for rolling the ingots): A term applied to money produced by the screw press which superseded the old method of hammering the coins by hand. The term has no connection with the "milling" on the edge of modern coins (see *Screw Press, Hammered Coins*). The method of producing milled coins was introduced from France in the time of Elizabeth, in 1561 (see *France, Coinage of*), but met with hostility from the English moneyers. The Frenchman who fabricated the milled money was eventually hanged for counterfeiting. Charles I and Cromwell produced some milled coins side by side with the hammered coinage, but it was not until the time of Charles II, in 1662, that the process of milling became permanent. In the reign of William and Mary the old hammered coins were called in. The advent of steam power in the time of George III actually marks the end of the "milling" process.

Mill-Sail Pattern: A geometrical pattern on the reverse of certain archaic Greek coins (e.g., on early coins of Aegina), where the punch mark (q.v.) assumes the shape of eight triangles conjoined.

Milreis (L. *mille*, a thousand, Port. *reis*, pl. of *real*, the royal coin): The unit of money used in Portugal and Brazil, 1,000 *reis*.

Minim or **Minimos,** pl. **Minimi** (L. *minimus*, smallest): Diminutive bronze coins, barbarous copies of Roman coins, with radiate or diademed busts, of the third and fourth centuries A.D. Some of these are no bigger than the head of a pin; in fact, more than fifty of such *minimissimi* (smallest *minimi*) would be needed to cover a modern halfpenny. In 1929 a hoard of many hundreds of these coins was found at Lydney Park, Gloucester. Most of the British minimi probably date from the fifth and sixth centuries A.D.

Mint: Like most mints of the Ancients, the old Roman mint was set up in a temple—the temple of Juno Moneta on the Capitoline Hill. As the Latin word for mint was *moneta*, it is possible that Juno obtained her title Juno Moneta, Juno of the Mint, from this word; many authorities, however, would have it that Juno Moneta meant Juno the Adviser, the Giver of Counsel (from *moneo*), and from the fact that the first Roman mint was set up in her temple, the title Moneta became the word for mint, and later for money. However this may be, it is from *moneta* (mint or money) that we derive our English words mint, money, monetary, etc.

The early mints, up to the time of George III when steam power was applied, were rough-and-ready work-sheds, employing no more than two to six artisans, equipped with a few hand tools. They were hardly more imposing to look on than the village smithy. There was a table on which bullion was weighed as it came in, and crucibles for melting the bullion into bars. These bars would be hammered on an anvil into sheets of the required thickness, then cut and trimmed into disks ready for striking between the dies (see *Die*). The whole process can be clearly followed in the accompanying reproduction of a German print of about A.D. 1500.

The modern mint has a number of machines, small and compact, for the different processes. The coining press itself, though elaborate, is by no means large, yet it can exert a pressure of up to 160 tons a square inch, and it is capable of striking coins at the rate of more than 165 per minute.

Mint Errors (Freaks): Mis-struck coins, originating in a government mint, that have slipped through inspection. They are of the following types:

(i) *Off metal coins.* Probably the rarest type of mint error. It occurs, for example, when a silver planchet intended for a dime is mixed with copper planchets and results in a silver penny.

(ii) *Double struck coins.* Two impressions on one planchet. The second striking is usually only a partial impression. Triple impressions are also known, though exceedingly rare.

(iii) *Off center coins* occur when the planchet is not properly centered between the dies. Generally, the further off from center such a coin is, the more desirable it becomes.

(iv) *Blank planchets* sometimes slip through the mint without passing between the dies to be impressed.

The most recently discovered mint error is the 1955 double die Lincoln cent. This was caused by a shifting of the hub in making one of the working dies.

Curious misspellings appear on some early American coins. Some of the 1796 cents carry the legend "LIHERTY," while "LIBETKY" appears on some 1800 half dimes. The 1801 cent has a variety with three errors, including "IINITED" for "UNITED." Some of the 1828 half cents have only 12 stars on the obverse.

For the curious story of the 1936 dot coinage of the Canadian cent, see *Rarities*.

Mint Mark: Various symbols, letters, or numbers were placed on many of the early Roman Republican coins, to denote the particular workshop in which they were struck, and in the later years of the Empire, from the time of Gallienus (260–68), when mints were established all over Europe and the East, it was necessary for the place of mintage to be clearly indicated. Under the monetary reform of Diocletian (A.D. 296) almost all the coins of the Roman Empire were marked with the place of mintage; in the case of important mints the actual *officina*, or workshop, was shown by a number or a letter.

This "mint mark," placed in the exergue of the reverse, often had the letter P (*pecunia*) in front, or SM (*sacra moneta*). The mint town is indicated by the initial letters; to this is added, when necessary, a letter showing the number of the workshop, i.e., P (prima), S (secunda), T (tertia), Q (quarta). Other workshops were indicated by the first few letters of the alphabet. The following are some common but puzzling mint marks:

Alexandria (Egypt)	Al, Ale, Alex
Ambianum (Amiens, France)	Amb, Ambi
Antioch (Syria)	An, Ant
Aquileia (Italy)	Aq, Aqvi
Arelatum (Arles, France)	Ar, Arl
Camulodunum (Colchester, England)	C*
Carthage (Tunis)	K, Kar, Kart
Constantinople	C, Con, Cons, Kon, Kons, Konst
Cyzicus (Turkey)	Cuz, Cuzic, Cyz, Cyzic, K, Kv, Kvz, Ky
Heraclea (Turkey)	H, Her, Heracl, Ht, Htr
Londinium (London)	L, Ll, Ln, Lon
Lugdunum (Lyons, France)	Ld, Lg, Lug, Lugd
Mediolanum (Milan, Italy)	Md, Med
Nicomedia (Turkey)	N, Nic, Nico, Nik
Narbo (Narbonne, France)	Nar
Ostia (port of Rome)	Ost
Ravenna (Italy)	Rav
Rome	R, Rm, Rom, Roma, Urb Rom
Serdica (Sophia, Bulgaria)	Sd, Ser, Serd
Sirmium (Yugoslavia)	Sir, Sirm
Siscia (Yugoslavia)	S, Sis, Sisc, Sm
Thessalonica (Greece)	TE, Tes, Th, Ts, Oes
Ticinum (Pavia, Italy)	T
Treveri (Trier, France)	Tr, Tre

On early medieval coins the inscription always begins, in the pious fashion of the Middle Ages, with a cross. This, however, gives us no indication of the place of mintage, nor of the particular mint where it was struck, so that, strictly speaking, it is not a mint mark at all, but an *initial mark*. Custom, however, has given it this name. From 1465 this initial mark became an heraldic symbol such as a crown, a sun, an annulet, a rose, a fleur-de-lis, and from the time of the Tudors served to differentiate one issue of coins from another. It became, in fact, a cryptic method of dating a coin.

An heraldic mint mark which serves to date a coin is known as a *privy mark*. On later coins we find initial letters beneath the bust serving as mint marks, as in William III's great recoinage of 1695, where the additional provincial mints of Bristol, Chester, Exeter,

* Some numismatists, however, ascribe this mint mark to Clausentum, (Bitterne) near Southampton.

Norwich, and York are indicated by the letters B, C, E, N, and Y, respectively. Similarly many eighteenth-century European coins are marked with a letter as a mint mark.

The locations of mint marks on U.S. coins can be summarized as follows:

Indian Head cents: on the reverse, at the bottom under the wreath.

Lincoln Head cents: on the obverse, under the date.

Three-cents silver: on the reverse, to the right of the "III."

Liberty Head nickels: on the reverse, to the left of CENTS.

Buffalo nickels: on the reverse, under FIVE CENTS.

Jefferson nickels: on the reverse, to the right of the building, or above it.

Liberty Seated half dimes: on the reverse, under the wreath or within it.

Liberty Seated dimes: on the reverse, under the wreath or within it.

Liberty Head dimes: on the reverse, under the wreath.

Winged Head Liberty ("Mercury Head") dimes: on the reverse, to the left of the fasces.

Roosevelt dimes: on the reverse, at the left bottom of the torch.

Twenty cent pieces: on the reverse, under the eagle.

Liberty Seated quarters: on the reverse, under the eagle.

Liberty Head quarters: on the reverse, under the eagle.

Standing Liberty quarters: on the obverse, above and to the left of the date.

Washington quarters: on the reverse, under the eagle.

Liberty Seated half dollars: on the reverse, under the eagle.

Liberty Head half dollars: on the reverse, under the eagle.

Standing Liberty half dollars: on the reverse, to the left of HALF DOLLAR.

Franklin half dollars: on the reverse, above the Liberty Bell beam.

Liberty Seated dollars: on the reverse, under the eagle.

Liberty Head dollars: on the reverse, under the eagle.

Peace dollars: on the reverse, at the bottom, to the left of the eagle's wing.

Trade dollars: on the reverse, under the eagle.

Gold dollars: on the reverse, under the wreath.

Ribbon Type quarter eagles: on the obverse, above the date.

Coronet Type quarter eagles: on the reverse, below the eagle.

Indian Head quarter eagles: on the reverse, to the left of the eagle's claw.

Three-dollar gold pieces: on the reverse, below the wreath.

Ribbon Type half eagles: on the obverse, above the date.

Coronet Type half eagles: on the reverse, below the eagle.

Indian Head half eagles: on the reverse, to the left of the eagle's claw.

Coronet Type eagles: on the reverse, below the eagle.

Indian Head eagles: on the reverse, to the left of the eagle's claw.

Coronet Type double eagles: on the reverse, below the eagle.

Liberty Standing double eagles: on the reverse, above the date.

The locations of mint marks on Canadian coins can be summarized as follows:

Large cents: on the reverse, under the date on the 1876, 1881, 1882, 1890 and 1907 issues; above the bottom rim on the 1898 and 1900 issues.

Five cents silver, Ten cents silver, Twenty-five cents silver, Fifty cents silver: on the reverse, below the center of the ribbon tying the wreath.

Gold sovereigns, Five dollars gold, Ten dollars gold: on the reverse, above the date.

Mint, The Royal: For some 500 years the London mint functioned in the Tower of London, but in 1810-12, the present spacious building on Tower Hill was erected, and was known as the Royal Mint. The architects were James Johnson and Robert Smirke. The presses were worked by steam power, in place of the old handturned screw presses, the engineers being Boulton, Watt, and Rennie.

In addition to coins and medals, the Mint produces the Great Seals of the Kingdom and seals of Government offices, as well as naval and military seals. There are branches of the Mint in Canada and in Australia. (See *London Mint, Tower Mint.*)

Mints, Canadian: Canadian coins have been struck at three mints:

Coins with the H mint mark were struck at the Heaton mint at Birmingham, England.

Coins dated between 1858 and 1907 which bear no mint mark were struck at the Royal Mint, London.

Coins dated after 1907 with the C mint mark or no mint mark were struck at the Royal Canadian Mint, Ottawa.

Mints, English: In Anglo-Saxon times the constant fighting with the Danes, and the consequent necessity for large sums of tribute, rendered a number of mints necessary for turning out quickly the coins that were needful. Athelstan (925–39) was the first English king to establish a variety of mints (28 or more). During the whole of the tenth century the number of mints steadily increased; over 75 mints are known to have existed in the reign of Athelred II (976–1016). The place of mintage was shown on the coins of Athelstan, and this was the practice up to the last year of Elizabeth I.

Dies were at first made locally; by the end of the eleventh century, however, all dies were issued from London. The number of provincial mints gradually decreased. Local mints, except those of Southwark, Bristol, and York, were suppressed by Henry VIII.

In the great recoinage of silver in the time of William III, when the old hammered coins were called in for restriking, provincial mints were necessary to relieve the pressure of work at the Tower Mint. For a period of two years (1696 and 1697) coins were struck at Bristol, Chester, Exeter, Norwich, and York. These mints have the initial letters of the town beneath the king's bust. After this time the last provincial mint was discontinued.

Mints, U.S.: The United States has operated seven mints at one time or another, as follows:

Mint		Mint Mark
Philadelphia, Pa.	1792 to date	none

(The only time that Philadelphia coins carried a mint mark was during World War II, the special contents of the Jefferson nickel being indicated by the "P" mint mark. See *Nickel Five-Cent Piece;* also *Mint Mark.*)

Dahlonega, Ga.	1838–61	D
Charlotte, N.C.	1838–61	C
New Orleans, La.	1838–1909	O
San Francisco, Cal.	1854–1955	S
Carson City, Nev.	1870–93	CC
Denver, Colo.	1906 to date	D

Missouri Centennial Commemorative Half Dollar: See *Commemorative Coins (U.S.),* p. 61.

Mis-strike: A coin that is "off-center." This is caused by shifting of the die so that it fails to come down centrally on the flan.

Mite (Old Dutch *mijte,* a minute coin): (i) Any small coin of trifling worth; (ii) old English weight, about $\frac{1}{20}$ grain Troy; (iii) in medieval money of account, one-sixth of a farthing. From its diminutive size and weight, and possibly influenced by its scriptural use (see below), the word "mite" obtained the signification of anything below normal size; thus we speak of a very small child as a "mite."

Mite, The Widow's: See Mark xii. 42:

"There came a certain poor widow, and she threw in two mites which make a farthing."

In the original Greek the word here rendered "mites" is *lepta,* and farthing, *kodrantes.* But such coins would be neither Greek nor Roman, for offerings to the Temple at Jerusalem had to be made in Jewish currency. The small Hebrew coin rendered in this passage as *lepton* at the time of Christ's ministry would be a rough copy of the Maccabean coins, especially those of John Hyrcanus and Alexander Jannaeus. These types would be: Obv/Hebrew legend: Rev/Poppyhead between two cornucopiae; Obv/Anchor; Rev/Spokes of wheel. (See *Lepton*.)

Mithraic Coin, Inscription, etc.: About the middle of the third century A.D., sun worship was introduced into Rome from the East, and became popular in that city. Thus, on coins of Valerian (253–59) we see the sun-god, or possibly the Emperor in the guise of the sun-god, radiate, bearing the whip of a charioteer. In the following century, sun worship became merged with the worship of the Persian God Mithras, a ritualistic religion especially popular with the Roman Soldiery, who spread the worship over the whole Empire. Dedications to Mithras, the sun, the Unconquered Comrade (*Soli invicto comiti*) are common both on altars and on coins. These Mithraic coins usually bear a representation of the sun-god.

Module (L. *modulus*, a small measure): The size of a coin as measured by the diameter.

Mohammedan Coins: The Mohammedan religion forbids any form of image making; the interest of these coins centers in the calligraphic art and the inscriptions. Often the coins bear the sacred legends "There is no God but God," "Mahomet is the Prophet of God," etc. (See also *Zodiacal Coins*.)

Mohammedan Dates: On coins of Morocco, etc., the dates are set out according to the Mohammedan calendar. The year 622 is the date of the Hejira or flight of Mohammed from Mecca to Medina, from which date the calendar is reckoned. There is a complication in comparing this calendar with our own in the fact that the Mohammedan year is a lunar one, and therefore eleven days shorter than the solar year. To convert the Mohammedan year to our own calendar, therefore, we should deduct 3 per cent and add 622 to the figure, and this will give the approximate year, A.D.

Mohur (derivation uncertain, perhaps Hindu *muhar*, a seal, a gold coin): Standard gold coin of India, struck by various princes of the native Indian states under the Mogul dynasty of the sixteenth century. Later the name was given to the gold coin struck for India under British rule, value fifteen rupees. In 1899 the silver standard was superseded by the gold standard and the mohur was replaced by the sovereign. (See *India, Coinage of*.)

Moidore, Moedore (Port. *moeda da ouro*, L. *moneta*, money, *aurum*, gold): A fine large gold coin of Portugal (and hence of Brazil), current in the latter part of the seventeenth century and the first half of the eighteenth century. It represented a value of 4,000 reis. It bore the arms of the country on the obverse, and a cross on the reverse with the motto IN HOC SIGNO VINCES ("by this sign shalt thou conquer").

Along with other Continental coins, the moidore circulated in England in the eighteenth century (see *Weights for Coins*).

Monastery Tokens: See *Nuremburg Tokens*.

Moneta: The surname the Romans gave to Juno, the "Giver of Counsel." The Roman mint was set up in her temple, hence Moneta became the name for a mint, and later the name for money. Coins were sometimes struck showing Moneta as a personification of money, holding scales and cornucopia. Commodus introduced three *Monetae* on the coins. (See *Mint*.)

Moneta Nova (L. new money): A term often found in the legends of a new issue of medieval European coins.

Monetarius pl. **Monetarii:** Latin for *moneyer*.

Monetary Convention: See *Latin Monetary Union*.

Monetary Union: See *Latin Monetary Union*.

Monetary Unit: The coin of any currency on which all other coins of that currency are based, e.g., the silver dollar, the mark, the franc, the sovereign.

Money (L. *moneta*, q.v.): In a popular sense "money" is synonymous with "coin"; in a broader sense it implies any medium of exchange. What exactly constitutes "money" is still a debated point in economics. All coins are money, and under the term we may include paper money and bank notes; credit documents, however, such as checks, promissory notes, and bills of exchange, are dependent on personal good faith and solvency, and these therefore would be ruled out of a strict definition. Bullion in one sense is money, and, in fact, foreign debts are often settled in bullion. Token coins are a borderline case, as some tokens are officially authorized as currency and others quite the reverse; in any case, their value is localized, as they cannot be used in settling foreign debts.

Money of Necessity: See *Necessity, Money of*.

Moneyer: The official in charge of a mint. The name of the moneyer, whether of the actual striker of the coin or of the official responsible for the striking, usually appears on all English coins up to the reorganization of the Mint under Edward I in 1279. After that date all the mints were placed under one authority, and the name of the moneyer is omitted.

In Anglo-Saxon and Norman times the moneyer was the actual

striker of the coin. His importance is indicated by that type of Anglo-Saxon coin where the name of the moneyer fills, in two lines, the whole of the reverse. Afterwards the moneyer, in place of a skilled craftsman, became an important government official or supervisor responsible for the efficient maintenance of the Mint. Such an official was, in fact, a mint master.

A belated, and, it would seem, somewhat irregular issue with the name of the moneyer (Robert de Hadeleie) continued to be struck by the Abbot of Bury St. Edmunds from 1280 till 1283.

For Roman moneyers see *Triumviri Monetales*.

Monroe Doctrine Centennial Commemorative Half Dollar: See *Commemorative Coins* (*U.S.*), p. 61.

Morgan Head Coins: Any coins or patterns designed by mint engraver George T. Morgan but used specifically to refer to the Liberty Head silver dollar of the 1878–1921 issue.

Mottoes on Coins: From the time of Edward III to that of Charles II, it was the custom for all English coins to bear a motto on the reverse. This, with the exception of the Commonwealth coins, was always in Latin. The motto was almost always of a religious character, though frequently it would bear some reference to the politics of the day.

On the groats and half-groats of Edward III appears the legend:

POSVI DEVM ADIVTOREM MEVM

("I have taken God to be my Helper")

This is evidently derived from Ps. lii. 7:

"Ecce homo qui non posuit Deum adiutorem suum; sed speravit in multitudine divitiarum suarum."

("Lo, this is the man that made not God his strength; but trusted in the abundance of his riches.")

It was an appropriate text to place on a coin, and, in fact, became the most popular of all coin mottoes until the time of Elizabeth I.

Sometimes a line was taken from an actual hymn of the day, for instance, the motto which appears on all the angelets:

O CRUX, AVE, SPES UNICA

("Hail, Cross, our only hope")

The motto on the *couronne d'or* of Louis IX (1226–70),

XPS VINCIT, XPS REGNAT, XPS IMPERAT

("Christ conquers, Christ reigns, Christ commands")

from the Easter Laudes, became a frequent motto on the Anglo-Gallic series.

Another text, the most popular on French coins up to relatively recent times, was that from the Vulgate version of Ps. cxiii. 2 (or from Job i. 21—the words are identical):

SIT NOMEN DOMINI BENEDICTUM

("Blessed be the name of the Lord")

It was introduced in the days of St. Louis on the *gros tournois*. This also appears on the Anglo-Gallic pieces. Such texts, of course, would be familiar from the missals of the Church.

Many of the mottoes seem to adapt the words of Holy Writ in an amuletic sense. On the *nobles* and *florins* of Edward III to Edward IV, and on the sovereigns and half-sovereigns of the Tudor monarchs, appears a text from the Vulgate version of Luke iv. 30:

IHS AUTEM TRANSIENS PER MEDIUM ILLORUM IBAT

("But Jesus, passing through the midst of them, went his way")

This may, it has been suggested, bear some reference to alchemy; more likely it was intended as a charm against thieves.

Often the mottoes on our coins have a direct historical reference, especially at such a stormy period of time as the Reformation. Thus on most of the shillings of Edward VI appears the text:

TIMOR DOMINI FONS VITAE

("The fear of the Lord is a fountain of life"—Prov. xiv. 27)

and on the groat of the Catholic Queen Mary,

VERITAS TEMPORIS FILIA

("Truth is the daughter of time")

a tag from an unknown Latin poet quoted by Aulus Gellius (*Attic Nights*, Book XII).

The quotation from Ps. cxviii. 23:

A DOMINO FACTUM EST ISTUD ET EST MIRABILE IN OCULIS NOSTRIS

("This is the Lord's doing, and it is marvelous in our eyes")

appears on various gold coins of Mary, Elizabeth, and James I, and served as a war cry to both Catholics and non-Catholics alike.

The coins of James I bear special reference in their mottoes to the union of England and Scotland, such as

FACIAM EOS IN GENTEM UNAM

("I will make them one nation"—Ezek. xxxvii. 22)

which appears on the *unites* and *laurels* of James I, and

QUAE DEUS CONJUNXIT NEMO SEPARET

("What God hath joined let no man put asunder"—Matt. xix. 6)

which appears on the silver crown and other silver pieces. The verse, taken from Ps. lxviii, which appears on the early coins of James I,

EXURGAT DEUS DISSIPENTUR INIMICI

("Let God arise, and let His enemies be scattered")

was apparently chosen for his coins by the king himself, and probably bears reference to one of the many conspiracies of the time.*

The characteristic and most popular motto of Charles I, ruler by "Divine Right," was

CHRISTO AUSPICE REGNO

("By the right of Christ do I reign")

The Commonwealth eschewed all Latin inscriptions as savoring of "Popery," and so for the first and only time in history a plain English motto was adopted:

GOD WITH US

Cromwell, however, had the learned Milton as his Latin secretary, so we find an echo of Classical writers on his own coins, as Protector, in the motto

PAX QUAERITUR BELLO

("Peace is sought by war"; cf. Statius, Thebais, vii, 554, "Saevis pax quaeritur armis")

It was, however, from the time of the Puritans that the idea of the coin motto being used as a prayer or religious charm completely faded out. In fact, Cromwell pushed the motto to the rim of the coin, where it became a mere warning to coin-clippers; thus, on his crowns and half-crowns, appears the threat

HAS NISI PERITURUS MIHI ADIMAT NEMO

the meaning of which is: the penalty for clipping this coin is death. This somewhat drastic legend was smoothed down in the time of Charles II to the milder

DECUS ET TUTAMEN

("An ornament and a safeguard")

This legend appears on the edge of the five-guinea and five-pound pieces and the crown from the time of Charles II to that of Victoria. The diarist Evelyn suggested this motto, which he had seen in a vignette in the Greek Testament of Cardinal Richelieu, though the actual phrase is that of Virgil (*Aeneid*, Book V, v. 262).

In U.S. coinage there are two familiar mottoes which appear over and over. These are E PLURIBUS UNUM ("many joined into one") and IN GOD WE TRUST. The first of these appears quite early, the initial instance apparently being on the reverse (with large eagle) on the 1797 eagle. The second motto originated on the Two-Cent Piece (q.v.) during the Civil War. On current coins both mottoes are used, one on each side of the coin.

---

* This motto, however, had appeared on earlier Scottish coins, namely on the *unicorn* and *half-unicorn* of James III (1486), as on those of James IV, and on some coins of Mary Queen of Scots.

Mule (Eng. a hybrid animal): A hybrid coin, medal or token, that is to say one having an obverse and a reverse that are not normally associated. Early English coins are frequently found where the head and title of a king are given the reverse of a previous monarch.

Mullet (O. Fr. *mollette*, the rowel of a spur): Heraldic term for a star.

N

Nail Marks (on Chinese and Korean coins): The mark of a crescent, or decorative spots, sometimes seen on Chinese and Korean coins. The Chinese term for these is "nail characters." They are formed by the workmen at the mint amusing themselves by pushing their nails into the clay molds while still moist. There is a story that when the soft clay model of a proposed coin was brought to the Chinese Empress in A.D. 620 Her Majesty accidently left the imprint of her thumbnail in the wax. This fortuitous imprint was carefully copied not only in the succeeding issue of coins but also in coins struck for some centuries afterwards.

Names, Roman: Every Roman citizen had at least two names: (1) the PRAENOMEN, the name of the individual, or "Christian" name as we should term it. Only about 30 *praenomina* were in common use, and they were usually indicated by the initial letter only (e.g., M. for Marcus); (2) the NOMEN GENTILICUM, which always ended in *ius* (e.g., Claudius). This was the tribal name, the name of the *gens*. Frequently a third name was added, the COGNOMEN, or hereditary name of the citizen's family. Often, like our own names "Brown," "White," "Little," etc., this name related to some physical peculiarity, for example, *Magnus* (big), and was frequently in the nature of a humorous nickname, e.g., *Brutus* ("Blockhead"), *Asina* ("Donkey"), *Naso* ("Big-beak"). The more important citizens bore a fourth name, the AGNOMEN. This was an honorary distinction, and usually commemorated some great achievement effected by them, or it related to the personage into whose family they had been adopted. *Agnomina*, such as *Germanicus*, *Britannicus*, commemorate victories in Germany and Britain.

Napoleon (From Napoleon Bonaparte): A French gold coin, bearing the head of Napoleon I; struck 1805–15; value, twenty francs. Applied also to any French gold twenty-franc piece.

Necessity, Money of: A term mainly applied to *Siege Pieces* (q.v.), though it actually embraces all unorthodox issues where the official mints for any reason have ceased functioning. See *Gun Money, Leather Money, Limerick Money, Nummus Castrensis.*

Newcomb Numbers: Specialists in collecting large cents refer to die varieties and attribute their coins according to listings in *United States Copper Cents 1816–1857*, by Howard R. Newcomb.

New England Money: A shilling, sixpence, and threepenny piece, issued by the Colony of Massachusetts in the mid-seventeenth century. This was the first money actually coined in America. They bear neither date nor legend. On the obverse are the letters N.E., and on the reverse Roman numerals indicating value in pence.

New Rochelle, N.Y. Commemorative Half Dollar: See *Commemorative Coins (U.S.)*, p. 67.

New Tenor—Old Tenor Notes: In Colonial America many issues of currency were recalled and replaced by a new issue. Sometimes this was occasioned by the circulation of an abnormally large number of counterfeit notes; at other times the replacement was necessitated by monetary revaluation. In such cases the old issue was referred to as "old tenor," while the new issue was "new tenor."

Nicked Coins: The middle issues of the coins of Henry I bear a small nick in the edge. According to William of Malmesbury, this was first done to test the worth of the coin, at a time when current coins were of dubious quality. People, however, looked askance at such coins, thinking them cracked in the making. To avoid discrimination, it was decreed that every penny issued should be nicked.

Nickel (abbrev. of Swiss *kopparnickel*; cf Ger. *kupfernickel*): As a medium of coinage, nickel is usually copper-nickel, or cupro-nickel, namely, an alloy of three parts of copper with one of nickel. Nickel coins were first struck by Switzerland in 1856. The Jamaica nickel penny and half-penny of 1870 were an attempt, with some degree of success, to bring this base-metal coinage to a higher plane of numismatic art than is usually attained, but the vast quantities of cheap, mass-produced coins that flooded Europe during and after the two world wars exhibit merely cheap and utilitarian designs and types.

In the United States, however, the five-cent nickel coin (q.v.) has proved highly successful since its introduction in 1866.

Abbreviation Ni.

Nickel Five-Cent Piece (U.S.): This coin has been struck from 1866 to date under authorization of the Act of May 16, 1866. The original weight of the coin—5 grams—has always been maintained. With one exception, all issues have had the following composition: 75 parts copper, 25 parts nickel. In the early part of 1942 nickels were struck with the standard composition, but after passage of the Act of March 27, 1942 the composition was changed to: 56 parts copper, 35 parts silver and 9 parts manganese. Beginning with the 1946 coinage the mint returned to the standard composition.

The following types of nickels have been struck:

Shield	1866–83
Liberty Head	1883–1912
Buffalo (or Indian Head)	1913–38
Jefferson	1938–

The official appearance of the Shield-type nickels was preceded by the usual patterns. During the first two years of issue, however, a great many additional patterns were tried—busts of Washington, Lincoln and Liberty, and several reverse designs. The original design was kept, with one exception. On the obverse there appears an ornate shield, with the motto IN GOD WE TRUST at the top and the date at the bottom. On the reverse of the 1866 nickels and some of the 1867 nickels a circular pattern of stars encloses a large "5." Rays are interspersed between the stars. Fairly early in 1867 the rays were permanently eliminated. The 1867 nickel with rays is the most valuable coin of the shield series in proof form. Only proofs were struck in 1877 and 1878.

The first Liberty Head nickels appeared in 1883, which was also the last year of the Shield nickels. The reverse featured a large "V" in a wreath, with UNITED STATES OF AMERICA along the upper curve and the motto E PLURIBUS UNUM along the lower curve. This gave some people the ingenious idea of gold-plating the coin and passing it off for a five-dollar gold piece. Later that year the motto was moved up and placed just under the upper legend. This made room for the word CENTS along the lower curve.

The only year in which Liberty Head nickels were struck at San Francisco and Denver was 1912. The mint mark appears on the reverse to the left of CENTS.

Nickel Five-Cents. *Left:* Shield type. *Right:* Liberty Head type.

The most valuable Liberty Heads are coins that were never officially struck by the mint. Congress had passed a law authorizing a new design for the 1913 nickel. But—so the story goes—some employees at the mint struck six Liberty Head nickels with a 1913 date and then disposed of the coins to a dealer. Eventually they found their way into the fabulous collection of Colonel Green, the son of the eccentric Hetty Green who had accumulated a huge fortune in Wall Street. Later the coins were dispersed into various collections. These rarities are valued at over $10,000 apiece.

NICK

The Buffalo nickel is also known as the Indian Head nickel. A finely modeled Indian head appears on the obverse. The word LIBERTY is seen at the upper right, with the date and the designer's initial ("F" for James E. Fraser). The 1913 coin has two varieties. In the first the buffalo stands on a mound. In the second the mound has been replaced by a noticeably thinner straight line. The second variety became the standard design for subsequent issues.

Nickel Five-Cents, Buffalo type.

These coins were struck regularly at Philadelphia, San Francisco and Denver. The mint mark appears on the reverse, under FIVE CENTS. The most valuable issue in the series is the 1918 D overstrike on the 1917 D nickel. The top of the "7" is quite perceptible in the overstruck "8." Of the later issues, the 1937 D nickel has the famous "three-legged" variety, caused by a portion of the die being filled in. Proofs were struck only in 1913–16 and 1936–37.

The Jefferson nickel first appeared in 1938. A fine portrait of Jefferson appears on the obverse, with IN GOD WE TRUST on the left curve and LIBERTY and the date on the right curve. The reverse features Jefferson's home, and the legend MONTICELLO underneath. The motto E PLURIBUS UNUM appears in the upper curve, with UNITED STATES OF AMERICA on the lower curve, and a curved FIVE CENTS directly above it. The "S" and "D" mint marks appear to the right of the building.

Toward the end of 1942 the quantity of copper in the coin was reduced; nickel was eliminated altogether, owing to wartime shortages, and replaced by silver. To indicate the change in composition, the mint mark was moved to the top of the reverse and a "P" was added for coins struck at Philadelphia. This is the only instance in the history of American coinage in which Philadelphia coins carry a mint mark. In 1946 the original composition and placement of the mint mark were resumed, and the "P" mint mark disappeared. See *Controller Coins*.

Nicknames: Money being something so near and dear to the human heart, and entering so intimately into the daily affairs of life, it is only natural that the vocabulary of numismatics should include a number of unorthodox designations, nicknames, or slang terms, some slighting and some semi-humorous. This was the case with the Ancients, more especially so with the Greek coins with their bizarre devices.

Thus we read of the "tortoises" or "turtles" of Aegina, the "colts" of Corinth, and the "archers" of Persia. We read in Plutarch that the Spartan general Agesilaus complained he was driven out of Asia by ten thousand of the Great King's "archers," meaning, of course, that he was compelled to retreat by the chicanery of bribery and corruption. The drachmai of Athens, from the bird of Athena stamped on the reverse, were known as "owls," hence "to take an owl to Athens" was the proverbial equivalent in Ancient Greece of our phrase "to carry coals to Newcastle." Aristophanes jests with the name in his comedy *The Birds*.

In modern times "quid," "bob," and "tanner" have been used in everyday conversation in England as frequently as "pound," "shilling," and "sixpence." The derivations of such words are much disputed, and give endless amusement to those who delight in linguistic research. "Bob" was apparently a "bobstick," "bob" meaning "small" and "stick" suggests a German origin "stück," a piece of money. "Tanner" is probably named from John Tanner, who was chief graver to the Mint 1741–75. The sixpence was formerly known as a "Simon" (perhaps from Acts ix. 43); John Tanner in 1738 counterfeited Simon's pattern coinage of Cromwell; hence the "Simon" became popularly known as a "Tanner." There is little doubt that "joey," the Britannia groat or silver fourpenny piece, was named from Joseph Hume, the Member of Parliament, who urged its introduction in 1836, for use in paying short cab-fares. The name "joey" was given in derision to this coin by the London "cabbies"; they took exception to the coin, as small fares were paid by this in place of the sixpenny piece. A "jimmy o' goblin" was a golden sovereign, but the origin of this word and that of the modern "quid" is unknown.

Among obsolete nicknames we find "hog," a word applied to coins of varying denominations, but the phrase "to go the whole hog" is still current, and is believed to be a gambling expression derived from this word. "Rhino" is a word occasionally met with in seventeenth-century literature, meaning money or cash, though the derivation is uncertain; thus Tom Brown, in *Letters from the Dead to the Living*: "wind-bound for want of the ready rhino." "Brass" is a current colloquialism for money; the explanation for this is given under *Brass*.

Nike (Gr. victory): A frequent device on Greek and Roman coins: the Goddess of Victory, a robed figure shown invariably with wings* and usually bearing a garland or palm branch. It may be either the principal device of a coin or a small accessory symbolic figure, either flying

---

* There is one exception, however, the Nike Apteros (wingless Victory) on a coin of Terina.

overhead to crown the victor (in some Ptolemaic coins crowning his name) or held, as a statuette (*victoriola*), in his hand.

In many Roman coins Victory plays a more active part, inscribing a shield, erecting a trophy, etc. Often the figure of Victory was modeled after some famous statue of the time, the most notable being that shown on a coin of Demetrius Poliorcetes, struck 306 B.C. Nike is standing on the broken prow of a war vessel, blowing a trumpet and holding a naval standard. This statue inspired the famous Nike of Samothrace, the original Greek statue, which is one of the greatest treasures of the Louvre.

Ninepence: The Irish shilling struck by Elizabeth I for use in Ireland, being of baser silver than sterling, was current in England as a nine-penny piece. This coin was a favorite love token; hence the old English proverbial sayings:

"As nice (or as nimble) as ninepence"

and

"A nimble ninepence is better than a slow shilling."

The only actual ninepenny pieces issued were money of necessity, namely, the Inchiquin ninepence (1643) and the lozenge-shaped Newark siege piece of 1645–46 (Obv/IX below crown and C.R.).

Noble (i.e., the noble, or excellent, coin, possibly so called from the fineness of the gold): The second gold coin of Edward III, struck 1344, and superseding the *florin*. The obverse shows the king, standing in a ship, and bearing a sword and shield. The type indicates symbolically the growing power of England on the seas, and probably commemorates

Noble of
Henry V.

in particular the great victory over the French off Sluys, in 1340. As a contemporary song says:

"Foure things our noble sheweth unto me,
King, ship and sword, and power of the sea."

On the reverse is the same motto as on the florin: IHS AVTEM TRANSIENS PER MEDIVM ILLORVM IBAT (see *Mottoes*). The coin was rated at the value of half a mark (6s. 8d.)*

---

* It is noteworthy that at one time a lawyer's fee in England was 6s. 8d.

A half-noble and a quarter-noble were also struck. These were of a similar pattern, but bore different mottoes. The noble was struck by succeeding monarchs, namely, Richard II, Henry IV, V, and VI, and Edward IV. (See *Angel, George Noble, Rose Noble, Sovereign.*)

Half-noble of Henry V.

Norfolk, Va. Bicentennial Commemorative Half Dollar: See *Commemorative Coins (U.S.)*, p. 67.

Northumberland Shilling: The first shillings of George III, dated 1763, are known as Northumberland shillings. The Earl of Northumberland was appointed Lord Lieutenant of Ireland in this year, and the shilling was intended to be a special issue commemorating the event, to be distributed among the people in Dublin. Owing to the scarcity of silver, no other shillings were struck until 1787. Two thousand of these coins (i.e., to the value of £100) were authorized to be struck. However, as this coin, though scarce, is by no means a rarity, it would seem that many more than this number were actually issued.

Numerals: Before the time of Henry III there is nothing on English coins to distinguish by the title one monarch from preceding monarchs of similar name. William II gives himself the same title on his coins as his father, "Willelm Rex"; Henry I and II both appear as "Henry Rex." Henry III, however, in his coinage of 1247, added TERCI or the Roman numeral III after his name. Succeeding monarchs, however, failed to adopt the idea, and there are no distinguishing numerals for the Edwards, the Henries, or Richards; it was not until the end of the reign of Henry VII that this became a general custom.

Numismatic Scrapbook Magazine: Published by Hewitt Bros., 7320 Milwaukee Avenue, Chicago 48. Annual subscription $4.

Numismatics (Gr. *nomismatikos*, relating to a coin, from *nomisma*, a coin): The science and study of coins and medals. Like "mathematics" and similar words dealing with complicated and laborious study, the word "numismatics" is a plural though used as a singular word.

Numismatist (derivation as above): A student of numismatics. Note pronunciation, num*i*smatist. To be distinguished from the mere coin collector, who hoards coins without bothering about their history, classification of types, nomenclature, etc.

Numismatist, The: See *American Numismatic Association.*

Nummus (L. a coin): The Latin name for any principal coin, sometimes applied to the *sestertius*, and sometimes to the Byzantine *follis*.

Nummus Castrensis (L. *Nummus*, a coin, *castrensis*, relating to a military camp): A term sometimes applied to Roman coins to denote money of necessity, or a special issue of money with which a general paid his troops in time of war, such as the legionary coins of Mark Antony. Also known as *moneta castrensis* (camp money).

Nuremburg Tokens: Small brass pieces, known also as Monastery tokens, or counters, originating in Nuremburg, where vast quantities were struck. The most prolific manufacturer was Hans Krauwinckel (1580–1610), whose name so often appears on them. The most common type on his counters is the emblem of the Holy Roman Empire, but as large numbers were made for the French monasteries, a very common device is the fleur-de-lis. These counters were used not only in the calculation of accounts but were also employed locally as unofficial small change. (See also *Counter, Jeton.*)

O

Obel, Obelos (pl. **Obeloi**), **Obeliskos** (pl. **Obeliskoi**) (Gr. a spit or sharp-pointed stake): Greek name for *currency bars* (q.v.), which, as in Early Britain and other primitive countries, served as currency before the introduction of coinage proper. According to Heraclides Ponticus, this spit money was abolished by Pheidon, King of Argos, in the seventh century B.C. The obsolete spits were set up in the temple of Argive Hera, and dedicated to the goddess. Within recent years, some of these actual spits have been excavated from the site of this temple. These obeloi were not unlike the African "spear-money" of today, with which it is possible they bear some affinity.

Obol, Obolus (Gr. *obolos*, a coin, a weight, connected with *obel*, as above): Small silver coin of Ancient Greece, one-sixth of the *drachma*, and, as such, representing the antique *obel* or spit (see above; see also *Drachma*). Later, during Roman domination, it became a bronze coin.

Obole (L. *obolus*, from the Greek, as above): The earliest European halfpenny, a small billon or base silver coin, a half-denier (see *Denier*), dating from the Merovingian Dynasty in France. In the Middle Ages it was known as a *mail* or *maille* (q.v.).

Obsidional Coins (L. obsidionalis, pertaining to a siege): *Siege Pieces* (q.v.).

Obverse: The "face" or "heads" of a coin; that side of the coin which has the more important device, on modern coins the side showing the face of the sovereign or some other portrait.

Old Spanish Trail Commemorative Half Dollar: See *Commemorative Coins (U.S.)*, p. 64.

Ore (Old Dan. allied to *ore*, mixed metal): An early Scandinavian coin (*ora* was the name of an Anglo-Saxon money of account), today one-hundredth part of the *krone* (crown).

Oregon Trail Memorial Commemorative Half Dollar: See *Commemorative Coins (U.S.)*, p. 62.

Ormonde Money: Money of necessity struck to pay the adherents of Charles I in Ireland, in 1643, under James, Marquis of Ormond, the Viceroy. This money consists of a series of silver pieces, a crown, half-crown, shilling, sixpence, groat, threepence, and half-groat. The obverse bears a crown above C.R., the reverse bears a large Roman numeral denoting the value. The flans were sheared by hand in an irregular circle.

Overdate: Until the early years of the twentieth century dates were placed on coins by means of an individual punch for each digit. It was thus possible to repunch a digit should the need arise. In the early days of American coinage it often happened that a particular die was still serviceable at the end of a calendar year. Rather than wastefully discard the still usable die the final digit was punched over, thus changing the date. Examples of this are the 1802/01 half cent, the 1807/06 large cent, etc. In the case of these overdates the original partially shows under the newer one.

Since the early years of the present century working dies have been made from a master hub bearing the total impression of the coin including a complete date. The modern overdate coins—1918/17 nickel, 1942/41 dime, 1918/17 quarter and 1909/08 double eagle—have resulted from a mixing of these hubs: the first blow from the earlier hub, the error detected, and the coin restruck with the hub bearing the proper date.

Overstrike: A coin freshly struck upon the flan of an existing coin instead of upon a blank is said to be overstruck. Examples of overstruck coins are found in the *gun-money* series, where the later crowns were overstruck on the large half-crowns, and the Limerick halfpennies and farthings were overstruck over the large and small shillings respectively.

Oxford Crown: A pattern crown in silver, struck by Rawlins at New Hall, Oxford, for Charles I. In the background of the obverse the King is shown on horseback, and below in the background is a view of the city of Oxford. Across the field of the reverse is the motto of the *Declaration Type* (q.v.). The reverse bears the legend *Exurgat Deus, Dissipentur Inimici* (Let God arise, let his enemies be scattered).

Pattern Oxford Crown of Charles I. (See Oxford Crown, page 173.)

P

P.: Abbreviation often seen in the titles of Roman emperors signifying PIUS. This Latin word denotes "dutiful" towards the gods, the fatherland, and one's parents.

PLN.: Mint mark on Roman coins which were struck in London. The letters are probably an abbreviation for *pecunia Londiniensis* (London money), or possibly for *percussum Londinio* (struck at London).

P.M.: See *Pontifex Maximus*.

P.P.: On Roman coins = *Pater Patriae* (q.v.).

PS: Found on Roman silver coins from the fourth century A.D. An abbreviation for *pusulatum* (*argentum*) ("refined" silver). As with the abbreviation OB, the letters are joined to the place of mintage, e.g., TRPS (refined silver of Triers).

Pagoda (from the figure of a pagoda on the reverse, although this is not an invariable type, especially with the earlier coins): Gold and silver coins of southern India, first struck at the end of the sixteenth century. They are mentioned in Hakluyt's *Voyages*, 1599. The obverse usually shows the image of some divinity. There are many varieties, not only in the native-struck coins but also in those struck by the East India Company and others struck by the French and the Dutch. Half- and quarter-pagodas were also issued.

Panama-Pacific Exposition Commemorative Coins: See *Commemorative Coins* (*U.S.*), pp. 60, 68, 69.

Papal Coinage: The ecclesiastical coinage of the Papal States begins with Pope Adrian I (772–95), who struck deniers of a Byzantine style. The early issues of the Papal series were usually issued in the joint name of Pope and Emperor. At the height of ecclesiastical power, in the twelfth century, the legend ROMA CAPUT MUNDI (Rome the head of the world) was proudly displayed on the silver coins. The Papal coins of the Renaissance period are celebrated for the great medalists that worked on them, such as Francesco Francia and Benvenuto Cellini. The series proper comes to an end with the annexation of the Papal States by Italy in 1871, but with the establishment of the Vatican City State in 1929 coins are issued once more by the Popes. (See also *Sede Vacante.*)

Paper Money: When the metals necessary for producing coins are in short supply, or the prices of them prohibitive, paper forms a cheap and convenient substitute. The purport of such notes is, of course, a promise to pay, but, unlike checks, bills of exchange, and promissory notes, there is no determined date for repayment. Paper money is said to have been in use in China as early as the ninth century A.D. (T'ang Dynasty). Marco Polo, who was at the Court of Kublai Khan, 1275–84, gives a long account of the system of producing notes. The Great Khan, he tells us, "may truly be said to possess the secret of the alchemists as he has the art of producing money" by a special process from the bast of mulberry trees. It is signed by officials and sealed in vermilion ink with the royal seal. Paper (or rather cotton) money is also alluded to by Rubruquis, a monk sent by St. Louis to the Mongol Prince Mangu-Khan, in 1262. This form of currency is mentioned by Sir John Mandeville as one of the marvels of the East. An example of this paper money, dating from the Ming Dynasty, (*c.* A.D. 1368) may be seen in the British Museum. In addition to the enormous issues of assignats in France during the Revolution, Russia and the South American states were the first countries to make use of paper money in modern times. The upheaval of two great world wars in recent years compelled all the countries involved to compromise with floods of paper money, much of it of very dubious value.

A curious form of paper money, current only in the spirit world, is found in China, where imitations of actual money are made in paper. These are burned so that their "doubles" may be used by friends and relations who have passed over—a much more economical method, and doubtless as effective, as burying metal coins with the body.

In the United States, distressing experiences with colonial currency and the Continental paper money during the Revolution made the Federal government very wary of entering this field. Up to the time of the Civil War the running expenses of the government were quite small and amply covered by land sales and import duties. The issue of paper money was left to state regulation, and the national government did not interfere despite the existence of serious abuses connected with the state-bank issues.

Colonial paper money printed by Benjamin Franklin.

However, the outbreak of the Civil War increased government expenditure to unprecedented heights. Even before the end of 1861 the U.S. Treasury had to take the drastic step of discontinuing the redemption of its Treasury Notes in gold or silver. In August 1861 Congress issued the first government paper money—the famous "Greenbacks," officially known as Demand Notes. They had no metal reserve and consequently their value fluctuated—sometimes violently—with the fortunes of war.

During the next two years more paper money poured from the government presses—the Legal Tender Notes, which had to be accepted in payment of debts even though they too had no metal reserve behind them.

The National Banking Act of 1863 was a great step forward in many respects. This act chartered "national banks" which bought United States bonds and then left them with the government as a reserve against the issue of their own currency. The government obtained badly needed funds while at the same time the money issued by the banks was backed by the government bonds they had purchased. Subsequent amendments to the Banking Act placed a prohibitive tax on the circulation of state-bank currency, which now permanently disappeared from circulation.

During the later years of the war the government issued Compound Interest Treasury Notes and Interest Bearing Notes which were redeemed after a fixed period. The Confederacy issued large sums of paper money which dwindled rapidly in value. The South never solved its financial problem and at the end of the war had to repudiate its outstanding notes.*

After the Civil War the government issued several other types of notes with substantial backing. The Silver Certificates, as the name indicates, were redeemable in silver. The Treasury Notes were issued to pay for silver bullion and were redeemable in gold or silver up to 1933, when gold redemption was dropped.

In 1913 the Federal Reserve System went into effect, and this led to the issue of Federal Reserve Notes. Currently three types of paper money are still being issued: Legal Tender Notes ($2, $5); Silver Certificates ($1, $5, $10); Federal Reserve Notes ($5, $10, $20, $50, $100, $500).

For the earliest Canadian paper money see *Playing-Card Money*. A great deal of merchants' fractional currency (the so-called *"Bons"*) was issued during the nineteenth century. A curious feature of early nineteenth-century Canadian currency was "phantom" notes purporting to be issued by organizations that were actually nonexistent.

The Province of Canada issued notes in 1866 in the denominations of $1, $2, $5, $10, $20, $50, $100 and $500. In 1870 and again in 1900 and 1923 the Dominion of Canada issued fractional currency in one denomination—25 cents. Other denominations issued by the Dominion were $1, $2, $4, $5, $50, $500, $1000, $5000. During the period 1935–50 the Bank of Canada took over the issue of paper money in these denominations: $1, $2, $5, $10, $20, $25, $50, $100, $500, $1000. At the same time the government-chartered banks paid over to the Bank of Canada all the balances due on their outstanding notes and the central bank assumed the liability for all the outstanding notes held by the public.

See *Assignat, Banknote, Broken Bank Note, Cancelled Note, Condition of Coins, Counterfeit Detectors, Fractional Currency Notes, Fractional Currency Shield, Friedberg Numbers, New Tenor—Old Tenor Notes, Playing-Card Money, Postage Currency Notes, Saddle Blanket Notes.*

Parthia: The almost invariable type of this long series of coins is Obv/ Head of the monarch; Rev/Figure (probably representing Arsaces I) holding the national weapon of the Parthians, the bow. The archery tactics of the Parthians have become proverbial. Although we have no identifiable coins of Arsaces, this name appears on nearly all the coins as the dynastic name of the reigning monarch. Identification of individual coins is therefore difficult. The inscriptions form a rough guide

---

* A detailed treatment of Civil War currency and coinage will be found in Reinfeld: *The Story of Civil War Money*, Sterling Publishing Company, New York, 1959.

to date, the later ones being longer and with more fulsome flattery. The series begins with Tiridates I (*c.* 248 B.C.) and ends about A.D. 220 with the subjugation of the kingdom under the Persian Sassanian dynasty.

Pater Patriae (L. *Father of his country*): A title of honor, and the highest, bestowed by the Senate. Cicero was the first living man to receive this title. On the legends of Roman coins it is usually abbreviated to P.P.

Pattern Coins: Pieces demonstrating a new denomination, a new design or a change in an existing design proposed for adoption as a regular issue. See Gobrecht Pattern Dollars under *Dollar, U.S. Silver; Piedfort; Stella; Transitional Pattern.*

Patina (pronounced *pat*ina, L. *patina*, a shallow bowl or pan; the connection of this derivation is uncertain): The incrustation on bronze formed by oxidation resulting in a change of shade or color. This change is caused by the action of atmosphere, soil, moisture, etc., and assumes a variety of shades, more particularly green. Considerable value is added to a coin when a fine patina is present. See *Cleaning Coins, Storing Coins.*

Pavilion d'Or (gold pavilion): A handsome gold coin of Philip VI of Valois (1328–50). The King is shown seated beneath an elaborate Gothic canopy or arch. Also known as a *royal.*

Pavillon, Pavilion (O. Fr. *pavillon*, a tent, canopy): A gold coin of Edward the Black Prince struck in the Anglo-Gallic series. A demi-pavilion was also issued. These were adapted from the Pavilion d'Or (see above).

Pax Penny (L. *pax*, peace): From Canute to Henry I a type of penny is found with the word PAX (variously spelled), either written across the field of the reverse, or with four letters (PAXS, etc.) in the separate

Pax Penny of William the Conqueror.

quarters. The word signalizes either some peace achieved or hoped to be achieved by accession to the throne, by some treaty, or any other means. The pax penny of Canute is extremely rare, as is the penny of Harold I. The penny of Edward the Confessor with the letters PAXS in the quarters is scarce, but not very rare. The only type of penny of Harold II is the penny with PAX across the field of the obverse. The commonest type of penny of William I since the Beaworth find (see *Hoards*) is the quartered "paxs" type. The pax penny of Henry I is rare.

Peace Type: See *Dollar, U.S. Silver.*

Penny (derivation uncertain): Originally a small silver coin of England. It was copied from the *novus denarius,* or *new denier* of Charlemagne (see *Denier*), and introduced into England in the time of Offa (757–96), or possibly a little earlier. It was the principal coin of the Middle Ages, and though later of minor importance, it continued to be issued as a silver coin up to the end of the reign of George I. The type still survives in *Maundy Money.*

The Anglo-Saxon penny weighed, on an average, 22½ grains, which was one two hundred-and-fortieth part of the Tower pound of silver (reckoned at 5,400 grains).

Penny of Edward the Confessor.

From the twelfth to the fourteenth century, pennies were known as easterlings or *sterlings* (q.v.).

In 1346 the weight of the penny was reduced to 20 grains though the fineness (92½ per cent) was maintained. Henry VIII reduced both weight and fineness (see *Debasement*).

The first English copper penny dates from 1797 (see *Cartwheel*), although copper farthings and halfpennies had been struck from the time of Charles II. This penny was a massive coin, weighing 1 oz. In that year Matthew Boulton, of the Soho Mint, Birmingham, was authorized to strike from his new improved coining presses 20 tons of twopenny pieces and 480 tons of penny pieces. Boulton intended his new coins should be used for gauging weights and measures, in addition to their utility as coins, as we see from a letter he wrote in 1797:

"I intend there shall be a coincidence between our Money, Weight and Measures, by making 8 twopenny pieces 1 lb, and to measure 1 foot; 16 penny pieces 1 lb and 17 to measure 2 feet; 32 half-pence 1 lb, and 10 to measure 1 foot."

The actual value of the metal of the penny was reckoned to be worth its face value; later, however, it became a token coin of more convenient size, the actual value of the metal being no more than about one-fourth of its face value. In 1860 the penny was further reduced in size, and struck, as it is today, in bronze in place of copper. From the conservatism of English speech, however, the coins are still familiarly known as "coppers."

For medieval pennies, see *Long-cross Penny, Short-cross Penny*. For the U.S. penny, see *Cent* (*U.S.*).

Penny, Gold: In 1257 Henry III struck a gold penny, to represent the value of twenty silver pennies. It was the first English gold coin to be struck since the time of the Anglo-Saxons, and was apparently intended to introduce gold coinage into England following the striking of the Continental florin. Only a few were struck, however, and it was not until the time of Edward III that a gold currency became popular.

Penny, New Testament: This was the *denarius*, or Roman silver penny, more correctly translated in the Revised Version of the Testament as "one shilling." As we see from Matt. xx, it was the usual day's wage for a laborer. (See *Denarius, Tribute Penny*.)

Periodicals, Numismatic: See *American Numismatic Association, Canadian Numismatic Association, Coin World, Numismatic Scrapbook Magazine*.

Peseta (Sp. diminutive of *pesa*, a little weight): A Spanish silver coin, originally representing two reals. In 1868 it replaced the *escudo* as the standard money of account.

Peso (Sp. a weight): The Spanish milled dollar, a piece representing eight *reales*. Primarily a silver ingot, based on the standard weight of 1 oz., it was first struck in Spain as a silver coin in the sixteenth century. The Spanish American dollar which figures so prominently in romances of the Spanish Main is popularly known as a "piece of eight" from the value /8 appearing in figures at the side of the coat of arms. It is also known as a *piastre*.

The *peso* current today in South American countries is equated to the metric system, being equal to 100 centimos, centisimos, centavos, etc. See also *Dollar*.

The famous peso was struck at Spanish and Spanish American mints for over a century. When other coins were lacking, a peso might be broken up into two halves (each one known as "four bits") or into four quarters ("two bits"). There was also a double peso, called a *Doubloon*—equivalent to 16 bits.

The peso was highly regarded throughout Europe and the New World, as it was made of pure silver in an age when much of the coinage was debased by being alloyed with cheaper metals. The seemingly inexhaustible silver mines of the Spanish colonies poured a steady supply into the mints, so that the Mexico City mint, for example, turned out well over a billion of these coins between 1732 and 1821.

Pesos were particularly in demand in the English colonies in the New World which were so short of coins that tobacco, nails, musket balls and other commodities were used as money. When the United States started its own coinage system in 1792 it modeled its dollar on the Spanish Milled Dollar, as the peso was sometimes called.

Even though the United States was coining its own silver dollars the peso was so popular in this country that it remained legal tender until 1857—the only instance in American history of a foreign coin receiving such recognition. (Incidentally, no U.S. dollars were struck during the period 1805–39.) At the time the peso lost its legal-tender status, more than two million dollars' worth of these coins was in circulation in the United States.

The origin of a peso struck in Spain is indicated by the legend on the reverse: HISPANIARUM REX ("king of the Spains"). Pesos struck at a Spanish American mint carry the legend HISPANIARUM ET IND. REX ("king of the Spains and the Indies"). There is still another difference; the famous "pillar and globe" dollars, described later on, were struck only in the New World. The two pillars on this design represent the Pillars of Hercules (Strait of Gibraltar).

The Spanish pesos carry a mint mark on the reverse (M for Madrid; S for Seville). On the early coins the mint mark appears to the left of the shield; on the later coins the mint mark appears in the inscription on the reverse.

Up to 1762 the pesos issued in Spain had a standard design: crowned shield on the obverse with quartered arms on the reverse. From 1762 until 1830 the obverse carried a bust of the king, with the crowned shield moved to the reverse. The obverse took several forms—sometimes a plain bust, sometimes laureated or draped or both.

Spanish Peso (Piece of Eight), Bust type from Bolivian mint.

Up to the reign of Ferdinand VII (1808–21) all Mexican pesos were struck at the Mexico City mint with the mint mark $\overset{\circ}{\text{M}}$. In 1732, during the reign of Philip V (1700–46) the obverse design was changed to two crowned globes with crowned pillars at the sides; the crowned arms of Spain appeared on the reverse. In 1772 the Bust type was introduced on the obverse; the reverse design was changed to the crowned Spanish arms and two elegant pillars, with scrolls or ribbons wound around them, at the sides. Thereafter the king's bust appeared on the obverse until Mexico gained its independence in 1821. After 1808 several other Mexican mints began operations. Their mint marks were CA, D or DO, Ga, Go, Z or Zs.

Spanish Peso (Piece of Eight), Pillar type.

Similar types prevail at the other Spanish American mints, with occasional variations. The pesos of Peru for 1809–12 have an interesting laureate bust which was struck only at the Lima mint (mint mark L or LIMA).

Pesos of the Potosi mint (Bolivia) carry the mint mark P or PTS or spell out the mint name in full. The pesos struck at Guatemala have a G mint mark. The city was destroyed by an earthquake in 1773 and rebuilt in 1776. After the latter date the mint mark becomes NG (for Nueva Guatemala). For pesos struck in Colombia the mint mark is NR (for Santa Fe de Bogota) or P or PN (for Popayan). The mint mark of the Santiago mint in Chile is $\overset{o}{S}$.

Petition Crown: In 1662 the mill-and-screw method of striking coins was reintroduced into England, and became a permanent process for striking coins. It necessitated new designs for the coinage. Thomas Simon, an Englishman, had been engraver to the Mint since 1646. A Flemish medalist, however, Jan Roettier, whose father had assisted Charles II in his exile, was brought over as a colleague of Simon, under the direct patronage of Charles. It seemed from the outset impossible for the Englishman and the Fleming to work together in harmony. The two rivals competed for the new designs for the coinage. The designs of Roettier were preferred, it would seem rather from personal favoritism than from any aesthetic appeal of art. In 1663 Simon struck his famous "Petition Crown," ostensibly as a pattern, but actually as a final and eloquent appeal to the King. The piece is magnificently engraved. Round the edge in two lines are these words in minute lettering:

"Thomas Simon most humbly prays your Majesty to compare this his tryall piece with the Dutch and if more truly drawn & emboss'd more gracefully order'd and more accurately engraven to relieve him."

Not more than twenty of these crowns were struck, and their auction value would today be well over $1,500. Simon's appeal, however, was unsuccessful. The more important coins of the realm were entrusted to the hands of the foreigner to produce, while the production of the lesser coins (groats, threepenny pieces, half-groats, and pennies) was handed over to Simon. (See also *Reddite Crown*.)

Pfennig, Pfenning (derivation uncertain, probably related to *penny*): The silver denier of Germany in the early Middle Ages; later (sixteenth century) a copper coin, the one-hundredth part of a *mark*.

Pheidon: King of Argos in Greece, probably in the early seventh century B.C. The Island of Aegina was part of his possessions, and here were struck the first European silver coins (see *Aegina*). Whether Pheidon himself actually struck these primitive coins or not is extremely doubtful. All that Herodotus tells us is that

"Pheidon, king of the Argives . . . established weights and measures throughout the Peloponnesus" (VI. 127),

hence instituting the famous Aeginetan standard. For the tradition that he abolished the antique "spit" money, see *Obel*.

Philippus: The gold stater (q.v.) of Ancient Greece. Originally struck by Philip II of Macedon (358–336 B.C.), the father of Alexander the Great, but which was struck and circulated over the Greek dominions for many centuries after the death of Philip. Obv/Laureated head of Apollo; Rev/Two-horse chariot (*biga*) and name of king. The coin became so popular that the word philippus became synonymous with any type of fine gold coin, and the Ancient Romans called the gold coins of the Emperors *philippi*. It was through the extensive trading of the Gauls with the Greek merchants at Marseilles (Massilia) that these coins became the prototype of our Ancient British gold coins. (See *Britons, Coins of the Ancient; Gaul, Coins of*.)

We can understand the immense coinage of Philip from the statement that the gold mines of Crenides yielded him 1,000 talents yearly—a sum equal today to $15,000,000.

Piastre (Fr., possibly from *plastra*, a thin metal plate): The standard unit of coinage in Turkey, Egypt, and many other countries in the Mediterranean regions. In Turkey 100 piastres are equal to the Turkish lira or pound. Piastre is also the name given to the Spanish dollar (see *Peso*).

Pie (Marathi, *pai*, a quarter): Small copper coin of the Mahratta (a

Hindu race), who gave it this name as it was originally a quarter of an anna, but from 1835 it has been one-twelfth of an anna.

Piece: In Elizabethan and Jacobean literature = a piece of eight. Frequently mentioned in the plays of Ben Jonson.

Pieces of Eight: See *Peso*.

Pieces of Silver, Thirty (New Testament): The *triakonta arguria*, or thirty pieces of silver, for which Christ was betrayed by Judas, would be the tetradrachms current in Palestine, and which were minted at Antioch. The "piece of money" of Matt. xvii. 27 is correctly named a "stater" in the Greek gospel and the translation of the Revised English Version.

Antioch, silver tetradrachm (about A.D. 30).

Piedfort (Fr. strong-foot): A sort of pattern coin, struck upon a thick flan. The earliest known are those dating from the time of Edward I. Various explanations as to the purpose of these have been put forward. It is possible that they were intended originally as patterns for the coiners to copy from when making the actual coins; the thickness of the flan would serve to distinguish the pattern from the coins themselves.

Pile (L. *pila*, a pillar): The lower die of the old hammered coinage, bearing the obverse of the coin. It was fixed by a spike into a wooden anvil. It is also known as the *standard* or *staple*. (See also *Trussel*.)

The obverse and reverse of a coin were formerly known as the *cross* and the *pile*.

Pilgrim Tercentenary Commemorative Half Dollar: See *Commemorative Coins (U.S.)*, p. 60.

Pistole (derivation uncertain, perhaps from Span. *pistola*, a metal plate, or from Fr. *pistole*, a small gun, from its small size as compared with the French crown): Name given by the French to the Spanish *double escudo*, a gold coin of the sixteenth and seventeenth centuries.

The name was afterwards transferred to the French *louis d'or* (q.v.), and similar coins circulating in Spain, Italy, Germany, etc.

It varied in value in different countries. In Germany the name was given to the gold five-taler piece. In France, where it was extensively circulated, it was valued at ten livres tournois.

A gold pistole was issued by Charles I in the Irish money of necessity series (see *Inchiquin Money*).

Pistrucci, Benedetto: Italian medalist, 1784-1855. He came to England in 1815, and succeeded Thomas Wyon as chief engraver to the Royal Mint. In 1817 he designed the new coins of George III,* and also those

Great Britain, silver crown with reverse showing St. George slaying the dragon.

of George IV. The famous design of St. George and the Dragon (q.v.) on the reverse of the English gold coins and silver crown was originated by him.

Planchet: See *Flan*.

Plate Money, Swedish: Great lumps of copper roughly cut up into squares, weighing up to 6 lb., and measuring up to 10 in. across, produced in Sweden originally in the early seventeenth century. They were occasioned by the fact that the country was depleted of silver after a disastrous war with Denmark. Copper, however, was plentiful and the attempt was made to give intrinsic value in weight of copper. The series ranges from the half-daler to the ten-daler piece, and was issued from 1644 to 1759.

Plated Coins: The art of plating coins was known to the Ancient Greeks, while numerous examples of plated Roman coins are found in abundance. Most of these plated coins, of course, were produced by counterfeiters, but undoubtedly some of the Roman issues had official sanction as a form of debasement of the currency, and from the time of Gallienus all the so-called "silver" coins were plated. The process of plating seems to have been similar to that used in the manufacture of Sheffield Plate. (See *Serrate*.)

Platinum Coins, Russian: Platinum was discovered in Russia between 1822 and 1823, and was thought very little of as a metal. During the reign of Nicholas I (1825–55) coins of certain denominations were

---

* Some of these coins are dated 1816, but they were not issued until the following year.

struck in small quantities. The dates of the coins and the number struck are as follows:

Twelve roubles (1830, 1831, 1832, 1834, 1835) . 1,501 struck
Six roubles (1829–35) . . . . . . 11,605 struck
Three roubles (1828–35) . . . . . 203,710 struck

The experimental coinage was not a success. Platinum was not found to be a practicable medium. It was difficult to melt, the metal was intractable, and the supply not plentiful. All these coins are now rare, particularly the twelve roubles of 1832.

In the 1860s and 1870s a few platinum coins were struck in Prussia. Here again, the experiment was not a success, and specimens are rare. Platinum patterns were also struck for Hawaii.

Playing-Card Money: A form of currency issued in New France (Canada) from 1685 to 1759. The first issue, made from playing cards cut into quarters, carried the signatures of the Governor and Intendant and the Treasurer's seal. There were three denominations: 4 francs, 40 sols and 15 sols.

Canada, playing-card money.

Further issues eventually resulted in 14,000,000 livres of these notes being outstanding at the time of the loss of the colony to England. The French government immediately repudiated the currency, but the British redeemed it at 25 per cent of face value.

Plugged Money: An issue of farthings and halfpennies struck in tin was made by Charles II and James II. These coins had a small plug of copper inserted in the center. The purpose of this was to prevent counterfeiting. (See *Farthing*.)

Plume: A small plume (or Prince of Wales' feathers) figured on an English silver coin usually signifies the metal came from the Welsh mines. On coins of James I and Charles I it is part of the heraldic charge, and appears as a provenance mark on coins of Charles II, William III, Anne, George I (in conjunction with roses), and George II.

Pontifex Maximus (L. High Priest): A title, usually abbreviated on Roman coins to *P.M.* or *Pont. Max.*, given to the head of the *pontifices*, or college of State priests at Rome. In imperial times the emperors were always *pontifices maximi*, except where more than one emperor was in office. In such a case one emperor only bore the title.

Portcullis Money: The first English colonial coins, struck at the Tower mint, and so called from the Tudor badge on the reverse, a portcullis surmounted by a crown. The obverse was a crowned shield with the royal arms. They were struck by Queen Elizabeth I in 1600–1, for the Eastern trade of the newly formed East India Company. The

Portcullis reverse.

coinage consisted of a crown, half-crown, shilling, and sixpence; the weights of the coins, however, were different from the corresponding English pieces, as they were adjusted to supersede the Spanish coins which had hitherto been used in India, namely, the peso and the four-and two-real pieces. It is significant no portrait appears on the coins, intended as they were for Mohammedan countries.

Portraits on Coins: (i) *Greek*. Alexander the Great (336–323 B.C.) boasted that he was descended from Hercules. The head of this divine ancestor, rather than that of Alexander himself, was honored on his

Tetradrachm of Alexander the Great, with head of Hercules.

Tetradrachm of Lysimachus, with head of Alexander the Great.

coins. A coin was still something connected with the temples, something almost amuletic; the place of honor (the obverse) was still held as something where the local god or divine hero could be shown or symbolized. After the death of Alexander, Lysimachus, one of Alexander's generals, who had then become King of Thrace, struck coins with the head of Alexander on the obverse. His example was copied by other generals of Alexander. It was, however, the head of Alexander deified that they displayed; to indicate this, horns of divinity were placed on the head of the portrait. They were the ram's horns of the god Jupiter-Ammon, whose adopted son Alexander himself had claimed to be. These were the first European coins on which a portrait of the human head was shown. The coins of Lysimachus achieved a great popularity, and were imitated in various parts of the Grecian world for nearly three centuries. It is noticeable that on later coins the divinity of the portrait lessens; the head of the god more and more becomes a likeness of Alexander as a man.

Ptolemy Soter (323–284 B.C.), founder of the dynasty which ruled Egypt for two and a half centuries, was the first to place his own head on coins purely as a portrait type of a ruler. He is shown no longer wearing emblems of divinity on his head; he bears the plain royal diadem. Ptolemy was deified after his death, as was his queen, Berenice. On the coins of their son, Ptolemy II Philadelphus, their portraits appear as *theoi* (divinities), and the deified portrait of Ptolemy Soter appears on all coins of the successive rulers of Egypt down to the time of the Roman conquest.

(ii) *Roman.* As in the case of Greek coins, whole centuries elapsed before the moneyers attempted to display contemporary portraiture on Roman coins. The earliest types of Roman coins were essentially religious. Later, on the family coins, some of the famous ancestors of the moneyers and their achievements are commemorated. It is not long before veiled allusions to contemporary events creep in, though without actual portraits; thus the elephant on Caesar's coins is an allusion to his conquests in Gaul. A vast field of obscure research still awaits the numismatist of today in this direction. Some of the moneyers go so far as to strike portraits of fairly recent celebrities; for instance, Caldus of the Coelian family issues a likeness of his own grandfather. It was not, however, until 44 B.C. that the first portrait of a living man appears on Roman coins. It was in that year that the Senate decreed Caesar should be honored by placing his own portrait on the denarius. This was in the nature of a challenge to the party hostile to Caesar. Soon the portraits of Brutus, Cassius, and others appeared, as it were, by way of propaganda. This was followed by realistic likenesses of Mark Antony, Octavian, and many other celebrities of the day.

Rome, denarius with portrait of Brutus on obverse and liberty cap and daggers on reverse (about 42 B.C.).

(iii) *Anglo-Saxon.* On the early Anglo-Saxon coins portraits rarely appear; geometrical motifs are predominant, but from the time of the later coins of Edgar (959–75), the portrait of the reigning monarch usually appears on the obverse.

(iv) *Medieval and Modern.* Medieval coins disdained egotism and individuality in their art; the obverse is merely a symbolic head of monarchy. Even when the king was a child, as in the case of Henry VI, the same type of crowned, impassive head appears.* This, to us, somewhat stereotyped form of art was not due to lack of artists or of initiative, but rather to the constricted method of striking coins. The set-up of the dies was limited to a few elementary geometrical designs (see *Die*), and the wonder is the moneyers achieved so much with so few resources.

In the latter part of the fifteenth century the new methods and the more ambitious spirit of the Italian Renaissance brought about a

---

* He came to the throne as a babe of nine months, and reigned for nearly fifty years.

complete change. Largely owing to the inspiration of the neo-classical medalists, the coin engravers of Italy brought an entirely new spirit of art into the coinage, an art that, like that of Ancient Greece and Rome, was both realistic and idealistic. Artists of genius, such as Benvenuto Cellini and Leonardo da Vinci, perfected this art, the influence of which was felt all over Europe. In France the coins of Louis XII began to carry portraits from life in place of the old stereotyped forms (see *Teston*); in Germany a painstaking and detailed realism was the keynote of numismatic art. The coins of Maximilian resemble medals rather than currency; in fact, the famous taler of A.D. 1479 (the "marriage-taler") was an actual copy from a medal. The coins of the English

Holy Roman Empire, marriage taler of Maximilian I (1479).

Renaissance, after a somewhat flamboyant beginning, more especially in the gold, settled down eventually to a fine classical restraint. Henry VII was happy in his choice of graver, the famous Alexander de Brugsal, and his profile portraits on the silver coins of the later years of Henry VII have never been excelled as works of fine portraiture. In the following reign the idealism faded away, but for realistic characteri-zation the portraits of Henry VIII in his advancing years are equaled only by the Ancient Roman portraits at their prime.

    (v) *United States.* See *Art; Cent (U.S.); Dime; Dollar, U.S. Silver; Half Cent; Half Dollar; Nickel Five-Cent Piece; Quarter Dollar; Symbols and Symbolism.* Also: *Dollar, U.S. Gold ; Double Eagle; Eagle; Half Eagle; Stella; Three-Dollar Gold Piece.*

Portraits on Coins, English: A curiosity of the English coinage is that from the time of Elizabeth I the portrait of the sovereign usually faces in an opposite direction to that of the preceding reign. From the time of Charles II this is so regular a proceeding that it gives color to the idea that the Merry Monarch inaugurated the tradition by turning his back on the hated Puritan regime.

Postage Currency Notes; Postage Stamps as Currency: Stamps are often sent through the mail to cover small debts; in times of national emergency they have sometimes been legalized as "small change."

During the First World War many European countries adopted the idea of using stamps to make up for a deficiency of small coin. Sometimes the stamps were encased in a celluloid front and cardboard back. In 1915 and 1917 Russia printed special stamps on thick paper, for use either on letters or for currency purposes. On the back they bore an official notice to the effect that the stamp had "circulation on a par with silver subsidiary coins." (See *Encased Postage Stamps, Fractional Currency Notes.*)

Russian stamp used as currency.

Potin (Fr. *potin*, pot-metal): A base, mixed metal, an alloy of copper, zinc, lead, and tin. Unlike *billon*, potin contains no silver. Certain coins of Ancient Gaul were composed of this alloy.

Pound (L. *pondus*, weight): Just as the *libra* of the Ancient Romans was a specified weight, and, as a monetary term, signified originally a pound in weight of silver, so the Old English "pound" was also merely a weight, and as a monetary term signified the amount of silver which could be coined into 240 silver pennies. In the Troy measure, still used by jewelers today, twenty pennyweights make 1 oz., and 12 oz. (240 pennyweights) make 1 lb. As a standard of weight the pound was based on the weight of 7,680 grains of wheat taken from the middle of the ear and well dried. The word was afterwards used to denote the sovereign. In 1816, when the silver standard was abolished in England, the unit of value was then the pound sterling, or sovereign. Its fineness was fixed at 22 carats. The first gold sovereign (q.v.) was struck under Henry VII.

Pound Notes: The first one-pound treasury note in England appeared in 1914. Gold coins gradually ceased to circulate from this date.

Premium Value: The price at which one can sell a coin (if above face value).

Private Gold: Gold coins or slugs (q.v.) issued in the United States by a source other than one of the government mints. During the nineteenth century gold coins or even ingots were issued to relieve a scarcity of government money. Many of these specimens were later melted down for their bullion value, and the comparatively small number that have been preserved are extremely valuable.

Templeton Reid struck gold coins in Georgia in the 1830's. In North Carolina Christopher Bechtler and his son and nephew struck gold coins starting in 1830 and continuing for over two decades. The design was extremely simple, carrying the name of the issuer, the value, weight and fineness.

Most of the private gold—or territorial gold as it is sometimes called —was issued in California during the period 1849–55. With thousands of fortune hunters streaming into the area and with very little U.S. coinage available, only the utilization of California gold made it possible to carry on buying and selling in a reasonably normal fashion. Some of these pieces were executed in a rough and ready manner; others are of surprising excellence. Collectors in this narrowly specialized field take a very keen interest in the private coins and ingots. For example, the $14.25 ingot issued by Moffat & Co. is valued at upwards of $10,000 in uncirculated condition.

California, privately struck 50 dollar gold piece (1851).

Oregon's state legislature provided for the issue of $5 and $10 gold pieces, although this was unconstitutional. Because these coins contained an 8 per cent excess of gold they proved self-defeating: holders of the coins melted them down to make a profit. This made the coins very rare, and the $10 "beaver" gold piece is now valued at over $5000 in uncirculated condition.

The equally isolated Mormon Territory suffered from the same lack of U.S. coinage and struck gold coins in several denominations. As the Mormons called their territory Deseret ("honey bee"), a beehive appears on the obverse of all the coins. All these pieces are rare and the $10 gold is valued at over $4000 in uncirculated condition.

Several Colorado firms issued gold coins in 1860–61. The greatest rarity in this group is the J. J. Conway & Company $5 gold piece issued in 1861. See *Slug*.

Proof: A coin with a mirror-like surface struck with polished dies on a polished blank. Usually sold at a premium by the mints. A matte proof is one having a dull frosted surface; in some cases this is specially put on after the coin has been struck.

Proof sets of American coins, including the cent, nickel, dime, quarter and half dollar for any given year, may be obtained from the Philadelphia mint. The Royal Canadian Mint supplies an analogous set of "proof-like" coins, consisting of the 1¢, 5¢, 10¢, 25¢, 50¢ and $1.00 denominations. Similar sets are available from other countries, notably Great Britain.

Provenance Mark: A symbol on a coin denoting the source whence the metal was obtained. The earliest English provenance mark dated from the third coinage of James I, in 1621. The Welsh silvermines in that year were leased by Sir Hugh Middleton; the silver from these mines was minted at the Tower of London, and the coins were struck with the Prince of Wales' plumes over the shield on the reverse. Similar symbols on coins are roses to indicate West of England silver, roses and plumes to indicate mixed Welsh and English silver, the elephant and castle to indicate gold or silver from the Guinea Coast. Sometimes letters are used, W.C.C. indicating silver from the Welsh Copper Company, or S.S.C. to indicate silver from the ill-fated South Sea Company; sometimes a name, such as *Vigo* or *Lima*, commemorates coins that were struck from treasure captured from Spanish galleons at those famous raids.

Providence, R.I. Tercentenary Commemorative Half Dollar: See *Commemorative Coins (U.S.)*, p. 65.

Puffin and Half-puffin: These were an unauthorized issue in bronze, corresponding to the English penny and halfpenny, for use on Lundy Island, in the Bristol Channel. They were brought out in 1929, to-gether with a series of postage stamps. The coins bear the portrait of the proprietor of the island, M. C. Harman, and on the reverse the figure of a puffin. The British Government declared them illegal, and a fine was inflicted on the "king" of Lundy Island.

Punch Marks: (1) the earliest Greek coins were uniface in type; the obverse was engraved on the anvil, but no design was engraved on the punch other than the rough pattern where (to ensure a secure grip) it was divided into a square, sometimes made up of four or more smaller squares. On some coins we can see a transitional stage between this utilitarian punch mark and a deliberate design on the reverse; the square on the reverse is quartered diagonally to form a pattern, or (as on early coins of Corinth) a rough form of swastika is engraved on the punch. (See also *Mill-Sail Pattern.*)

(2) A small mark in the form of a symbol or of letters punched on the field of an Ancient Greek coin. They are supposed to have been placed there by merchants, after the coins had become obsolete, to signify that such coins were to be treated merely as bullion.

Punctuated Date: Varieties of the 1795 *half cent*, and 1811 and 1817 *half dollars*, show what appears to be a punctuation mark in the dates (a comma in 1,795; a period in 18.11; and a period in 181.7). In all these cases the "punctuation" mark resulted from a chip in the die.

Pyx, Trial (Gr. *pyxis*, box or vase with lid): Out of every 15 lb. Troy weight of gold and every 60 lb. Troy weight of silver minted in England, a coin is put aside in the *pyx*, or special box for the annual testing by weight and assay which is known as the "Trial of the Pyx." This takes place in the Hall of the Goldsmiths' Company in London, and is called a "trial," as the ceremony is conducted in the presence of a jury of goldsmiths, who must deliver their verdict in writing to the Lord Chancellor. The Trial was introduced from France in the reign of Edward I, and formerly took place in the "Chapel of the Pyx" in Westminster Abbey. Before the reign of Edward VI the ceremony was held every three months.

In addition to coins from the Royal Mint, the goldsmiths assay specimens from mints of the Dominions and Colonies. (See *Remedy.*)

The United States also conducts a traditional "trial of the pyx" pursuant to a law passed by Congress in 1792. Two quarters and two half dollars are taken from every 50,000 of these coins, as well as two dimes from every 100,000 struck. These coins are weighed on sensitive scales calibrated to 1/500th of a milligram.

The coins are then cut up and dissolved in acid to determine whether they conform to the prescribed degree of fineness (900 parts silver to 100 parts copper, with an allowable deviation of 6/1000ths. See *Tolerance*).

This annual inspection is held at the Philadelphia mint by the National Assay Commission. The members, who serve without pay or expenses, receive a commemorative medal known as the Annual Assay Medal.

Q

Quadrans (L. a quarter): Ancient Roman bronze coin, the fourth part of the *as* (q.v.). Usual type, Head of Hercules, Rev/Prow of vessel, and three dots representing three *unciae*. In imperial times it was the smallest of the Roman bronze coins, and still represented the fourth part of the *as*. (See also *Farthing, Biblical*.)

Quadriga (L. L. singular form of L. plural word *quadrigae*, a chariot drawn by four horses abreast (cf. *biga*): This is a frequent type of the agonistic Greek coins (commemorating athletic contests), especially those of Sicily. The early coins of Syracuse indicated their value by the number of horses; four horses and a chariot indicated the tetradrachma or four-drachma piece, and two horses a didrachma or two-drachma piece. The drachma had a single horse with its rider.

Quadrigatus (L. stamped with the figure of a quadriga): Early type of Roman silver coin, for use probably in southern Italy, figuring Jupiter in a quadriga. It was current down to the end of the second Punic War (202 B.C.). The corresponding half-denarius was the *victoriatus* (q.v.).

Quarter Dollar: Authorized by the Acts of April 1792 and October 1794, these silver coins were first issued in 1796. Early issues were somewhat sporadic, no quarters being issued in 1797–1803, 1808–14, 1816–17, 1826, 1829–30. From 1831 the coins have been struck regularly to date. The following types have appeared:

Bust	1796–1807
Turban	1815–38
Liberty Seated	1838–91
Liberty Head (Barber)	1892–1916
Liberty Standing	1916–30
Washington	1932–

The Bust type features Liberty facing right on the obverse. Most of the reverse is taken up by an eagle—a design that has continued on our quarters to this day. The 1796 coin had no indication of value, but "25c." was added to the bottom of the reverse on the 1804 quarter, and this was continued until early in 1838.

The Turban Head type (Liberty facing left) was introduced in 1815. An additional item on the reverse was a ribbon over the eagle, with the motto E PLURIBUS UNUM. There are quite a few restrikes, overstrikes and varieties among the early issues, resulting in a number of rarities. The outstanding one is the original quarter of 1827 with a curled-base 2 in the value. In 1831 the size of the quarter was reduced and in order to avoid overcrowding on the reverse, the ribbon and motto were eliminated.

On the introduction of the Liberty Seated type in 1838, the value was changed from "25c." to QUAR. DOL. In 1853 the weight of the quarter was slightly reduced. To indicate this change the 1853 quarter has arrows at the date on the obverse, and rays above the eagle on the reverse. The rays were omitted on subsequent quarters but the arrows remained on the 1854 and 1855 coins and were then eliminated.

Quarter. *Left:* Turban Head type. *Right:* Liberty Seated type.

The first New Orleans quarters were struck in 1840; at San Francisco the first quarters were minted in 1856. During 1870–78 quarters were also struck at the Carson City mint, and several of them are quite valuable. The mint marks on the Liberty Seated quarters are found on the reverse, under the eagle. Despite the reduced size of the quarter, the ribbon above the eagle on the reverse was restored in 1866 to carry the motto IN GOD WE TRUST.

The slight increase in the weight of the quarter in 1873 was indicated by arrows at the date on the obverse of the 1873–74 issues. In 1875 the arrows were removed.

The Liberty Head type, also known as Barber type from the name of the designer, was first struck in 1892. This was the first quarter to have the full name, QUARTER DOLLAR, spelled out on the coin. The motto IN GOD WE TRUST appears along the upper curve of the obverse, while the other motto, E PLURIBUS UNUM, is set in a ribbon above the eagle on the reverse. The designer's initial "B" is at the base of the neck on the obverse.

The "S," "D" and "O" mint marks are found on the reverse under the eagle. The "O" mint mark appears for the last time on the 1909 quarters.

Quarter, Liberty Head (Barber) type.

The Standing Liberty type (1916–1930) was first issued only a year before the United States entered World War I. The troubled spirit of the times is reflected in the design on the obverse which shows Liberty holding a shield in the left hand and an olive branch in the right hand. The initial "M" (for the designer, Herman A. MacNeil) appears above and to the right of the date. A graceful eagle in flight dominates the reverse.

On the 1916 quarters the usual 13 stars appear on the reverse. In 1917 the stars were arranged somewhat differently and the eagle was raised a bit. These changes give the reverse a less crowded look.

An impractical feature of the original obverse design was maintained for some time, however. On the coins of the early years, the date was placed somewhat too high to wear well. In 1925 a mound was placed below Liberty and the date was lowered a bit. As a result the dates stood up to wear much better.

The motto IN GOD WE TRUST appears on the obverse, with E PLURIBUS UNUM on the reverse. The "S" and "D" mint marks appear on the obverse, above and to the left of the date. The most valuable coin of this series is the 1918 S overstrike on 1917—one of the most valuable items among comparatively modern coins.

Left: Quarter, Liberty Standing Type. *Right:* Quarter, Washington Type.

The current quarter (Washington type) has been issued since 1932, no coins of this denomination having been issued during 1931. The first appearance of the Washington quarter was timed to coincide with the bicentennial of Washington's birth. The designer's initials ("JF" for John Flanagan) appear at the base of the neck on the obverse. The chief features of the design are a noble head of Washington on the obverse and a standing eagle with outstretched wings on the reverse. As is customary on this denomination, the motto IN GOD WE TRUST appears on the obverse and E PLURIBUS UNUM on the reverse. The "S" and "D" mint marks appear above and to the left of the obverse. See *Controller Coins.*

Quarter Eagle: This $2.50 gold coin, authorized by the act of April 2, 1792, was issued from 1796 through 1929. These types were struck:

Liberty Cap	1796–1807
Turban Head (Round Cap)	1808–34
Ribbon	1834–39
Coronet	1840–1907
Indian Head	1908–29

QUARTER EAGLE

The Liberty Cap type (Liberty facing right) had no stars on the obverse on the early 1796 coins. Later on, stars were added. An eagle above a shield appeared on the reverse. The value is absent from all the coins of this type. All the coins in this series are valuable, the coins being rarer than would seem to be warranted by the mint records of the quantities issued. The explanation seems to be that after 1834 the price of gold bullion increased about 6 per cent. Consequently, holders of gold coins realized a handsome profit by having their gold coins melted down and recoined.

In 1808 the Turban Head type (Liberty facing left) made its appearance. The value ("2½D.") was introduced on the reverse. No quarter eagles were struck during 1809–20. No coins were struck in 1822–23, 1828. The motto E PLURIBUS UNUM appears in a ribbon over the eagle on all the coins of this type. The 1834 issue is the most valuable of the Turban Head quarter eagles.

Quarter Eagle. *Left:* Liberty Cap type. *Right:* Turban Head type.

In 1834 this type was replaced by the Ribbon type (Liberty facing left, with hair bound in ribbon). The reverse is unchanged except for the elimination of the motto. Most dates of this and succeeding issues are considerably lower-priced than the earlier quarter eagles. The "C," "D" and "O" mint marks are found above the date on the obverse.

In 1840 the Coronet type started, with a somewhat smaller head of Liberty facing left. An outstanding rarity in this group is the 1841 proof in prime condition. Another exceedingly valuable coin is the 1854 S quarter eagle. In addition to the Philadelphia coinage, quarter eagles of this type were struck at Charlotte, Dahlonega, New Orleans and San Francisco. The mint mark is under the eagle on the reverse.

Quarter Eagle. *Left:* Ribbon type. *Right:* Coronet type.

Some of the first gold that reached the mint from California was used to strike quarter eagles. They have a special mark (CAL.) above the eagle on the reverse; they are valuable, particularly so the proofs, of which only two are known. The motto IN GOD WE TRUST appears on the quarter eagle for the first time with the 1866 issue. The Coronet type was unusually long lived, lasting through 1907.

Coinage of the quarter eagle ended with the Indian Head type (1908–29). This and the same type of half eagle, designed by Bela Lyons Pratt, are the only U.S. incuse coins (that is, with the design sunk into the flan). Both mottoes (E PLURIBUS UNUM and IN GOD WE TRUST) appear on the reverse. The "D" mint mark may be found to the left of the eagle's claw on the reverse.

Quarter Eagle, Indian Head (Incuse) type.

Quarter-farthing: A very small British copper coin, struck in the time of Queen Victoria, for use in Ceylon.

Queen Anne Farthing: The popular tradition was that only three of these were ever struck; the story went that the British Museum had two of them, and the fortunate (?) possessor of the hitherto missing third one was entitled to a reward of £1,000. Many tragico-comic anecdotes are told regarding these little elusive coins, and the delusive hopes of those who "discovered" them. Actually the one type that was circulated (1714), with Britannia on the reverse, is by no means rare, but those dated 1713 are patterns only, of which not many were struck. Collectors should beware of forgeries (usually cast).

Queen Anne farthing (1714).

Quinarius (L. containing five, i.e., five *asses*): The half-denarius of the Ancient Roman coinage, a small silver coin of the Republican and the Imperial period, and first coined in the second century B.C. Unlike the denarius, the issue was somewhat sporadic. The name was also applied to the gold half-aureus, representing 12½ silver denarii.

R

Radiate: With beams or rays emanating from the head—usually a symbol of divinity, real or assumed. The Roman emperors' heads on the

Peace-type dollar with radiate head.

antoniniani are always radiate. (See also *Barbarous Radiates.*) This is also true of the dupondius, to distinguish it from the *as.*

Rarity, Degrees of : In a catalogue of coins a common type of coin is indicated by the letter "C" and a rare coin by "R." Very rare and extremely rare coins are indicated by "RR" and "RRR" respectively, while "RRRR" would indicate a coin or medal almost unique.

Rarities in U.S. Coinage: Three factors have played prominent roles in the collecting of American coins. These are (a) the stress on trying to assemble a complete series of a given type; (b) the strength of the demand for the coins, often expressed in a lifelong specialization in a single series; (c) variations in the annual amounts issued by the mints, making some dates and/or mint marks much more inaccessible and expensive than others. For these reasons American numismatics abounds in glamorous rarities which are now well beyond the reach of the ordinary collector. Here is a partial list of some of the outstanding rarities:

Cent: 1793 Wreath type; (strawberry leaf variety); 1856 Flying Eagle; 1914 D Lincoln Head.

Two cents: 1864 small motto.

Nickel five-cents: 1913 Liberty Head (unofficial issue).

Dime: 1894 S Liberty Head.

Twenty cents: 1876 CC.

Quarter dollar: 1827 Turban type; 1873 CC Liberty Seated type.

Half dollar: 1838 O Turban Head type; 1853 O, 1866 (unique proof) Liberty Seated type.

Dollar (silver): 1794, 1804 Bust type; 1836–39 Gobrecht design; 1851; 1866 (no motto), 1870 S Liberty Seated type; 1884, 1885 Trade dollar.

Dollar (gold): 1849 C Liberty Head type.

Three-dollar gold: 1870 S (unique); 1875.

Four-dollar gold: All issues (Stella patterns).

1804 dollar, one of the outstanding U.S. rarities.

Half eagle: 1818, 1822, 1829 (large and small dates) Turban Head type; 1854 S Coronet type.

Eagle: 1798 overstrike on 1797 Liberty Cap type; 1858 Coronet type.

Double Eagle: 1849, 1861 S (Paquet's reverse) Coronet type; 1907 plain edge, large lettering on edge—Saint-Gaudens type.

Real (L. *nummus regalis*, royal money): A small Spanish coin, one-eighth of the *peso*, first struck in the middle of the fourteenth century. It was current up to the Revolution of 1869–70. The eight-real piece, or Spanish dollar, is the famous "piece of eight."

Recut Dates: These are often encountered in American coinage, particularly on issues of the 1840's and 1850's. These differ from *overdates* in that they are a repunching of the same digit to correct a weak or out-of-place impression. The double outline on such a recut digit or date is clearly visible. Letters can also be recut.

Reddite Crown: The pattern crown, struck by Thomas Simon, similar in all respects to the *Petition Crown* (q.v.), but the edge, in place of the famous petition of Simon, is inscribed REDDITE QUAE CAESARIS CAESARI (Render unto Caesar the things that are Caesar's).

Reducing Machine: A machine used in modern mints, whereby, from one large plaster model, a number of metal dies can be produced to any small size or sizes as required. The process, though saving time and money, is not conducive to fine numismatic art.

Reeded Edge: A coin edge with lines running across the thickness of the edge from obverse to reverse. The purpose of this is to prevent clipping (q.v.). The coins of Charles II struck by Blondeau were the first in the English series to have reeding, though the larger coins bore the motto DECUS ET TUTAMEN round the edge in place of reeding. (See also *Engrailed, Lettered Edge, Milled Edge, Wire Edge.*)

Relief: A design or legend is said to be in relief when it is raised. The opposite of relief is *incuse*.

Religion: For various aspects of numismatics concerning religion see *Portraits on Coins, Mottoes on Coins.*

To the religious mind of early man, a coin is not merely a token of wealth; the signs and symbols it bears are amuletic in character. The world's earliest coins were usually issued by and stored in temples, and for that reason bore either the image or the symbol of a divinity. Often a god or goddess will appear under different aspects, frequently localized, as in the case of the famous "Diana of the Ephesians." An interesting numismatic divinity appears on Roman coins—Juno Moneta, the divine patroness of the Roman mint. Demigods, heroes, and nymphs are abundant, especially on the more imaginative coins of the Greeks. On the later Roman coins (third century A.D. and on) faith in the ancient gods seems to wane, and in place of divinities we find frigid personifications of virtues, such as Hope (*Spes*), Valor (*Virtus*), Peace (*Pax*). Often a deceased emperor, sometimes a living one, is represented as translated into a divinity. Of particular interest on coins are the various cults that are represented, mostly of Eastern origin, such as that of Mithras in the third century A.D. (See *Mithraic Coin.*) For the beginnings of Christian types, see *Christian Types on Roman Coins.*

Remedy: In English coinage, a small margin or allowance for loss of weight and fineness incident in the minting of coins. In the case of gold coins the remedy is extremely fine, a sovereign being permitted a remedy of only $\frac{1}{5}$ grain in weight and $\frac{1}{5}$ per cent in fineness. (See *Tolerance.*)

Republican Coins, Roman: Roman coins struck from *c.* 264 B.C. up to Imperial times. They may be conveniently divided into *consular coins* and *family coins* (see these titles). In the year 2 B.C. Augustus abolished the office of the monetarii and reserved for himself all rights connected with the coinage of the gold and silver.

Restitution Coins: These Roman coins, known also as RESTORED COINS (not a very happy designation), have the letters REST. or RESTITUIT in the legend, and appeared under the emperors from Titus to Lucius Verus. Barring these letters and the added name of the emperor "restoring" the coins, they are faithful copies of coins that had appeared in earlier ages. A great number were issued by Trajan. Restitution coins are usually of bronze.

Restrike: A coin struck from original, official dies at a time later than the date of the coin would indicate. Several U.S. coins, such as the 1856 Flying Eagle cent and several years of the Gobrecht dollar, are believed to have been restruck in the 1860's.

Retrograde (L. *retrogradus*, going backwards): An inscription is said to be retrograde when it has to be read backwards, i.e., from right to left.

Reverse (L. *reversus,* turned back): The back of a coin, the side popularly known as the "tail"; opposite to the *obverse* or "head" of a coin. The earliest coins have no proper reverse (see *Punch Marks*). The first to bear a distinct reverse are those of Athens. On some coins of Magna Graecia (Caulonia, Crotona, Metapontum, etc.) the obverse type is repeated incuse on the reverse.

Rex Franciae (L. King of France): At the outbreak of the Hundred Years' War (1337) Edward III assumed this title, which first appeared on his gold coins issued in 1344. With the exception of the period from the Treaty of Bretigny, 1360 to 1369, this phantom title remained on English coins until 1800.

Ribbon Type: See *Half Eagle, Quarter Eagle.*

Richard I (Coeur-de-Lion, 1189-99): No coins were struck in England which bore his name, though short-cross pennies were struck during his reign bearing his father's name HENRICUS; they can be distinguished only by the type of portrait. Anglo-Gallic coins, however, were struck bearing the name RICARDVS. It is likely that his absence from England may account for the name not being changed.

Rider: An ancient Scottish gold coin, so called from the obverse of the king riding a galloping horse. First issued 1475 (James III). Name also given to a similar gold coin of the Netherlands.

Right and Left: In descriptions of coins, these directions are always from the spectator's point of view. Thus, a portrait profile described as "facing right" would be facing toward the spectator's right.

Ring-dollar or **Holey Dollar:** In the early days of Australia the Spanish dollar (piece of eight) was freely circulated, but the need for

Left: Holey dollar of New South Wales (1813). *Right:* Original center of Spanish coin, over-stamped with crown and value.

smaller pieces was felt. By a proclamation of 1813, the center of the Spanish dollar was stamped out, thus forming two separate coins, one, a sort of ring money, was stamped "New South Wales 1813, Five Shillings"; the other was a small round token, known as a *dump*. This was re-stamped with a crown on one side and the words "fifteen pence" on the other. The ring-dollar and dump came to an end in 1829.

Ring Money: A popular form of currency, serving both for ornament and use, from the earliest days up to today. Egyptian wall paintings show it was the national currency of that country in early days.

The Celts made extensive use of ring money in Ireland down to the twelfth century. In the Anglo-Teutonic epic of Beowulf, Hrothgar, the Danish king, is the "Keeper of the ring-hoard" and distributes rings at the feast of warriors.

Celtic gold currency ring, late Bronze Age.

Roanoke Island, N.C. Commemorative Half Dollar: See *Commemorative Coins* (*U.S.*), p. 67.

Roll: A standard quantity of identical coins, all of the same type, same date, same mint, and generally in uncirculated *condition*. Purchase of rolls of American coins has increased substantially in recent years, undoubtedly for speculative reasons.

The standard number of coins in a roll according to denomination is as follows:

> 50 cents
> 40 nickels
> 50 dimes
> 40 quarters
> 20 half dollars

Rolls of current "select uncirculated" Canadian coins can be obtained from the Royal Canadian Mint. Earlier years are available from dealers.

Roma: The head of the "genius" of Rome, as she appears on the Republican denarii—a rather grim-looking female bearing a winged Phrygian helmet adorned with a griffin, though some would have it the head is that of Bellona, the Amazon goddess of war.

Roman Coins—Some Common Abbreviations:

AVG: Augustus. A title of honor first assumed by Octavius. This title was reserved exclusively for emperors.

AVGG, AVGGG, etc.: Signifies two Augusti, three Augusti, etc.

BRIT: Britannicus. Title of honor commemorating a victory over the Britons.

C., CAES: Caesar. Originally the family name of Caius Julius Caesar. Later it became a title of honor of the reigning emperor, but after the death of Hadrian (A.D. 138) it was applied to the heir to the imperial throne.

CENS: Censor, a magistrate, entrusted with assessing property and superintending the conduct and morals of the State.

COS: Consul. Originally one of the two magistrates entrusted with supreme power. The title and power were taken over by the emperor from the time of Augustus. As the consulship was an annual office, the years were dated by the existing consul; thus COS III on a coin would indicate the emperor was consul that year for the third time, thus effectively dating the coin.

D.N.: Dominus noster (our Lord). A title of the emperor dating from the decadence of Rome.

DIC: Dictator.

DIC. TER: Dictator tertio, dictator for the third time. This abbreviation occurs on coins of Julius Caesar. The dictator was a person endowed by the Senate with supreme power for some special emergency measures. After the death of Caesar the office was abolished.

F: Filius (son). Sometimes Filia (daughter).

FEL: Felix (happy, fortunate). First appears on coins of Commodus.

GERM: Germanicus: Title of honor commemorating a victory over the Germans.

IMP: Imperator. Originally one on whom the *imperium* was conferred, a commander-in-chief; later, a title of supreme power, conferred on the emperor.

IVN: Junior.

P.F: Pius felix. Pius (gracious) was a title given to emperors after Marcus Aurelius on coins and inscriptions.

P.P: Pater Patriae (Father of his country). A title of honor first bestowed on Augustus.

PONT MAX: Pontifex Maximus, High Priest. Augustus took over the office of high priest, and from then well on to Christian times the office was an imperial dignity.

PRIN: Princeps, leader, chief.

S.C: Senatus consulto, by order of the Senate. These letters appear on all copper coins minted at Rome, these being considered to be under the control of the Senate.

TR(IB). POT: Tribunetia potestate (functus), endowed with the tribunitian authority. This office, like that of the consulship, was taken over by the emperor, and the numeral affixed to the title affords a certain method of dating a coin.

IIIVR: Triumvir, one of a board of three men invested with power for some special occasion.

VOT V, X, XX, etc. VOT XX MULT XXX, etc.: These abbreviations signify various public vows taken up (*vota suscepta*) or accomplished (*vota soluta*) on some special occasion, or for the general welfare of the emperor or state.

Roman Coins Relating to Britain: The Roman occupation of Britain dates from A.D. 43, when, acting under the orders of Claudius, the General Aulus Plautius landed there with four legions. The conquest was commemorated by Claudius by a series of aurei and denarii showing his triumphal arch at Rome. The reverse type shows clearly the equestrian statue of the emperor between trophies and the arch bearing the legend DE BRITANN. Hadrian celebrated the building of his wall between the Tyne and Solway, by bronze coins showing Britannia with spear and shield seated, her right foot resting on a pile of stones. A similar type was issued by Antoninus Pius, celebrating his more northerly defenses between the Forth and the Clyde. This coin seems to have been the prototype of the reverse of the modern English penny (see *Britannia*). Many subsequent emperors commemorated on their coins various victories over the rebellious Northern tribes. The most remarkable allusion to the interest the Romans took in British affairs is the unique gold medallion struck by Constantius Chlorus at Treves. Here we see the "genius" of London, plainly designated by the letters underneath LON, outside the gates of the city. She is kneeling, and welcomes with open arms the advancing figure of the emperor on horseback. Below is a galley with armed troops being rowed across the waves. The legend REDDITOR LUCIS AETERNAE (Restorer of the light eternal) is a proud boast that the civilization of Rome had returned to save the country from the bane of usurping emperors and the turmoil of civil war. See *Britain, Allusions to on Roman Coins*.

Roman Influence on U.S. Coinage: This influence has come down in two ways—in some cases directly, in other cases by way of English, French and Spanish coinage.

As early as the first decade of American coinage, a Latin motto made its appearance on the coins of the young republic. This was E PLURIBUS UNUM (see *Mottoes on Coins*) which may be rendered as "many joined into one"—very suitable for a federal union of the original 13 colonies.

The custom of curving inscriptions to follow the shape of the circular edge is likewise derived from Roman coinage. The use of mint marks similarly imitates Roman usage.

But it is in the pictorial sphere, with its emphasis on eloquent symbolism, that U.S. coinage most clearly reveals its debt to the Romans. The liberty cap, a favorite device on early American coins, was a popular symbol for freedom during the French Revolution, and this in turn may be traced back to the distinctive cap worn by Roman freedmen to show that they were no longer slaves.

Throughout the history of U.S. coinage, some representation of an eagle has been the favored theme for the reverse. This too is a direct imitation, as the eagle often appeared on Greek and Roman coins; being associated with Jupiter (Jove), the eagle was a religious symbol in the age of antiquity. The standards of the Roman legions were topped by the figure of an eagle—an idea that Napoleon took over for his armies many centuries later. On some American coins the eagle holds a scroll or a cluster of arrows or an olive branch in its talons. All these devices stem directly from Roman coins. A magnificent eagle on a sestertius struck during the reign of Hadrian gives one an uncanny sense of the kinship between Roman and American coins.

Roman Empire, eagle reverse on a coin of Hadrian.

The custom of using wreaths and stars on U.S. coins is likewise copied from the Romans. It was customary to crown victorious Roman generals with a laurel wreath during the celebration of a triumph. Later on it became customary to picture Roman emperors wearing a laurel wreath on their coin portraits.

The Goddess of Liberty who appears so frequently on U.S. coins is descended from the goddesses Roma and Libertas. The diadem wreath is also of Roman origin.

One of the most fascinating of numismatic sequences started with an ancient Greek coin issued by Lysimachus, a king of Thrace who had been one of Alexander the Great's outstanding generals. On the reverse of this coin there appears an impressive seated figure of the goddess Athene. Several centuries later the same figure appears on coins of two Roman emperors, Hadrian and Antoninus Pius. Over a thousand years later the same figure turns up on British coins as Britannia. And almost two centuries later this same figure is seen on the Liberty Seated obverse of U.S. silver coins.

Roman Empire, Pieta reverse on a coin of Hadrian.

The famous octagonal Panama-Pacific commemorative piece of 1915 involves an equally interesting historical analogy. For the helmeted Athene on the modern coin is copied from the ancient staters of Corinth, while the owl on the reverse is an allusion to Athene's favorite bird, a symbol for wisdom. The most famous coin of Athens was the one commemorating the victory of the Athenians over the Persians at Marathon. This coin had an owl on the reverse, and so the American engraver seems to be drawing a parallel between the glorious victory of the Greeks and the superb feat of completing the Panama Canal.

The striking "radiate" headdress on the Peace Dollar of 1921 is copied from a style often seen on Roman imperial coins. This headdress reflected the popularity of the cult of Mithras the Sun god which started in Persia and spread rapidly throughout the Roman Empire.

The American coin which has the most Roman feeling of all is the Winged Head Liberty dime, first issued in 1916 and generally if erroneously known as the Mercury Head dime. The device on the obverse—a head with a winged helmet—closely resembles a design used by the Romans for 600 years on their denarius, a coin of about the same size and composition as the dime.

There is a close family resemblance here between the modern Liberty and the ancient Roma. There are more parallels on the reverse. The fasces (an ax and a bundle of rods) was the Roman Lictors' symbol of authority, their function being to escort and protect the Consuls. (See *Fasces*.) It is such frequent and unmistakable borrowings that highlight the role played by coinage in maintaining a link between two cultural traditions seemingly separated by many centuries.

Roman Mints in England: Mints were established at London and Colchester in the time of Carausius (A.D. 287–93). These coins bear the mint marks L and C respectively. Other mint marks, however, occur, such as S, SC, SP, RSR, R, OPR. Some of the coins with these mint marks have been attributed, on grounds of style, to London, and Colchester. Mint marks incorporating an R are supposed to have emanated from Richborough (Rutupiae). (See also *London Mint*.) The Colchester Mint issued no more Roman coins after the defeat of Allectus, but the Roman Emperors continued the supply of coins from the London mint until the time of Magnus Maximus (d. A.D. 388).

Romano-Campanian Silver: The first Roman silver coins, struck in the third century B.C. in south Italy, probably at Capua. They were based on the weight standard of Magna Graecia (didrachma, etc.) and were intended for purposes of trade with that region. Greek in style, the fine art of the coins seems to indicate they were struck by Greek moneyers. The obverse bears the head of some god or demigod (Minerva, Apollo, Mars, Hercules, Janus), and the reverse shows a horse or horse's head, or a figure of Victory. They bear the single word ROMANO or ROMA. They were superseded *c.* 269 B.C. by the denarius.

Rome, Coins of Ancient: The study of the antique Roman coinage, Republican and Imperial, is such a vast subject that there is little point in inserting an inclusive article under this heading. Readers are referred to the main cross-references, as follows: *Aes, Antoninianus, Art (ii), As, Aureus, Consecration Coin, Consular Coins, Cos, Denarius, Dupondius, Family Coins, Follis, Janus, Legionary Coins, Moneta, Portraits on Coins (ii), Quadrans, Quinarius, Republican Coins, Restitution Coins, Sestertius, Siliqua, Solidus, Victoriatus.*

Roosevelt Type: See *Dime.*

Rosa Americana (L. American rose): A series of coins in Bath metal (a combination of copper and zinc) consisting of a twopenny piece, a penny, and a halfpenny, struck under royal patent by William Wood (the inventor of Bath metal) between 1722 and 1724, and intended for circulation in the colonies of North America. The scarcity of coinage made these tokens popular in the colonies. The obverse bears a bust of George I. On the reverse is a large Tudor rose with the legends ROSA AMERICANA and UTILE DULCI. The latter legend is taken from Horace's *Art of Poetry*:

> "Omne tulit punctum qui miscuit utile dulci,
> Lectorem delectando pariterque monendo."

(He has achieved everything who has united pleasure with profit, by delighting the reader, at the same time teaching him.)

Owing to the softness of the metal in which these coins were struck, they are usually found in rather poor condition, the surface being rough and irregular, as if scorched by fire. Patterns of these coins exist, but are very rare. As was the case with Wood's halfpence (q.v.), the issue was withdrawn in 1725.

Rose: On certain coins from Charles II to George II a small rose is found, either under the portrait or in each angle of the cross on the reverse; this indicates that the silver was from the west of England mines.

Rose Noble: The noble was slightly altered by Edward IV; a large rose appeared on the side of the ship figuring on the obverse; the reverse bore a small rose in the center of a radiate sun. The rose and the sun were the badges of the Yorkist dynasty. This coin was rated at a value of ten shillings. Another name for the Rose Noble is RYAL. (See also *Noble.*)

Rose noble (Ryal) of Mary Tudor.

Rose Pennies and Halfpennies (so called from the obverse, a full-blown rose, with the initials of the monarch and the motto ROSA SINE SPINA—a rose without a thorn): Small coins of much debased silver, struck in the later years of Edward VI and the early years of Mary. The proportion of alloy to pure metal was 3 to 1. They were probably regarded as a token currency to remedy the shortage of fine silver. An unsuccessful attempt was made to foist them on to the Irish; by proclamation in 1556 they ceased to be lawful money in all parts except in Ireland. They could be redeemed at only half their nominal value.

Rose-Ryal: A gold sovereign of James I first struck 1605, and worth thirty shillings. The obverse showed the King on a throne; on the reverse was a shield with **XXX** (i.e., thirty shillings) above.

Roses (Elizabeth): The sixpence, threepence, three-halfpence, and three-farthings were distinguished from the groat and the penny by a rose placed behind the queen's bust. It was a scandal of the times that rogues would often erase the rose so that the coin might appear to be of a higher value than it really was.

Roses and Plumes: Certain silver coins of Anne, George I, and George II were struck with roses and plumes placed alternately in the angles of the cross on the reverse. This indicated that the silver was obtained from the "Company for melting down lead with Pitcoale and Seacole," and was of mixed Welsh and west of England origin.

Rouble or **Ruble** (Russ. *rubitji*, a piece cut off): A silver coin first struck in Russia in the seventeenth century. It was divided into 100 kopecks and became the standard coin of Russia under Peter the Great in his reorganization of the coinage in 1704. Klippe, or square, roubles were issued under Catherine I (1725).

Round Cap Type: See *Half Eagle*, *Quarter Eagle*.

Royal: Name given to various gold coins, such as the *pavillon*, the *ryal* or *rose-noble*, the Spanish *real*, etc.

Rubbings of Coins: To make an effective copy of a coin on paper by rubbing, cover the coin with thin blank paper, slightly moistened; rub over with a finger until the outline of the coin shows through, and finally shade over the design with a lead pencil, lightly rubbed over the whole design.

Runic Alphabet (Icel. *run*, a mystery, secret): Early coins of the Anglo-Saxon period sometimes bear runic lettering, and English coins of this period, up to a comparatively late century, often have some runic letters intermingled with the ordinary Latin lettering. The runic lettering is supposed to have originated with a form of the Greek alphabet, and it was adapted by the Scandinavian races to angular shapes that could easily be carved on wood, stone, iron weapons, etc. In the days when reading and writing were considered a form of white magic, the runes became associated with spells and charms, and, as such, they were more or less outlawed by orthodox Roman Christianity. The Runic alphabet is sometimes called the *futhorc*, from the order of the first six letters, as will be seen from the diagram below.

The runic form of "W" appears like the Latin "P" on our Norman

coins, i.e., "PILLELM" for "William," and the letter "thorn,"𝖯 , later mistaken for a "Y" accounts for the current pseudo-antique "Ye," as in "Ye Olde Curiosity-Shoppe."

Rupee (derivation uncertain, perhaps Sanskrit, "wrought silver"): Silver coin of India, formerly with a nominal value of 1*s*. 4*d*. Originating from the *tankah*, under the Mogul dynasty it became the standard silver coin of India. It is now a common coin not only in India but also in parts of Africa and certain Eastern countries.

Russia: The earliest coins of Russia date from the end of the tenth century, and were greatly influenced in their style by Byzantine art. Peter the Great reformed and modernized the whole system of coinage, along with everything else. This reorganization dates from 1704. Gold coins were struck in this year. After the time of Catherine the Second (1726–96) portraits ceased to figure on the coins until the nineteenth century; it is believed that the emperor Paul, the son of Catherine, suppressed this feature, owing to his own unprepossessing appearance. (See also *Kopeck, Leather Money, Platinum, Rouble*.)

Ryal: See *Rose-noble, Rose-ryal*.

S

S.C.: Abbreviation on Roman bronze coins for *senatus consulto* = by order of the Senate. In the year 2 B.C. Augustus abolished the office of the *monetarii*; he took over the coinage of gold and silver, but left to the Senate the privilege of striking the bronze. This privilege was denoted by the letters S.C. These letters also served another purpose—to differentiate the bronze coins of Rome from those issued in the provinces.

S.M.: Abbreviation found on late Roman coins for *sacra moneta* (sacred mint or money). (See *Mint Mark*.)

S.C.C. (South Sea Company): These letters are found in the field of the reverse of most English silver coins struck in 1723. The South Sea "Bubble" had burst in 1720, but the South Sea Company was re-formed, and carried on an active trade with the West Coast of South America. These coins were struck from Peruvian silver which the Company acquired by trading.

Sacrificial Implements: Where the family of a moneyer had pontifical connections, it was customary to place a group of sacrificial instruments

Rome, coin of Julius Caesar with reverse showing sacrificial implements.

on the reverse. Thus on this coin of Caesar's we see the *simpulum* (ladle for making the libation), the *aspersorium* or *aspergillum* (used for sprinkling altars and the people with lustral water), and *praefericulum* (metal vase for holding the libation), and the *lituus* (augural wand). Caesar was *pontifex maximus*, hence these symbols on his coin.

Saddle Blanket Notes: Any large-size U.S. paper money issued before 1929, the year in which a reduction in the regulation size of notes went into effect. The change involves a saving of millions of dollars in the government's annual paper bill.

Saint George and the Dragon: This famous design modeled by Pistrucci after the famous "George" of the Order of the Garter first appeared on the sovereign of 1817 and on the silver crown of 1818. It is said the design was originally intended for a gem that the artist was engraving at the time. (See *Pistrucci*.)

Saint Patrick's Money: A copper halfpenny and farthing, struck at Dublin in the time of Charles II (probably 1678). On the obverse is King David kneeling and playing on a harp, and on the reverse St. Patrick blessing the people. The halfpenny bears the obverse legend FLOREAT REX (May the King flourish) and the reverse legend ECCE GREX (Behold his flock); the farthing bears the legends FLOREAT REX and QUIESCAT PLEBS (Let the people be still). Irish emigrants brought the coinage over to New Jersey in 1681, and it was legalized as currency for that colony. Both types of this coin are found with a plug of brass, with a crown impressed on the plug.

San Francisco-Oakland Bay Bridge Commemorative Half Dollar: See *Commemorative Coins (U.S.)*, p. 66.

Sceat (akin to Ger. *schatz*, treasure): A small Anglo-Saxon coin, in use mainly in southern England from *c.* A.D. 600 to 750. It was mostly of silver, but sometimes contained an admixture of gold, and weighed about 15 grains. It was probably an adaptation of the Frankish *tremissis*. The earlier types are derived from Roman (e.g., the Wolf and Twins) and from Merovingian coins. Runic inscriptions are found on some. A late and debased form of the sceat, circulating in Northumbria, is often called a styca.

From this Anglo-Saxon word "sceat" the word "shot" is derived, meaning money owing ("to pay one's shot"), as is also the term "scot-free."

Schild (Dutch, a shield): The crown or dollar of the Netherlands, circulating there in the seventeenth century (see *Ecu*).

Scilling, Scylling (A.S. *scill, scilling, scylling*, possibly from Teut. root *skil*, to divide): Although this was the word which gave us our modern word "shilling," the Anglo-Saxon *scilling* was not an actual coin, but merely money of account.

Scissel (Fr. *cisaille*, clippings): The scraps of metal which remain after the blank for a coin has been cut.

Scottish Coinage: The Scottish coinage began at a much later date than that of England; there was no national coinage in Scotland until the reign of David I (1124–53). He struck coins similar in type to those of the contemporary English King Stephen. The coinage in course of time became debased, and was consequently lowered in value. Although the coins of Scotland and England were equal in value until the reign of David II (1355), by 1390 the value of the Scottish coinage was only half that of the English; by 1475–1544 it was a quarter, by 1579, one-eighth, and when James VI of Scotland became James I of England the Scottish coins were found to be exactly one-twelfth that of the corresponding English coins—i.e., a Scottish shilling was worth no more than one English penny. Consequently what appears to us to be a Scottish shilling is really a silver twelve-shilling piece of the period.

Scotland continued to strike her own coins until the Union with England in the time of Anne. The later coins previous to the Union had become more and more assimilated in type to the contemporary English types. After the Act of Union in 1707, until the closing of the Scottish Mint in 1709, coins similar to the English were minted at Edinburgh. They bear the letter E below the queen's bust (see *Act of Union*).

References to Scottish coins will be found under *Hardhead, Merk*.

Screw Press: The screw press was probably invented in Italy in the fifteenth century, where it was originally used in the striking of medals. It was employed in France and Germany for minting coins in the sixteenth century. Queen Elizabeth appointed a Frenchman, Mestrell, to the English Mint to strike coins by this new method. A number of coins and some patterns of coins were struck, but, either from professional jealousy or because the Frenchman was alleged to have used his influence as a means to enrich himself, the experiment came to an untimely end. It was not until the time of Charles I that *milled money* (q.v.) was produced in any quantity, although hammered silver money continued in current use until 1695 and hammered gold until 1733.

Scudo (L. *scutum*, a shield, from the original obverse design): The Italian form of the *écu* (q.v.) or silver crown, dating from the late sixteenth century, and abundant in various Italian States in the eighteenth and nineteenth centuries. Occasionally it was struck in gold. The Papal scudo was divided into 100 *baiocchi*.

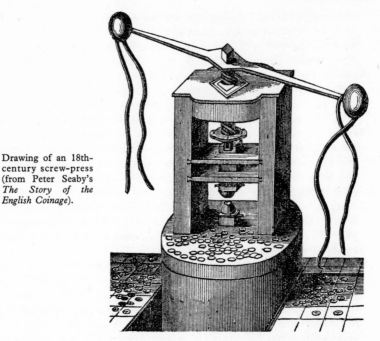

Drawing of an 18th-century screw-press (from Peter Seaby's *The Story of the English Coinage*).

Scyphate, Nummi Scyphati (Gr. *scyphos*, a cup): Any coin that is in the shape of a shallow cup or bowl, i.e., concave-shape, is termed "scyphate." Such coins are found among the early Germanic tribes, the Gauls, the Ancient Britons, and are very common in the Byzantine series where they appeared in the time of Basil II and Constantine XI (A.D. 976–1025); they became the principal type of Byzantine coins until the end of the eleventh century.

Secular Games: (L. *saecularis*, relating to an age or period; Latin term: LVDI SAECVLARES): The thousandth anniversary of the foundation of Rome fell in the reign of Philip I, in the year A.D. 248. For three days and three nights, without intermission, games were celebrated with unprecedented magnificence in the Circus Maximus: various animals that took part in these *Ludi Circenses* are shown on many of the coins struck during this reign. The ceremony itself was ancient, but judging from Philip's coins, it must have been presented at that time with particular splendor.

Sede Vacante (L. the seat being vacant): This phrase is sometimes seen on ecclesiastical coins, such as the Papal issues from the sixteenth century (1521), and signified that the see was vacant at the time the coin was struck. It is the custom that from the death of a Pope until the actual coronation of his successor, no coin is struck with a portrait. The obverse bears the arms of the pontifical chamberlain.

Seignorage (O. Fr. from L. *senior*, lord): A royalty, or charge, levied upon bullion, etc., when it was turned into coins, or upon old or foreign coins when exchanged for new coins; the difference between the value of bullion and the value of the coins which are struck from that bullion.

Semée (Fr. sewn, p. part., fem. form): An heraldic term, signifying a pattern of little pieces, of an indeterminate number, sewn or sprinkled over the field; thus the English shilling and the sixpence of 1787 are said to be either semée or without semée. Although an adjective, this word is often used as a noun, e.g., "a semée of hearts."

Semis (L. *semi-as*, half an *as*): An ancient Roman copper coin, half an *as* (q.v.). On the obverse was the head of Jupiter, and on the reverse the prow of a vessel with the mark "S." It originally weighed 6 oz. (6 *unciae*).

Sequin: See *Zecchino*.

Serrate, Serration; Serrate or **Serrated Coins** (L. *serratus*, saw-shaped, from *serra*, a saw): Certain coins, especially some of the Republican series, have indented edges, or "nicked" as they are sometimes called, presumably to show that the coin was of pure silver and not merely plated.

Series-collecting: Collecting a complete series of a specific design—as for example, the Jefferson nickel from 1938 to date—by seeking to obtain one coin of each date and from each mint and including any significant variety. Several makes of albums are available for this purpose.

Collecting in this manner is most appropriate for current designs or for series that were issued up to fairly recently. When this method is applied to series that were discontinued a long time ago, costs mount steeply. Of the older series, the Indian Head cent is the one most readily within the reach of the average collector.

American coinage is the most popular field for series-collecting, but Canadian coins are gaining in appeal, partly because of the moderate expenditure involved. For more detailed information, see *U.S. Coinage*, *Canadian Coinage*, *Mint Marks* and the individual entries on various denominations.

Sestertius (L. *semis tertius*, two and a half): In 269 B.C. (or thereabouts) the Romans, imitating the coinage of Sicily and Magna Graecia, instituted a silver coinage based on the *denarius* (ten *asses*); this included the sestertius, a small silver coin (infrequently issued), worth two and a

Roman Empire, sesterce commemorating Emperor Titus as the conqueror of Judea.

half *asses* or one-quarter of the denarius. It bore the symbol II.S (i.e., two and a half, the "S" standing for *semis*, a half). In the time of Augustus the monetary system was reorganized. The sestertius became an important coin, but was now struck in orichalcium. It took the place of the *as* as the unit of reckoning sums of money. The denarius by this time was valued at sixteen *asses*, consequently the sestertius was reckoned as four *asses*. It was popularly known as the *nummus* (i.e., the "coin"). To numismatists the sestertius is known as *first* brass, abbreviated to Ae. 1. The sestertius was last struck by the emperor Postumus (A.D. 259–67).

Sextans (L. one-sixth): One-sixth of the *as* (q.v.), or two *unciae* (indicated on the coin by two dots). The obverse shows the head of Mercury; on the reverse the usual prow of vessel with the legend ROMA.

Shekel (Heb. *sheqel*, a shekel by weight): A unit of weight, first used in Babylonia, and later adopted by the Phoenicians, Hebrews, and other Semitic races. The principal silver coin of the Jews. As a Hebrew coin, it was probably struck at the time of the first revolt in the reign of Nero, A.D. 66. Obv/A chalice, ornamented with gems; Hebrew inscription "Shekel of Israel," with the year of the Revolt (one to five); Rev/Three-branched flower or rather buds (the supposed "Aaron's rod"); Hebrew inscription "Jerusalem Kedushah" (Jerusalem the Holy). Half-shekels were also struck with similar devices.

Sheldon Numbers: Specialists in collecting large cents refer to die varieties and attribute their coins according to listings in *Early American Cents,* by William H. Sheldon. The new edition of this book is retitled *Penny Whimsey.*

Shield Type: See *Nickel Five-Cent Piece (U.S.).*

Shilling (derivation uncertain): Originally money of account (see *Scilling*). It was first struck as an English silver coin by Henry VII some time after 1504, and was then known as a teston from the Italian *testone* which inspired its design. It was produced by the master-graver Alexander de Brugsal, and was the first English coin to bear a

Silver shilling of
Edward VI.

realistic portrait of the monarch. The portrait is in profile (see *Portraits on Coins (iv)*). The shilling was worth intrinsically twelve pence until 1816, when it became a token coin. (See *Teston*.)

"*To cut off with a shilling*" was a form of disinheriting a person. The custom probably originated from the idea that a will was not valid unless at least some small consideration was left to the heir; it was also a proof that the testator had not overlooked the heir, and that therefore the disinheritance was intentional.

"*To take the King's (or Queen's) shilling*" means to enlist in the Army. (See also *Lion Shilling, Northumberland Shilling*.)

Shooting Festival Coins: These 5-Franc coins issued by Switzerland were intended primarily as prizes but they were also used in general circulation for a time.

Short-cross Penny: A type of English silver penny, bearing the legend HENRICVS REX, and on the obverse a voided cross extending only to the inner circle of the design. A small cross pommé is displayed in each of the four angles of the voided cross. The obverse bears a conventional full-face head with crown, intended not as a portrait but merely as a symbol of kingship. Short-cross pennies were the only coins current in England from 1180 (tempo Henry II) and throughout the reigns of Richard I and John, until the introduction of the long-cross penny in 1247 (in the reign of Henry III). It is only by variation in the bust, in the lettering, and other minor details that these coins can be assigned to their respective reigns, and to the different periods of those reigns. The

Short-cross penny of Henry III.

reason why the short-cross penny was replaced by the long-cross is explained under *clipping* and *long-cross penny* (q.v.).

Shovel-boards: The game of shovel-board, or "shuffle-board," was immensely popular in Elizabethan times. The popular coin for playing this game was the thin broad shilling of Edward VI, and this coin became known as a "shovel-board" or "shove-groat shilling"; see Shakespeare's *Merry Wives of Windsor*, Act I, Scene 1, where Master Slender grumbles that Pistol had picked his pocket

"of seven groats in mill-sixpences, and two Edward shovel-boards that cost me two shillings and two pence apiece."

Siege Piece: Sometimes called *obsidional coins* and *money of necessity* (q.v.). In time of war the armies must be regularly paid; sometimes if no actual coin is available, as may happen in the case of a beleaguered city, an emergency coinage has to be improvised. An easy method of doing this was to cut up pieces of silver plate, or even gold, into small pieces of a recognized pattern and usually stamped with the value. The greatest issue of English siege pieces was during the time of the Civil War, 1642–49. They often bear the abbreviation OBS (city or town *obsessa* or *obsessum* = besieged). Such pieces were issued at Carlisle, Newark (the commonest of existing coins), Pontefract (including a piece struck after the execution of Charles I, bearing the name of Charles II), Colchester (these are rare), and Scarborough. For references to Irish siege pieces see under *Inchiquin, Kilkenny, Ormonde*.

Newark siege piece.

Siglos (Greek form of "shekel"): The silver *daric* (q.v.) of Persia. Twenty *sigli* represented one gold daric.

Signatures on Coins: Occasionally an artist's name is indicated on a coin, usually by small initials; on modern coins these must be distinguished from the manufacturer's initials; see, for instance, "H" (Heaton). The very finest Greek coins were sometimes signed by the artist; for instance, the famous dekadrachms of Syracuse (415–405 B.C.) by Euainetus bear the letters EY behind the neck of the goddess on the obverse. Coins of Charles I struck by Briot have a very small "B" underneath the mint mark. The St. George and Dragon type of Pistrucci bears the letter B.P. The last bust of Queen Victoria on the sovereign and half-sovereign by Brock has the initials T.B. beneath it. The current (Queen Elizabeth II) coins bearing the initials W.G. were designed by William M. Gardner. For engravers' initials on American coins, see the entries on individual denominations.

Siliqua (L., a carob-bean, cf. *carat*): Originally a small weight, in fact, like the *carat*, it was the weight equal to that of the locust bean (i.e., nearly 3 grains). In 312 Constantine I reorganized the Roman monetary system, basing it on the gold *solidus* and the silver *siliqua*, the latter being one twenty-fourth of the solidus. These coins were current in Byzantium as late as the mid-seventh century. The siliqua was issued abundantly in the reign of Constantine's son, Constantine II. A common reverse of this coin is *Urbs Roma* (the City of Rome), showing Rome, as a female figure, seated and also *Virtus Romanorum* (Valor of the Romans). (See also *Miliarensis*.)

Silly Head: (1) The popular contemporary name given to the first coin struck by George III, namely, the Irish halfpenny of 1766. (2) A certain type of the American 1839 cent, so termed from the rather vacant expression of the Head of Liberty. Another variety of the 1839 cent is nicknamed a "Booby Head."

Silver (numismatic abbreviation Ar = L. *argentum*): One of the "noble" metals, easily worked, capable of taking a brilliant polish, and harder than gold. Though ancient silver was purer than modern for the rough usage of coinage, it is now usually alloyed with $7\frac{1}{2}$ per cent copper. It tarnishes easily from atmospheric sulphur. As practically all English coins up to the time of Edward III were of silver, the word "silver" became a term for money in general, and, in fact, is still in popular use to denote the present cupro-nickel coins.

Silver Standard: Up to the middle of the fourteenth century, nearly all English coins had been struck in silver. Later, and prior to 1816, the currency had been bimetallic, i.e., it was based on a gold and a silver standard. Owing to the expansion of trade in the eighteenth century, gold had increased in importance. The Napoleonic wars tended to upset the ratio between gold and silver; moreover, at that period and for some time after, silver coins were short and were of varying quality. In 1816, therefore, it was decided that the currency should become monometallic; silver coins were henceforth issued merely as token currency. The weight of the shilling was reduced from 93 grains to 87 grains. Owing to the high price of silver, from 1920 the

English coins were 50 per cent silver, and in 1947 the so-called "silver" coins ceased to have any silver in them. Silver of the *old standard* contained 11 oz. 2 dwt. of fine silver to 18 dwt. of alloy. This standard was maintained in the English coinage from the days of the Saxons until the time of Henry VIII.

Silverling (*silver* + dimunitive *ling*): Elizabethan word meaning a coin or a small piece of money. Biblical, a shekel or half-shekel; see Isa. vii. 23, "A thousand vines at a thousand silverlings."

Simon, Thomas: The greatest of English medalists and coin engravers. In 1633 Briot, who was then Chief Engraver, introduced Simon to the Mint. Simon in 1646 succeeded him as Chief Engraver. He had already distinguished himself in cutting the Great Seal of the Commonwealth, and in 1649 he designed the gold and silver coins of the Commonwealth. He engraved the pattern coins of Cromwell. His later years were embittered by quarrels with his more favored rival, Roettier (see *Petition Crown*). He died of the plague in 1665.

Skilling (Scandinavian): In Scandinavia and Northern Germany both money of account and a copper coin of low value (value about ¼ of a cent). The larger multiples of the skilling were in silver.

Slug (derivation uncertain): Unofficial gold coin, issued privately in California during the days of the gold rush. It was a heavy mass of metal, weighing sometimes more than 2½ oz., usually octagonal in shape, sometimes (though rarely) round; the value was fifty dollars. See *Private Gold*.

Small and Large Eagle: Varieties of early American silver and gold coins are described as having a large or small eagle. The small eagle (1794–1798) appears as an eagle standing on a rock, wings displayed, the head turned to the right. The large eagle (1796–1807) is a heraldic type of eagle with a large shield on its breast and 13 arrows grasped in its right claw. This eagle faces left toward an olive branch.

Small Cents: See *Cent* (*American*) and *Cent* (*Canadian*).

Sol (M.L. *solidus*, thick, i.e., *solidus nummus*, a thick coin): Old French coin, originally, like the English shilling, money of account. Twelve *deniers* were equal to one *sol*, and twenty sols amounted to one *livre*. The sol was at first a gold coin. Under Louis XI it became silver, and in the time of Louis XV it was a copper coin. At the Revolution, when it was known as the *sou*, the value was fixed at one-twentieth part of the franc.

Soldo (derivation, as above): A small Italian coin of copper or billon. Twenty soldi are equal to one *lira*.

Solidus, Solidi (L.L. *solidus*, thick): From the time of Augustus the *aureus* was the principal Roman gold coin, but about A.D. 312 Constantine struck the solidus (i.e., *solidus nummus*, or "thick coin") in place of the aureus, the former being a gold coin of slightly lighter weight than the aureus. Seventy-two were struck to the pound. The solidus, known later as the *bezant* (q.v.), became the standard gold coin of early Europe, before the florin and zecchino were minted, and it was current until the fall of the Byzantine Empire (1453). The name *solidus* became transferred to money of account, and was reckoned to contain twelve denarii or silver pennies (see *L.s.d.*). The *triens* (q.v.) was one-third of the solidus. The solidus gave its name to the Italian *soldo* and the French *sol* and *sou*. (See also *Siliqua*.)

Sou (L. *solidus*, see *sol*): Popular name of the French halfpenny, or five-centime piece. From 1914 the coin was a small nickel piece, with a hole in the center. In 1938 it was found that the production of the coin was costing more than double its nominal value.

Sovereign or **Pound Sovereign:** So called from the representation of the monarch sitting on a throne. Originally a fine large gold coin, in fact larger than any English coin previously produced, first struck just after 1489 by Henry VII. It was intended as a double *rose noble* or double *ryal*, i.e., a twenty-shilling piece. Hitherto the pound had been merely money of account. (See *Pound*.) The coin was of standard gold and bore on the reverse a large double Tudor rose charged with the English shield. Under Edward VI (period 1550–53), Mary and Elizabeth, the sovereign became a thirty-shilling piece. Under James I the *unite* took the place of the sovereign. The modern type of sovereign, a smaller, and more insignificant piece, was first struck by George III in 1817. It bore the device of St. George slaying the dragon. After 1917 no sovereigns were issued for internal currency.

Sovereign of Henry VII.

Spade Guinea: So called from the shield of arms on the reverse, which resembles the "spade" of a playing card. It was struck in the reign of George III, 1787-99. The spade half-guinea was struck 1787-1800, with the exception of the years 1792 and 1799.

Spade guinea of George III (1798).

Spade Money: An early form of Chinese currency cast in the shape of a spade. Like *knife money* (q.v.), it marks an intermediate stage between a barter implement and an actual coin. The most ancient are uninscribed.

Spanish Milled Dollar: See *Peso*.

Specie (L. ablative case of *species*, from the M.L. term *in specie*, "in coin"): Metallic money of any kind, as opposed to paper money, etc. Coined money regarded as a class.

Spurious (L. *spurius*, of illegitimate birth, false): The original Latin word *spurius* signified a bastard, and hence came to mean anything of questionable origin, or not what it purported to be. A "counterfeit" is a close imitation of something. In days when coins all over Europe were much alike, it was difficult, especially for illiterate people, to distinguish the true from the false. Thus we find numerous types of base foreign coins in circulation in England in the Middle Ages masquerading as sterling, in spite of repeated legislation, backed by heavy penalties, to put them down.

In the fourteenth century vast numbers of base-metal coins from Luxembourg, known as *lushburgs* or *lushborows*, found their way into the English currency.

Legislation was enacted against the spurious coins in 1346, 1347, 1348, and 1351. Copper coins struck at Tours were circulated at this time in Ireland. In the fifteenth century we hear of suskins, crocards, galley-halfpence, and pollards, which were manufactured in the Low Countries, and brought over illegally by the merchants of the day. Thus Stow tells us that in the time of Henry V "there was at that time forbidden certaine other coynes called seskaris and dodkins." The dodkin (doitkin, or little *doit*) was a small Dutch coin of practically worthless value. From Italy the merchants ("galley-men") brought over silver coin from Genoa.

A general term for base-metal spurious "silver" coins was "black money," from the color of the metal. (See also *Counterfeit, Evasions*.)

Standard of Currency: The amount, authorized by law, of precious metal and alloy in a coin. See *Crown Gold, Silver Standard.*

Stars: These have been significant features in the design of many American coins and their number has varied from 1 to 48 stars. Most of the coins issued from about 1799 to the early years of the twentieth century carried 13 stars representing the 13 original colonies.

Curiously enough our first silver coins, issued in 1794, had 15 stars because by that time Vermont and Kentucky had joined the Union. At that time it was apparently the intention of mint officials to add a star for each new state. Following the admission of Tennessee in 1796, for example, some varieties of half dimes, dimes and half dollars were produced with 16 stars.

As more states were admitted to the Union, however, it quickly became apparent that this scheme would not prove practical and the coins from 1798 on were issued with only 13 stars—one for each of the original colonies. Due to an error at the mint, one variety of the 1828 half cent was issued with only 12 stars. There is also a variety of the 1808 large cent with only 12 stars, but this is the result of a die break and is not a true error.

The 1934 Texas commemorative half dollar in honor of the Lone Star state's centennial has one large star on the obverse. The "Stella" patterns (q.v.) have a five-pointed star on the reverse. On the obverse of the Saint-Gaudens double eagle and on the edge of the Indian Head eagle, 46 stars appear from 1907 through 1911. Starting with 1912, after the admission of Arizona and New Mexico, two more stars were added. Perhaps some future coins will have 50 or more stars. Both 5- and 6-pointed stars have been used.

Stater (Gr. *stater*, a standard of weight, etc.): The name given to any standard gold or silver coin of an Ancient Greek city or State. As such, of course, it varied in size and value. (See *Philippus.*) The gold and silver coins of the Gauls, for want of a better name, are known as staters.

Stella (L. *star*): The $4 pattern gold piece struck at the Philadelphia mint in 1879 and 1880. There were two obverses—a Liberty with flowing hair (designed by Barber) and with coiled hair (designed by Morgan). The reverse in both cases is a five-pointed star.

All the stellas are valuable, but the coiled hair type (10 struck in each year) are much more so. In addition to the stellas struck in gold, others were struck in aluminum, copper and white metal. The work on these pattern pieces was an outgrowth of Dr. W. W. Hubbell's work with his "goloid" metal. See *Experimental Pieces.*

Stemless Wreath: This is a feature of varieties of the 1804, 1805, 1806

half cents and 1802 and 1803 *large cents*. The laurel wreaths on the reverse lack the stems that appear on normal varieties. On one variety of the 1801 large cent the left-hand laurel has a stem while the right-hand branch is stemless.

Sterling (O. Fr. *esterlin*): Seems to have been applied to any small silver coin of fine quality, especially pennies. The derivation of this word is sometimes given as from Easterlings (the Hanse merchants), but the Medieval Latin word *sterlingus* occurs in a document drawn up before the time of the Hanse merchants, and the French word *esterlin* occurs in a metrical romance written by Wace, the Anglo-Norman poet (died *c*. 1174). Other suggested derivations are from *star*, or *starling*, from the devices of early pennies. From its use as standard currency, the word came to mean anything of fixed, authorized value. Hence we talk of a "pound sterling," meaning of the fixed authorized national value.

Stiver (Dutch *stuyver*, *stuiver*, name of coin): English form of *stuiver*, a small copper coin of the Netherlands, one-twentieth of the *gulden*.

Stone Mountain Memorial Commemorative Half Dollar: See *Commemorative Coins* (*U.S.*), p. 61.

Storecards: See *Civil War Tokens*.

Storing Coins: Once a collector advances beyond the dilettante stage he wants to have his coins stored in some orderly manner. This serves several purposes: easy access, display value, protection.

For a general collection a cabinet with long trays is very satisfactory. This is also good for a U.S. type collection, crowns or a highly specialized collection for which there are no albums. As some woods aid the tarnish process, steel is the safest material for a cabinet. The cabinet trays are usually 12 inches in length and just the right size to hold two rows of 2×2 coin envelopes.

Coin envelopes are made of kraft paper, glassine or cellophane. The last two materials, being transparent, enable the collector to see the obverse and reverse without having to handle the coins. Any of these materials will give good protection against moisture, tarnish and dust.

Another advantage of transparent envelopes is that the collector can place all relevant information on a slip of paper or part of an index card and then staple it to the appropriate envelope. It is also a good idea to divide up the envelopes according to country or type or other classification scheme which makes it easy to find any desired coin.

Some collectors use portable storage boxes which are considerably cheaper and serve the same function as a cabinet with trays.

For those who specialize in series-collecting of American or Canadian coins, special albums are available which are devoted to a single series.

In most of these albums each coin slit is clearly labeled with the proper date, mint mark and sometimes the quantity issued. In the higher-priced albums the coins, once inserted, are kept in place by a section of transparent plastic which can be removed or put back as desired.

Series-collectors can also use coin folders which are much less substantial; these do not have the plastic to keep the coins in place, but they have the virtue of being very inexpensive. They are particularly suitable for the beginning collector.

Plastic holders make a fine background for beautiful coins and they are very popular with collectors of proof sets. Collectors of rolls can store their coins in plastic tubes which are sealed at the top to afford maximum protection. Some collectors prefer to store rolls in storage boxes designed for that purpose.

Strawberry Leaf Variety: This variety of the 1793 Wreath type large cent is the outstanding rarity in the whole series of large cents.

Striated (L. *striatus*, scored or furrowed): A coin is said to be striated when it is marked with a number of lines or streaks. Some of the earliest coins of Greece have a striated surface on the reverse in place of a pattern or device.

Sweating Coins: To sweat coins is an illegitimate means of obtaining from them particles of precious metal without the too obvious method of clipping. It is effected by jostling the coins together in a confined space such as a box or a bag. Naturally it is only gold coins that are worth the time and trouble of sweating.

Symbols and Symbolism: A symbol is a conventional sign or pictograph with some esoteric meaning, representing something greater or beyond itself. Thus the simple sign of the Cross can represent Christianity, or a dot within a circle (the "solar disk" of Neolithic races) can represent the sun. In numismatics, however, a symbol is usually understood to be some minor device in the field of the coin, such as an olive branch, the club of Hercules, the eagle or thunderbolt (symbols of Zeus), a lyre, a dolphin, a wolf, or a tripod, signifying the god Apollo; such symbols of divinities are termed their *attributes*. Such attributes abound on Greek coins, but they should be distinguished from many of the so-called symbols on later Greek coins which are really a form of signature of the issuing magistrate. Ancient Celtic coins abound in symbols, mostly of a solar type, many not yet interpreted. These leave wide scope for research. On medieval coins the monarch's head is, in a sense, a symbol, the symbol of kingship, for there is no pretense to portraiture. Thus Henry VI, the infant king, figures on his coins as a mature monarch with his crown.

In the early ages of the world, symbolism was not only applied to coins as something simply ornamental and pretty: it was a living reality. Coins were struck not only to please the eye, but as a concrete emblem that could approach at times to amuletic power. In Mediterranean regions beads of amber were used as currency. Amber was regarded as endowed with amuletic power. Ingots were frequently cast in the shape of the sacred double ax of the Mycenaean cult. It was by such symbolism that trade and commerce were brought under the protection of the divinities. On Greek and Roman coins the figures of the various divinities were not chosen arbitrarily, but were selected usually for some definite religious or even quasi-mystical purpose. Sometimes it may be merely political propaganda that is concerned, and here again, though perhaps not apparent to us, symbolism is present. Thus the various leagues of the Greek City States often placed their symbols on various types of coins, expressive of some common ambition or ideal. A striking instance of this occurs on coins of the so-called Anti-Spartan League. About the years 394–387 B.C., a number of coins were struck by various Greek cities with an obverse showing the infant Hercules strangling serpents. This type appears to have been the recognized device issued by various Leagues that were engaged in struggling to regain their lost freedom. This symbolic type of coin was struck by Thebes, Ephesus, Rhodes, Samos, Cnidus, Iasus, and Byzantium— cities that were struggling to shake off the Spartan yoke (see *Alliance Coins*). Coming to medieval coins, the cross, the triangle (symbol of the Trinity), the Hand of Providence are all forms of religious symbolism found on coins. In the case of the Florins and Nobles struck by Edward III and others the amuletic symbolism of the legend IHS AUTEM TRANSIENS PER MEDIUM ILLORUM IBAT is mentioned in *Mottoes on Coins*. A late example of this language of symbolism may be found on the gold ducats of Frankfurt. The usual type showed a representation of the city with the sun's rays issuing from a triangle; after the capture of the city by Napoleon, it is shown overshadowed by a cloud.

On U.S. coins, the repeated use of Liberty for over a century on many obverses was a staunch allusion to the ideals of the Founding Fathers. The absence of any portrait of an actual person on the regular coinage up to the issue of the Lincoln Head cent in 1909 is indirect confirmation of this view.

The Indian motif in American coinage (Indian Head cent, Indian Head nickel, Indian Head gold pieces) is a symbolic allusion to the settlement of the West, the pioneering spirit, the steady pushing back of the frontier.

The eagle, that outstanding symbol of the fierce desire for freedom, is perhaps even more common on American coins than Liberty. There is a remarkable variety of styles in these eagles, ranging from the rudimentary creatures on the earliest coins to the graceful birds on the Gobrecht pattern dollar, the Flying Eagle cent, the Trade dollar, the Saint-Gaudens double eagle—to mention only a few.

Stars are another favorite symbolic device in American coinage. Generally 13 are used, to refer to the original 13 states. But sometimes all the states in the Union are represented, as on the Saint-Gaudens double eagle and the Indian Head eagle. See *Art, Britannia, Stars.*

T

Tael (Malay *tahil*, a weight): European name of the *liang*, or Chinese ounce, weighing a little over the English ounce; formerly an ounce of silver and a unit of reckoning or money of account. The tael was divided into ten mace or 100 candareens.

Talent (Gr., *talenton*, a balance or pair of scales): As the name suggests, this was a weight rather than a coin. It originated as such in the metrology of Babylonia, and was adopted by various Semitic races, including the Jews. It seems likely that originally it represented the value of one ox, the standard of measurement of value so popular in primitive races. Later the value varied considerably according to the different systems of ratio. It also became a unit of value in Ancient Greece, and large tablets of bronze have been found in Greece, shaped like the hide of a flayed ox. They are over 3 ft. long, and are presumed to be early talents. The parable of the talents (see Matt. xxv) gave a special meaning to the word; thus the word came to signify some mental gift or aptitude.

Taler (Ger. *Joachimstaler*, relating to St. Joachim's Valley): Towards the end of the fifteenth century silver began to be plentiful in Europe, and the increasing volume of trade required heavier pieces of silver than had been current hitherto. Large silver mines in Tyrol and Bohemia were opened up, and in 1516 the famous mines of Joachimstal

One of the earliest Joachimstalers (1525).

were exploited, resulting in the broad and heavy silver dollars which began to be struck in 1518, with the figure of St. Joachim (Father of the Blessed Virgin) on the obverse. They became popular all over Europe, and were imitated under the names of *dollar, daler, tallero,* etc. Other names given to this type of large silver coin are *peso, écu, crown, scudo, piastre,* etc. For some 400 years, the thaler was the standard type of European silver coins.

The thaler (now spelled *taler*) became the unit of the German Monetary Union until 1871, when it was decreed to be replaced by the mark, the minting of which began in 1873.

Ten Cents Silver (Canadian): Issued from 1858 to date. For years of regal types see *Cent (Canadian).* The reverse design is the same as on the five-cent piece through 1936, and the mint mark is located in the same position.

Some of the Queen Victoria issues are much rarer and more valuable than one would expect from the mint records of the quantities issued. These dates are: 1872 H, 1875 H, 1883 H, 1884, 1889, 1893. In the case of the 1893 date the price of the round top 3 variety has skyrocketed far above that of the flat top 3 variety. There is a similarity, though not so marked in the case of the 1913 coin; the broad leaves variety is much more valuable than the small leaves variety.

The ten-cent coin, like the cent (q.v.) has its 1936 "Dot Coinage" rarities, only 8 of which are known. The fishing schooner reverse starts with the 1937 issue and has been maintained to date.

Tessera, *pl.* **Tesserae** (L. a die for gaming, token, tally): (i) A ticket or token of bronze or lead in use among the Romans, entitling the holder to a stated quantity of food (*tesserae frumentariae*) or money (*tesserae nummaria*). The ceremony of the distribution of the tesserae was called a *congiarium,* and this took place usually on such occasions as the accession of an emperor or on his birthday. Special coins were often struck to celebrate a congiarium, and these depict the emperor in person seated on a platform distributing the tokens. Sometimes the tesserae were scattered among the crowd to be scrambled for (*missilia*). The *congiarium* should be distinguished from the *annona,* which is also often commemorated on Roman coins. The *annona* was the regular yearly distribution of corn or bread at a subsidized rate or even gratuitously.

(ii) A ticket of admission to the theatre, the circus, etc. It was a small disk, not unlike a coin; it stated the number and position of the holder's seat.

Teston, Testune, Testoon (O.Fr. *teston, teste,* a head): A silver coin, struck by Galeazzo Maria Sforza, Duke of Milan, in 1468, and in

France by Louis XII, in 1513. So called from the importance given to the head of the king, in place of the stereotyped symbolical bust of royalty that had previously figured on medieval coins. It took the place of the *gros tournois*.

The shilling of Henry VII (third coinage, 1504), from its resemblance to the French coin and from being of an equivalent value to it, is also known as a testoon (see *Shilling*, also *Portraits on Coins*).

The words *teston* and *testoon* are loosely applied to both these two types of coins, but the former is better used for the Continental coin, and the latter for the English coin.

The Elizabethan *tester* is derived from the testoon, though, owing to the depreciation of the currency, it was applied (up to fairly recent times) to the English sixpence.

Tetradrachm (Gr. *tetradrachmon*, four-drachmae): The four-drachmae piece of Ancient Greece, distinguished by its size from the smaller *drachma* (q.v.), and often by its superior art. The tetradrachm was equal in value to three Roman denarii.

Texas Centennial Commemorative Half Dollar: See *Commemorative Coins* (*U.S.*), p. 63.

Thaler: See *Taler*.

Third-farthing: First struck in the reign of George IV, for use in Malta. It was also issued in the reigns of William IV and Victoria. The last Victorian third-farthing was struck in 1885. There was an issue in 1902 and 1913, also for use in Malta.

Thistle Crown, Thistle Dollar: See *Merk*.

Three-Cent Piece (Nickel): This coin, issued from 1865 through 1889, was struck from a kind of "German silver" attributed to Dr. Lewis Feuchtwanger and made up of nickel, copper and a small proportion of zinc. The coins originated as a replacement for the three-cent silver coins (q.v.). The nickel coins, like the twenty-cent piece, had a smooth edge instead of the usual reeded edge. From 1877 on, most of the issues were limited to proofs. The most valuable coin of the series is the 1877 proof.

Only one design was used throughout: a Liberty Head for the obverse and a Roman numeral III, enclosed in a wreath, for the reverse.

Nickel Three Cents.

Three-Cent Piece (Silver): This coin, the smallest ever issued by the United States, was struck from 1851 through 1873. The initial appearance coincided with the first issue of three-cent stamps in 1851. However, the inconvenience of handling the tiny coins eventually turned the public against them, and from 1863 on, only proofs were struck. It seems that this coin was to be called a "trime" (analogous to the dime), but the new name was never actually used.

The design for the 1851–53 issues was a six-pointed star on the obverse and a Roman numeral III on the reverse. In 1854 the silver content of the coin was modified somewhat; to indicate the new composition the border of the star was changed to three lines, while on the obverse the value was enclosed in an olive sprig, with a bundle of three arrows below. Thereafter the reverse remained unchanged, but beginning with the 1859 issue, the three lines of the star on the obverse were replaced by two lines.

The rarest year of regular issue is 1855. Only one issue carries a mint mark—the 1851 O.

Silver Three Cents.

Three-Dollar Gold Piece: Authorized by the Act of February 21, 1853, this coin was first issued in 1854. Like the silver three-cent piece, it was intended mainly for buying three-cent stamps. Neither coin received popular acceptance and a change in postal rates brought about the disappearance of these coins.

During the period of issue (1854–89) there was only one type: on the obverse an Indian princess with a feathered crown. This is the same design as on Type II of the gold dollar, also first struck in 1854. The

$3 gold piece.

word LIBERTY appears on the crown. The reverse features a wreath of tobacco, wheat, corn and cotton. The value and date are inside the wreath. Branch-mint coinage of three-dollar gold terminated in 1870, when the San Francisco mint struck only two of the coins. The mint mark is below the wreath on the reverse. Today only one of these coins is known to be in existence; the second was put in the cornerstone of the old San Francisco mint and could not be found when the building was demolished.

The next rarest coin of the series is the 1875 issue, of which 20 proof coins were struck all told.

Three-Error Large Cent: A die variety of the 1801 large cent on which three separate errors were made on the reverse. (1) The fraction appears as $\frac{1}{000}$ instead of $\frac{1}{100}$; (2) the right-hand branch of laurel does not have a stem; (3) the "U" in "United" appears as "II."

Three Farthings and Three Halfpence: Very small English Elizabethan silver coins, struck at various dates between 1561 and 1581. Like the sixpence and the threepenny piece, they were distinguished from the other small coins of the time (the penny, half-groat, and groat) by a rose behind the queen's head.

Three Halfpence: Small silver pieces, struck in the reigns of William IV and Victoria, for use in certain British colonies. The coins may be distinguished from the Maundy coin of similar value by the reverse. The colonial pieces have the figure 1½ beneath a crown.

Threepence: The silver threepence was first struck in the third coinage of Edward VI, in 1551. Recently it has been suppressed in favor of the brass twelve-sided threepence, with a clump of thrift on the reverse, first struck in 1937.

Tical, also **Tecal, Tecul, Tycal, Tickal, Tekal** (Anglo-Burmese): An odd-shaped coin, popularly known from its size and appearance as *bullet money*. The standard silver coin of Thailand, worth about 2 shillings. The coin, with its fractions and multiples, has its value based on weight. It consists of a small silver ingot, hammered into horseshoe shape, and roughly flattened at the sides. The tical is sometimes countermarked for currency in Burma. The native name of the coin is *bat*.

Tin: Tin is more used in coinage as an alloy (bronze, pewter, etc.) rather than in the pure state. Though silver-like in luster and very malleable, it is too soft to stand up to the wear and tear of currency. The so-called "tin" of the Ancient British coinage (see next article) is a misnomer. The tin coins of Syracuse are alluded to under *Depreciation of Currency*, but as none of these pieces has come down to us, we cannot tell if they were of pure tin or not. In the seventeenth century, in addition to a few traders' tokens, farthings and halfpennies of tin were struck in England (see *Farthing, Plugged Money*).

Tin Money (Ancient British): The so-called "tin" money of the Ancient Britons is presumed to be the earliest native British coinage, and is probably contemporary with the Gallic gold coins of the Bellovaci, namely, *c.* 100–75 B.C. In the second century B.C. the Greek bronze coins of Massilia (Marseilles), with head of Apollo obverse, and on the reverse a charging bull, were circulating and freely copied in Gaul. The Ancient Britons copied these coins in their crude native manner, using an alloy of one part tin and three parts copper. The coins were cast in a strip, and usually a portion of the runlet still adheres to the rim where they were cut apart. Large quantities of these coins have been dug up, nearly all in southeast England.

Titles of English Kings on Coins: The big-wigged Georges loved long and pompous inscriptions attached to their names. The coins were, of course, too small to set out the inscriptions in full, but, giving the letters and abbreviations their full significations, we find such titles as the following on their gold coins from 1714 to 1798:

"Georgius, Dei Gratiae Magnae Britanniae Franciae et Hiberniae Rex, Fidei Defensor, Brunsviciensis et Luneburgensis Dux, Sacri Romani Imperii Archithesaurius et Elector."

(George, by the Grace of God King of Great Britain, France and Ireland, Defender of the Faith, Duke of Brunswick and Luneburg, Arch-Treasurer and Elector of the Holy Roman Empire.)

Tobacco as Currency: In many parts of the world tobacco has proved a useful bartering medium, and, indeed, as an unofficial form of currency, but in Maryland, Virginia, and other American states is was authorized currency in the seventeenth and eighteenth centuries. In the *British Empire in America*, Oldmixon, 1708, we are told of the inhabitants of Maryland

"Tobacco is their Meat, Drink, Cloathing, and Money,"

and Daniel Defoe in his *Colonel Jacque* (published 1722) tells us that in Virginia:

"As Tobacco is their coin as well as their product, so all things are to be purchased at a certain quantity of tobacco, the price being so rated."

Tobacco in Virginia was officially rated from 1618 at three shillings the pound. A brisk trade was done there in imported wives, the price per head being 100 lb. of tobacco in weight, though subsequently the price was raised to 150 lb.

Token (A.S. *tacen*, a sign, symbol): (i) A token in numismatics is a piece of metal, in size, shape, and type resembling a coin, issued usually without government authority, and generally at a time when coin of the realm is in short supply; it is intended as a pledge to be redeemed either in goods to the value it represents or in corresponding coin of the realm. It is usually of lower intrinsic value than a coin. In the Middle Ages base-metal spurious coins were imported into England from the Continent (see *Spurious*) and the brass *jetons* or *Nuremburg Tokens* (q.v.) would serve as small local change in the neighborhood of a monastery. Owing to the growth of trade in the sixteenth century, considerable inconvenience was experienced in the lack of small change. To remedy this, traders themselves started to strike small token coins in base metal.

In the time of James I, the Government took things in hand, and issued *Harrington farthings*, as an official token coinage.

These, however, were extremely unpopular. They showed a handsome profit to the instigators and no small loss to those who had to use them. During the whole period of the Commonwealth no copper coins were issued, but an enormous number of private tokens were struck by municipalities, traders, tavern keepers, etc. It is estimated that over 20,000 different types were issued from 1648 to 1672. In Evelyn's *Diary* we read of the tokens issued by every tavern
"payable through the neighborhood, though seldom reaching farther than the next street or two."
Such common inscriptions on them as FOR Y^e BENEFIT OF Y^e POORE show that they were essentially a poor man's coin. They are usually circular, but square, heart-shaped, lozenge-shaped, and octagonal tokens are common. Penny tokens are known, but the usual values are halfpennies and (more frequently) farthings. They are usually dated, and give the name and town of the issuer. Often they bear the initials of the issuer and of his wife, sometimes joined by a "true-love" knot. In 1672 Charles II issued the first regal copper coins, and the making of private tokens was prohibited by proclamation, in August of that year.

(ii) *Eighteenth-century Tokens.* Between 1755 and 1769 no regal copper coins were struck. Halfpennies and farthings were struck 1770–75, but in no great quantity, and no more copper coins were struck until 1797. In 1787 local issues by private companies and corporations began with the Anglesey penny and halfpenny (q.v.). About the same period, John Wilkinson struck his well-known "Iron-Master" Tokens, bearing his portrait, and on the reverse, a steam forge.

Eighteenth-century tokens abound in mythical types (Bladud, Prince of Bath, Lady Godiva), historical (King Alfred, John o' Gaunt, Queen Elizabeth, Isaac Newton), contemporary notorieties (Nelson, Earl Howe, William Pitt), literary characters (Shakespeare, Dr. Johnson), politicians (Thomas Hardy, Horne Tooke).

On the social side we find bathing machines, mail coaches, and ships of all types depicted. Some tokens are in the nature of advertisements (Lackington the Bookseller and his "Temple of the Muses"), vendors of boots, gloves, umbrellas, fireplaces displaying their wares. Some are architectural in type (cathedrals, shire halls, guild halls, bridges, canals,

Eighteenth-century token
(political).

town crosses, Newgate Jail). Many of these were evidently struck more as collectable curiosities and souvenirs rather than as currency. For this reason it is easy to find pieces in uncirculated condition. PRIVATE TOKENS were also struck in limited numbers by individuals as numismatic oddities, and for gifts to friends. The large issue of regal pennies and twopenny pieces in 1797 brought the series of eighteenth-century tokens to an end.

(iii) *Nineteenth-century Tokens*. As the Industrial Revolution swept over the country, so supplies of copper coins, needed to pay the thousands of workers entering the new factories, dwindled, and in 1811 a number of private firms began striking the larger penny tokens. Such tokens were declared to be illegal in 1817, though tokens of the Birmingham Workhouse and Sheffield Overseers of the Poor were allowed to circulate for some years after this date, owing to the great quantity which had passed into circulation. Silver tokens began to be issued as early as 1804, but most of these are dated 1811 and 1812. They are mostly sixpences and shillings, though pieces of higher value were sometimes issued. (See also *Bank of England Dollars; Dollars, Countermarked.*)

In the United States large quantities of privately issued tokens were struck during the economic distress of the 1830's (see *Hard Times Tokens*). Several decades later thousands of different kinds of tokens made their appearance during the Civil War because the official coinage was hoarded (see *Civil War Tokens*).

Private tokens were widely used in Canada even after the introduction of official coinage in the nineteenth century (see *Canadian Tokens*).

Token Coinage: A coinage consisting of pieces which have not the full intrinsic value they purport to represent. In England the shilling became a token coin in 1816 and the penny in 1817. Until then gold and silver coins were presumed to be worth their actual metal value, though copper coins (with the exception of the *cartwheel* (q.v.) penny and twopenny piece of George III) were considered token coins.

Tolerance: All United States coins are alloys with a specified proportion of the amounts of metal that go into the composition of each coin. This proportion is called "fineness." The legally allowable degree of deviation from the stipulated grade of fineness—known as "tolerance"—is as follows:

Silver (dime, quarter dollar, half dollar): 900 parts silver to 100 parts copper; tolerance is a deviation of 6 parts of silver per thousand parts.

Cupro-nickel (nickel): 750 parts copper to 250 parts nickel; tolerance is a deviation of 25 parts of nickel per thousand parts.

Bronze (cent): 950 parts copper to 50 parts zinc and tin; no legal definition of tolerance.

See *Pyx, Trial.*

Touch Piece: A coin or medalet distributed by a person of royal blood to sufferers from scrofula (the "king's evil"), in the ceremony of healing by touch. According to both Tacitus and Suetonius, the Emperor Vespasian effected miraculous cures at Alexandria by his touch. (Tacitus, *History,* IV. lxxxi; Suetonius, *Vespasian,* VII.) Edward the Confessor is the first English king on record who "touched" for the king's evil (1058); the last English sovereign to perform the ceremony was Anne. Among those she "touched" was Samuel Johnson, then a child of two and a half. The original medalet placed round his neck is now in the British Museum. The ceremony of "touching" is alluded to by Pepys, and Evelyn gives curious details of it in his diary (6 July 1660, 28 March 1684).

The Tudors and the Stuarts used the gold angel in touching, doubtless from the symbolical type showing St. Michael defeating Satan. After the issue of angels had ceased, a special small gold medalet was struck for the purpose, in the time of Charles II. This bears the same type of St. Michael and the Devil; on the reverse is a ship with the legend SOLI DEO GLORIA (To God alone be the glory). Both coins and medalets are always found with a hole pierced in them for suspension. They were not merely mementos of the occasion, but were considered as amulets, intended to be worn around the neck of the sufferer until a cure was effected.

Tournois (L. *Turonensis,* relating to the city of Tours): Adjective, applied to medieval French money, such as *gros tournois, livre tournois,* etc. French money of the Middle Ages was based on two standards, that of Tours and that of Paris. From the time of the Carlovingians, coins were struck at the Abbey of St. Martin of Tours; later this Abbey became a royal mint. Deniers were struck here bearing the head of St. Martin, and, later, the well-known and abundant denier bearing what is supposed to be an image of the Abbey, though highly conventionalized. The *monnaie parisis* was later in date and was established by Philip Augustus 1180–23. These coins were heavier and worth about 25 per cent more than the *monnaie tournois*. (See *Châtel Tournois*.)

Tower Mint: This was the royal mint of the City of London, from A.D. 1300 to the beginning of the nineteenth century. The site of the mint was between the inner and outer walls of the Tower, on the west side. Old plans of the Tower mark the spot as "Mint Street." In 1810 the Mint was moved to Little Tower Hill. The new buildings were planned by Boulton (q.v.) who supplied the machinery. The new mint was regarded as a model of its kind, and the machinery was not superseded until 1881–82. (See *London Mint*.)

Tower Pound: Before the Troy pound was introduced by Henry VIII in 1526, this was the standard of weight employed at the Royal Mint. The fractions of the pound were the same as in Troy weight, but the pound itself was ¾ oz. under the pound Troy.

Trade Dollar: See *Dollar, U.S. Silver*.

Transitional Pattern: A coin issued at the time of a design change incorporating features of both the old and new designs. The best-known transitional pieces are the half dime and dime of 1859 and 1860 combining the old obverse and the new reverse. See *Pattern Coins*.

Treasure Trove: A hoard of gold and silver, either of coins or other valuables of these metals, which has been deliberately buried in the soil, and the owner of which cannot be traced, is known as treasure trove. Copper coins, however rare and valuable, would not constitute treasure trove, nor would gold or silver casually lost or thrown away with no intention of reclaiming later. In England in the event of a hoard being deemed treasure trove, the local coroner and a jury hold an inquest on it, and it is claimed on behalf of the monarch. It is customary, though not obligatory, to give recompense to the full value to the finder.

Treasury Note: Paper money, issued by the Treasury under Government legislation, as a substitute for metallic coinage. (See *Paper Money*.)

Tree Money: From the year 1652 coins were struck in Massachusetts, with representations of various trees (oak, pine, and willow) on the obverse. Massachusetts was always a thorn in the side of the English

Massachusetts, Pine Tree Shilling.

kings, and the fact that coins should have been struck there offended Charles II, as this was an infringement of the royal prerogative. Sir William Temple, however, succeeded in pacifying the King by maintaining that the trees depicted on the coin must surely be a symbol of the Royal Oak. The dates on these coins are delusive. Though minted for some thirty years, the date of the threepence, the sixpence, and the shilling was always 1652, and the oak-tree type of the twopence was always dated 1662. The pine-tree shilling is familiarly known as the Boston or Bay shilling.

Tremissis (L.L. *tremis, tremissis*, a three-*as* coin): Gold coin of the Byzantine Empire, also known as the *triens* (q.v.). From this coin was derived the Merovingian tremissis (*c.* A.D. 500–750). A few of the latter coins have been found in southeast England.

Tressure (Fr. *tresser*, to plait, weave): Heraldically a framework of a shield; numismatically it is applied to the florid and ornamental border framing the device of a coin.

Tribute Penny: The common denarius of Tiberius, with inscription TI.CAESAR DIVI AVG.F.AVGVSTVS; reverse, female, seated in chair, presumed to be Livia, the mother of Tiberius, legend PONTIF. MAXIM. In A.D. 6 Judaea was declared to be a Roman province, and an annual poll tax of one denarius was levied on the inhabitants. This tax had to be paid in Roman coin. This denarius would be the current type used in Judaea in the time of our Lord when the question was put to Him:

"Is it lawful to give tribute unto Caesar ?" (Matt. xxii. 19, Mark xii. 15, Luke xx. 24).

Rome, denarius of Tiberius (the "tribute penny").

Trial Pieces: Impressions made to test completed or partially finished dies. A soft metal is generally used for this purpose.

Triens, *pl.* **Trientes** (L. *tres*, three): Ancient Roman coin of the Republic representing one-third of the *as* (q.v.); also a gold coin, one-third of the *solidus* (q.v.), first struck by Valerian (254–60) in the Byzantine series, and imitated by the Merovingians as the *tremissis* (q.v.).

Triple Unite: See *Unite*.

Tri. Pot.: Abbreviation found on the legend of Roman imperial coins, signifying TRIBUNITIA POTESTATE (*functus*), "functioning with tribunitian power." The tribunitian power was one of the many offices taken over by the emperors from the earlier and more democratic government of Rome. Officially it was conferred by the Senate annually; as the number of the year in which the office was conferred is indicated also in the legend (TRI. POT. III, etc.), the exact date of a Roman coin may be ascertained from this title.

Triquetra (L. *triquetrus*, having three corners): In heraldry and art a device of three symmetrical interlaced shields, or shield-shaped lobes, their points turned outwards; numismatically, the word is often used to denote the TRISKELION or TRISKELES (Gr. *tri = treis*, three, *skelos*, a leg), a device of three bent legs radiating from a common center. This device appears on certain Greek coins (Sicily, etc.) and on the well-known copper coins of the Isle of Man (see *Man, Isle of*).

Isle of Man with triquetra reverse (1839).

Triumviri (or **Tresviri**) **Monetales** (L. financial board of three men): Officers entrusted with the supervision of the coinage in Ancient Rome, in other words, Masters of the Mint (see *Family Coins, Roman*). This office was abolished by Augustus in 2 B.C.

Troy Weight (from *Troyes*, a French town): The town of Troyes was of considerable commercial importance in the Middle Ages, largely owing to the great fair held there twice yearly. The standard of weights used at Troyes became popular in many parts of Europe for weighing bread, silk, gold, silver, and precious stones. The scale was based on the "grain." This was a weight equal to a grain of corn "round, dry, and taken from the middle of the ear" (statute of Edward II, 1324). Troy weight is still used among jewelers for weighing gold, silver, coins, and precious stones.

The table of weights is:

    24 grains = 1 pennyweight (dwt.)
    20 dwt.   = 1 ounce (oz.)
    12 oz.   = 1 pound (lb.)

The Troy pound of 5,760 grains superseded the Tower pound at the Mint in 1526. (See *Tower Pound*.)

Truncation (L. *truncatus*, cut off): The truncation of a bust is the line at the base of the neck, where it appears "cut off." This usually takes the form of a narrow scroll, where often the initials or the name of the designer of the coin appear.

Trussel (O. Fr. trestel, a bar, etc.): The upper die of the old hammered coinage, which was engraved with the design for the reverse of a coin. It was held in the hand and hit on top with a heavy hammer. As the trussel bore the direct force of the blow, it naturally wore out sooner than the lower die, the pile (q.v.), so usually two trussels were supplied to one pile.

Turban Head Type: See *Cent (U.S.)*, *Dime*, *Half Cent*, *Half Dime*, *Half Dollar*, *Half Eagle*, *Quarter Dollar*, *Quarter Eagle*.

Twenty-Cent Piece: This silver coin was first issued in 1875 pursuant to the Act of March 3, 1875. But it was so close to the familiar quarter in size and design that the public expressed strong dislike for the coins, which were discontinued after 1878. The Liberty Seated is very similar to the obverse on the quarter; the eagle has a close resemblance to the eagle on the reverse of the Trade Dollar. A peculiarity of the twenty-cent pieces is that they have a smooth edge instead of the usual reeded edge.

Despite the fact that 10,000 1876 CC pieces were struck, this coin is an outstanding rarity, being valued upwards of $3000 in uncirculated condition.

20-Cent piece.

Twenty Cents Silver (Canadian): This coin was struck only once—in 1858—and thus proved an even bigger failure than the U.S. coin of the same denomination. The reverse is similar to that of the Canadian five-cent piece.

Twenty-five Cents Silver (Canadian): Issued from 1870 to date. For years of regal types see *Cent (Canadian)*. The reverse design is the same as on the five-cent piece through 1936, and the mint mark is located in the same position. Rare dates of the early period are 1875 H, 1880 H (wide O), 1885, 1887, 1889, 1891, 1915, 1927. The "Dot Coinage" of 1936 has considerable premium value, but is nowhere near the prices commanded by the cent and ten-cent piece. The caribou head reverse was first struck in 1937.

Two-Cent Piece: United States coin issued from 1864 through 1873, under the authorization of the Act of April 22, 1864. This law provided for a bronze two-cent coin of 95 per cent copper, with tin and zinc making up the remaining 5 per cent. The weight was 90 grains, slightly less than double the weight of the bronze cent authorized in the same legislation.

In the first year of issue, almost 20,000,000 two-cent coins were struck, doubtless in answer to the severe coin shortage that developed during the Civil War. Thereafter the popularity of the coin declined very sharply, only about 3,000,000 being struck in 1866. The annual mint figure continued to dwindle, and in the final year of issue (1873) only proofs were struck.

2-Cent bronze.

Nevertheless this coin is of outstanding interest to collectors, as it was the first to carry the familiar motto, "In God We Trust." It is believed that the Rev. M. R. Watkinson originated the idea, suggesting "God, Liberty, Law" to Secretary of the Treasury Salmon P. Chase in 1861 in the hope that this "would relieve us from the ignominy of heathenism." Secretary Chase liked the idea and authorized designs for a coin to carry a motto for expressing this theme "in the fewest and tersest words." One of the mottoes submitted was, "God, Our Trust," which Chase modified to the form which was actually adopted.

The design for the obverse of the two-cent coin was a shield (very similar to the one subsequently used on the shield nickel), encircled by leaves and topped by a wavy scroll containing the motto. The issue of 1864 is made up of two varieties—"small motto" and "large motto." The small-motto type is by far the more valuable, having been issued in such small quantities that some authorities think it may have been a pattern coin.

The two points of difference between these varieties aside from the difference in the sizes of the motto lettering, are: (a) the space inside the "D" of "GOD" is noticeably narrower on the large motto; (b) on the small motto there is a stem to the right of "WE" leading to a leaf; on the large motto the stem is missing.

Type (L. *typus*, a figure, an impressed mark): The distinguishing characteristic of either obverse or reverse. It may include a portrait (e.g., the "bonnet" type of William I), or some device (e.g., St. George and the Dragon), but always with the idea of classification or division, distinguishing it from other but kindred classes or divisions.

Type-collecting: Collecting coins on the basis of the design on the obverse. Example: Indian Head cent, Shield nickel. This involves obtaining one coin of each design type. Any date or mint will do. This comparatively inexpensive form of collecting is particularly suitable in the case of the older, sometimes prohibitively costly American coins. Contrast this with *Series-collecting*.

Type Parlant (Fr. *parlant*, speaking): A canting device, a sort of rebus or picture-pun; a type punningly allusive to the name of some person or place. Thus Selinus, in Sicily, was named from the wild parsley or celery (*selinon*) which grew in abundance on the riverbanks. Many of the coins of Selinus show a spray of this plant. Rhodes was named from the rose which bloomed there in profusion, and thus the flower figures on the coins of Rhodes. Similarly, coins of Melos show a pomegranate (*melon*), Phocaea, a seal (*phoca*), Ancona, a bent arm (*angkon*, a bend, from the bend of the coast). All these types parlants are allusive to the places where they were struck. On Roman coins, Q. Voconius Vitulus struck a coin with a calf (*vitulus*) on it, and L. Aquillius Florus a coin with a flower (*florus*). P. Fourius Crassipes ("Fat-foot") shows a wry sense of humor in displaying on his coins the small effigy of a distorted foot.

Luneberg silver taler (1547). Man in the moon ("Luna") is used to represent Luneberg.

U

Uncia (L. a twelfth part): In Ancient Rome originally an ounce in weight, twelve unciae forming the *libra* or pound. As a coin it was of copper, representing one-twelfth of an *as* in the *aes grave* series. The obverse of the earliest coins has a head of Roma (supposed by some numismatists to be that of Bellona), and the usual reverse of the prow of a vessel. It usually bears a single boss or pellet as mark of value. (See *As*.)

Uncirculated: Another name for "in mint condition," or F.D.C. (See *Condition of Coins*.)

Unicorn: Gold coin of Scotland, issued during the reigns of James III (in 1486), James IV, and James V. The obverse bears the figure of a unicorn, with a crown around his neck, supporting the Scottish shield; legend, on reverse, EXVRGAT: DE: ET: DISIPENT: NIMICI:E.

Uniface (L. *unus*, one, *facies*, face): A coin or medal having the device, legend, etc., on one side only, the other being a blank.

Unite: So called from the motto FACIAM EOS IN GENTEM VNAM (Ezek. xxxvii. 22) ("I will make them one people"), referring to the Union of England and Scotland: a gold coin, resembling in type the previous sovereign, and first struck by James I of England in 1604. The mark of value, XX indicates the value, twenty shillings. A splendid TRIPLE UNITE (three-pound piece) was struck during the Civil War by Charles I at Shrewsbury (1642) and later at Oxford (1642–44). On the reverse is the Declaration motto and the Exurgat legend. (See *Declaration Type*, *Mottoes*.)

Up-grading: A continuous process of improving a collection and increasing its investment value by replacing inferior specimens with superior examples of the same coins. See *Condition of Coins*.

Urbs Roma Type (L. City of Rome): In A.D. 330 Byzantium, under the new name Constantinople, was solemnly dedicated by Constantine the Great to the Blessed Virgin. To commemorate the election of the capital of the new Eastern Roman Empire, small copper coins were struck either by Constantine himself or by his immediate successors. There are two types of these coins, one bearing the helmeted head of Rome on the obverse, the other that of Constantinople. The usual inscription of the first is VRBS ROMA, the other bears the name CONSTANTINOPOLIS.

U.S. Coinage: See *Adams-Woodin Numbers; Altered Dates; Architecture; Art; Barber Head Coins; Beistle Numbers; Bolender Numbers; Broken Die; Browning Numbers; Bungtown Coppers; Cent; Cent (U.S.); Civil War Tokens; Colonial and Pre-Mint Coinage; Commemorative Coins (U.S.); Condition of Coins; Confederate Coinage; Controller Coins; Crosslet 4; Dime; Dollar Sign; Dollar, U.S. Gold; Dollar, U.S. Silver; Double Eagle; Eagle; Elephant Coin; Engraver; Fasces; Feathered Crown; Feuchtwanger Composition; Fugio Cent; Gilbert Numbers; Gold Order; Half Cent; Half Dime; Half Dollar; Half Eagle; Hard Times Tokens;*

Legal Tender; Lettered Edge; Lord Baltimore Coins; Mint Errors (Freaks); Mint Marks; Mints (U.S.); Morgan Head Coins; Mottoes on Coins; Newcomb Numbers; New England Money; Nickel Five-Cent Piece (U.S.); Overdate; Portraits on Coins; Private Gold; Proof; Punctuated Date; Pyx, Trial; Quarter Dollar; Quarter Eagle; Rarities in U.S. Coinage; Recut Dates; Restrike; Roll; Roman Influence on U.S. Coinage; Rosa Americana; Saint Patrick's Money; Series-collecting; Sheldon Numbers; Silly Head; Slug; Small and Large Eagle; Stella; Stemless Wreath; Strawberry Leaf Variety; Symbols and Symbolism; Three-Cent Piece (Nickel); Three-Cent Piece (Silver); Three-Dollar Gold Piece; Three-Error Large Cent; Token; Tolerance; Transitional Pattern; Tree Money; Twenty-Cent Piece; Two-Cent Piece; Type-collecting; Valentine Numbers; VDB; Vines and Bars.

U.S. Mints: See *Mints, U.S.*

V

Valentine Numbers: Specialists in collecting half dimes refer to die varieties and attribute their coins according to listings in *The United States Half Dimes*, by D. W. Valentine.

Value: See *Face Value, Market Value, Premium Value.*

Value of Money: The further we go back in history, the greater is the value of money compared with the value of today. Thus the Roman denarius, represented by the *"d."* of the English *"£ s.d.,"* and, in fact, translated in the Authorized Version of our Bible as "penny," is usually reckoned at 10¢ to 15¢ in numismatic works. We see, however, from the Parable of the Vineyard (Matt. xx. 2) that this sum represented the average wage of a laborer for a day's work. It was also the daily pay of the Roman legionary. To realize the value of money in ancient times, the so-called "value" must be multiplied many times. Coins of the time of Edward III (1312–1377) should be multiplied at least fifteen times their face value to give some idea of their contemporary buying power, and those of the time of Elizabeth I by at least six times.

VDB: See *Altered Dates*, and "Lincoln Head Cents" under the entry *Cent (U.S.).*

V.E.I.C.: Initials of the United East India Company. Seen on the "bale marks" which figure on early coins of Bombay. The "bale mark" was a relic of the medieval "merchants' mark" and not the official arms of the Company.

Vermont Sesquicentennial Commemorative Half Dollar: See *Commemorative Coins (U.S.)*, p. 63.

Victoriate, Victoriatus (L. *victoriatus nummus*, coin with figure of Victory): An Ancient Roman silver coin, smaller than the denarius, first struck during the Second Punic War (218–201 B.C.), and intended for oversea trading. The obverse bears the head of Jupiter; on the reverse is a figure of Victory (giving the coin its name) crowning a trophy. The value was three-quarters of the denarius, though later it was reduced to a half-denarius.

Victory, Victoriola: See *Nike*.

Vigo: In 1702 Admiral Sir George Rooke, in conjunction with the Dutch, attacked the French and Spanish fleets in the port of Vigo. Vast treasures were taken from the captured galleons, which had just returned loaded from South America. The treasures included bullion, plate and over 11 million "pieces of eight." These were melted down at the Royal Mint, and, in commemoration of the victory, some shillings of 1702 and many gold and silver coins of 1703 were stamped with the word VIGO.

Queen Anne shilling with "Vigo" inscription.

Vines and Bars: A device on the edge of 1793 chain *cents* and some of the 1793 wreath-type *cents*. Sections of vertical bars alternate with sections showing a slender vine with leaves. This device is also occasionally referred to as "stars and bars."

Vis-à-vis (pronounced *vee-zah-vee*: O. Fr. *vis*, face): Face to face. Two busts on a coin are said to be *vis-à-vis* when they face each other (cf. *jugate*). In imitation of the coins of Ferdinand and Isabella of Spain, the heads of Philip and Mary are placed *vis-à-vis* on their English coins.

V.O.C.: In monogram form; signifies *Vereenigde Oostindische Compagnie* (United East India Company). This monogram appears on coins of the Dutch East India Company.

Voce Populi (L. by the voice of the people): Irish halfpenny and farthing tokens struck in Dublin in the reign of George II (1760), to remedy the scarcity of copper coins. Obv. Head of king (?), legend VOCE POPULI; Rev. HIBERNIA (Ireland); Hibernia seated, with harp. On some coins the obverse bears the letter P.

Voided Cross: A cross consisting of double lines, so that it appears as if the limbs were hollowed out. The voided cross appears on the English penny from 1180 (tempo Henry II) until the time of Edward I. It was placed on the reverse of the penny so that it could be easily and equally divided into half-pennies and farthings. (See *Cut Halfpennies and Farthings.*)

Votive Coins (Roman): In 27 B.C. Octavius (the future Emperor Augustus) took command of the Provinces. He promised that in ten years' time all the world would be at peace. At the beginning of the year solemn vows were made both for the past, the VOTA SOLUTA (vows performed) and for the future, VOTA SUSCEPTA (vows to be taken up). Such vows were made for the prosperity of the whole Roman Empire; the Emperor was presumed to hold the Empire as Imperator (Military Commander) not, as a king, for his whole lifetime, but for a determinate number of years. On coins of various emperors who commemorated these public vows we find such inscriptions as:

VOTA PUBLICA

VOTA SUSCEPTA

VOTA SOLUTA

VOTA V (*Vota quinquennalia*, vows for five years)

VOTA X (*Vota decennalia*, vows for ten years)

VOTIS X. MVLTIS XX (*Votis decennalibus solutis, multis vicennalibus susceptis*, vows for ten years having been performed and with many others taken up for the succeeding twenty years).

Such legends are usually accompanied by a sacrificial scene, or a pair of Victories are shown inscribing such words on a shield. On later types the inscription appears on the field of the reverse encircled with a wreath.

Votive legends are particularly common on coins of the late Constantine period.

W

Wales: If Wales ever struck any national coins, none seems to be extant. There is a coin, however, struck in the reign of Athelstan. It is of the ordinary contemporary Saxon type, but bears the name HOWAEL REX on the obverse. This is presumed to be Howel (or Huel) Dda, Howel the Good, the great Welsh legislator (*c.* 913–48). Some coins of William I and Henry III were minted at Rhuddlan.

Wampum (*wompam*, Indian word meaning "white"): A form of currency used formerly by the North American Indians and other primitive races, consisting of beads or disks made from seashells. The name is properly applied to the white beads only, the black beads being known as *suckauhock* (*suki* = black), though wampum is usually seen today with white and black beads threaded together alternately. A string of wampum beads was known as *wampumpeag* (*peag*, an Indian word for beads threaded together). Like other forms of primitive currency, such beads were not merely used for trade, but also as ornaments for personal adornment. In fact, wampum was something of a great deal more than mere money; it was regarded as talismanic or even semi-sacred. Wampum was no longer regarded as legal tender after 1661, but in the regions of the South Sea Islands beads and shell disks are still used as currency. (Cf. *Cowrie.*)

Washington (Booker T.) Birthplace Memorial Commemorative Half Dollar: See *Commemorative Coins (U.S.),* p. 67.

Washington-Carver Commemorative Half Dollar: See *Commemorative Coins (U.S.),* p. 68.

Washington Type: See *Quarter Dollar.*

Weights: In many instances the names of coins were originally the names of actual weights, or were derived directly from the names of weights. Such was the case with the *talent* (originally a Babylonian weight), the shekel, and the Roman *as.* The English word *pound* and the French word *livre* can either mean a specific weight or else an actual coin. Similarly, the *mark* and the *peso,* and many other names of quite modern coins, were originally merely the names of weights.

Weights for Coins: The amateur collector is often puzzled by certain small thick pieces of brass, marked with values as though they were coins, and yet appearing more like tokens or counters. Actually they are weights for weighing coins. They are often found as a set in a box complete with a balance. We may distinguish two sorts: (i) In the days when clipping (q.v.) was rife, both gold and silver coins were liable to be diminished gradually in weight and therefore in value. It was, of course, necessary to check if they could still be accepted at face value. In the time of King John (1205) the records of the assize state that

> "for discovering lack of weight there was issued from the Mint a penny poise wanting one eighth of a penny, to be delivered to any one who would have it" (Ruding).

Henry V in 1421 commanded certain persons

> "to make weights for the Noble, Half Noble and Farthing of gold sufficient for the several cities and boroughs" (Ruding).

Elizabeth I in 1587 ordered

> "cases of Wood, Leather and Latten to be made with weights to weigh all manner of Gold Coins current within the Realm, to be sold to all persons who should have cause to use the same."

By the Statute of 1773, passed for the

> "better preventing the counterfeiting, clipping and other diminishing the coin of this kingdom,"

the revenue officers were ordered to break and deface guineas minted before the accession of George III if they did not weigh at least 5 dwt.

3 grains, and those minted between that time and 1772 if they did not weigh at least 5 dwt. 6 grains, while those minted after 1772 had to weigh at least 5 dwt. 8 grains. The half-guinea had to be of a proportionate weight. With these elaborate enactments a proper set of weights would be a necessity for every businessman.

(ii) Formerly Continental coins were allowed to circulate freely as part and parcel of English currency. Portuguese gold coins especially abounded during the eighteenth century, owing to the favorable trade balance with Portugal. According to Ruding, such quantities were brought over that at the beginning of the eighteenth century very little gold coin other than Portuguese was to be found in the western counties of England. To arrive at an exact value of the foreign coin it was, of course, necessary to know the weight. To simplify matters, weights were manufactured to correspond with the exact values of certain foreign coins. Thus we find a weight inscribed NINE SHILLINGS; this was for use in weighing the escudo of John V of Portugal. There are also weights for assessing the Johannes, or eight-escudo piece; these are inscribed with the value THREE POUND TWELVE. From other coin weights we can tell what foreign coins were current, and their respective values, such as:

Spanish moidore   27s. (also half moidore, 13s. 6d., quarter moidore, 6s. 9d.).

Portuguese dobra   72s. (also the half, quarter, one-eighth, one-sixteenth, 36s., 18s., 9s., and 4s. 6d. respectively).

French Pistole   18s. 6d. (also half-pistole, 9s. 3s.).

A collection of coin weights going back to the time of James I can be formed. This makes an interesting series, as it shows portraits of the monarchs different from those on the contemporary coins. Such weights can be purchased at very small cost.

The earliest weights were square, but as these were easy to file down fraudulently to lessen the weight, from the time of Charles I they were usually made circular.

Window Tax: In many old English houses one can see windows which have been bricked up to avoid, or lessen, the unpopular "window tax." This was a tax levied on all houses which had six or more windows. It dates from 1695 (William III), and the purpose of it was to defray the enormous expense of the great recoinage that was necessary owing to the clipping and defacing of the old hammered coinage. The window tax was not repealed until 1851.

Winged Head Liberty Type: See *Dime*.

Wire Edge: When a coin has a sharp rim around the perimeter it is said to have a wire edge. Some of the 1907 Saint-Gaudens eagles and double eagles have a wire edge.

Wire Money: An issue of Maundy money of George III, dated 1792. The name is given to the issue of this year because of the numerals, 4, 3, and 2 on the coins, which have a very distinctive thin and wiry appearance.

Wisconsin Territorial Centennial Commemorative Half Dollar: See *Commemorative Coins (U.S.)*, p. 65.

Wolsey's Groat: The notorious groat struck 1514–30 by Cardinal Wolsey, as Archbishop of York. This coin figured in his impeachment. To stamp his archiepiscopal signature on a coin of the value of a groat would have been deemed an infringement of the royal prerogative.

Wolsey's Groat with portrait of Henry VIII.

Wood's Irish Halfpence and Farthings: These coins were struck under patent by William Wood, an ironmonger, 1722–24; Obv/Head of the King (George I); Rev/Hibernia seated, holding a harp. They were of good quality and well-struck; in fact, they were better coins than the contemporary English copper coins. Unfortunately for the English Government, however, it came to light that the patent had, in the first place, been granted to the King's mistress, the Duchess of Kendal; she had sold the patent to Wood, and there was no doubt that it showed considerable personal profit at the expense of Ireland, the country for which it was intended. In 1724 Swift, in his famous letters which appeared under the mysterious name M. B. Drapier, furiously attacked the whole system. A substantial reward was offered by the British Government for the discovery of the writer. Swift, however, continued his polemical campaign, with even increased ferocity. Although the patent had been originally granted for a period of 14 years, in 1725 the defeated Government was forced to withdraw the issue. Wood's Irish halfpence and farthings were eventually sent over to British North America, where they were made current and circulated along with the Rosa American coins (q.v.).

Wreath Type: See *Cent (U.S.)*.

Wyon, William: The best known of a long and distinguished family of coin designers and engravers. In 1828 he succeeded Pistrucci as Chief

Engraver at the Mint. The portrait on the coins of William IV was designed by him, and to his genius we owe the principal coins of Queen Victoria, until his death in 1851.

Y

Yap: One of the Caroline Islands, in the South Pacific. Apart from a few modern European and American coins, the ordinary native currency is shell money. The capital wealth of the island, however, is reckoned in FEI, a curious relic of Stone Age currency. Fei are enormous disks of limestone, resembling millstones, with a hole in the center to facilitate transport. The smallest is 6 in. across, the largest 12 ft. The latter weigh up to nearly 5 tons. They are not from local quarries, but come from the Pelew Islands, over 200 miles to the south. This fact seems to suggest they are of semi-sacred origin.

Yen (Chinese *yuen*, something round): The standard monetary unit of Japan. There is a gold yen, equaling 100 silver *sen*, and a silver yen, the size and value of the American dollar. The sen comprises ten copper or nickel coins called *rin*.

York County, Maine Tercentenary Commemorative Half Dollar: See *Commemorative Coins (U.S.)*, p. 65.

Z

Z: A contraction found on medieval inscriptions for the Latin *et*, meaning "and."

Zecchino (from *"La Zecca,"* the name of the palace which was the Venetian Mint): The ducat of Venice, one of the earliest gold coins of medieval Europe. It is also known by its French name of *sequin*. First struck about 1280. Obv/Christ in glory; Rev/The Doge, kneeling, and receiving the sacred banner (the *gonfalone*) from St. Mark. The first type of zecchino bore the same legend as the first *ducat* (q.v.) SIT TIBI, CHRISTE, etc. The type of the zecchino persisted until 1797, when the Venetian Republic came to an end.

Zinc (Ger. *zink*, zinc, spelter): The Germans struck coins of zinc during the First World War for use in occupied zones. These coins bore inscriptions in French and Flemish. Coins were also struck in this metal by the Germans for the Netherlands in 1940–44. Zinc coins have of late been issued in Yugoslavia and Austria, but in both these countries they have been superseded by aluminum coins. Coins of zinc for low values are still in use in Denmark.

The metal costs little to produce, and the coins have the advantage of being light in weight. The metal, however, is subject to a slow but certain oxidation, and the surface soon crumbles into a chalky powder. It can therefore be regarded only as a makeshift metal in coinage. The abbreviation for zinc is Zn.

Zodiacal Coins: A series of twelve gold *mohurs* and twelve silver *rupees*, struck by the Mogul emperor Jahangir (1605–27). On each of these coins is a sign of the zodiac. This was against the strict tenets of the Mohammedan religion, which forbade the representation in art of any form of living creature. This emperor, however, seems to have deliberately flouted orthodoxy, for he struck a *mohur* showing himself imbibing from the wine cup forbidden by his creed.